TEXTUAL SOURCES FOR THE STUDY OF RELIGION
edited by John R. Hinnells

Islam

TEXTUAL SOURCES FOR THE STUDY OF RELIGION

Judaism ed. P. S. Alexander
Zoroastrianism ed. Mary Boyce
Hinduism ed. Wendy Doniger O'Flaherty
Sikhism ed. W. H. McLeod

Further titles are in preparation

TEXTUAL SOURCES FOR THE STUDY OF

Islam

edited and translated
by Andrew Rippin and Jan Knappert

The University of Chicago Press

The University of Chicago Press, Chicago 60637
Copyright © Andrew Rippin and Jan Knappert 1986
All rights reserved.
Originally published by Manchester University Press in 1986.
University of Chicago Press edition 1990.
Printed in the United States of America

99 98 97 96 95 94 93 92   6 5 4 3 2

Library of Congress Cataloging-in-Publication Data

Textual sources for the study of Islam / edited and translated
    by Andrew Rippin and Jan Knappert.
        p.   cm.
    Reprint. Originally published: Totowa, N.J.: Barnes &
Noble, 1987, c1986. (Textual sources for the study of
religion).
    Includes bibliographical references and index.
    ISBN 0-226-72063-2 (pbk.)
    1. Islam.   I. Rippin, Andrew, 1950–   II.
Knappert, Jan. III. Series: Textual sources for the study of
religion.
BP161.2.T43   1990
297—dc20   90-44300
                                               CIP

∞   The paper used in this publication meets the minimum
requirements of the American National Standard for Information Sciences—Permanence of Paper for Printed Library Materials, ANSI Z39.48-1984

CONTENTS

GENERAL INTRODUCTION

This series is planned to meet a fundamental need in the study of religions, namely that for new, reliable translations of major texts. The first systematic attempt to provide such translations was the monumental *Sacred Books of the East* in the nineteenth century. These were pioneering volumes but, naturally, are now somewhat out of date. Since linguistic studies have advanced and more materials have come to light it is important to make some of these findings of twentieth-century scholarship available to students. Books in this series are written by specialists in the respective textual traditions, so that students can work on the secure foundation of authoritative translations of major literary sources.

But it is not only that linguistic and textual studies have advanced in the twentieth century. There has also been a broadening of the perspective within which religions are studied. The nineteenth-century focus was largely on scriptural traditions and the 'official' theological writings of the great thinkers within each tradition. Religious studies should, obviously, include such materials; but this series also reflects more recent scholarly trends in that it is concerned with a much wider range of literature, with liturgy and legend, folklore and faith, mysticism and modern thought, political issues, poetry and popular writings. However important scriptural texts are in a number of religions, even the most authoritative writings have been interpreted and elucidated; their thoughts have been developed and adapted. Texts are part of living, changing religions, and the anthologies in this series seek to encapsulate something of the rich variety to be found in each tradition. Thus editors are concerned with the textual sources for studying daily religious life as exemplified in worship or in law as well as with tracing the great movements of thought. The translations are accompanied by generous annotation, glosses and explanations, thus providing valuable aids to understanding the especial character of each religion.

Books in this series are intended primarily for students in higher education in universities and colleges, but it is hoped that they will be of interest also for schools and for members of some, at least, of the religious communities with whose traditions they are concerned.

John R. Hinnells

The editors and publishers regret that it has not been possible to incorporate all the corrections and changes that may have been desirable for this reprint.

FOREWORD AND ACKNOWLEDGEMENTS

When the general editor of this series set out his notions for the scope of this book, he stipulated a number of requirements. An attempt was to be made to provide a wide geographical coverage and to include aspects of popular Islam as well as official Islam. Such requirements are not easy to meet; they take a combination of linguistic skill and area knowledge seldom found in individual scholars. The attempt has been made in this book, therefore, to reap the benefit of scholarly collaboration between an Islamicist with conventional classical Arabocentric interests and an Africanist with widespread interests in contemporary manifestations of popular Islam throughout the world. The result may not take into account every aspect of Islam that would be desirable but that is due more to the restraints of space than to a lack of desire to include as much variety representative of the Islamic phenomenon as possible.

In trying to meet the aims of this book, we made a number of decisions concerning the material to be presented. The passages were to be of substantial length so that there would be sufficient material available for a student to analyse a given author's train of thought; this seems far preferable to the practice of providing snippets of ideas, which happens so frequently in books of this type. This procedure has, of course, led to a smaller number of authors being represented in the book; indeed, the absence of many figures who may be considered pivotal in the development of Islam will be noted. Instead, we have favoured less well known authors for the most part, which has the benefit of drawing students' attention to the depth of the Islamic phenomenon – a depth which has barely been scratched by scholarship. Ironically, perhaps, the one place where the intention of using long extracts has not been put into practice is with the text of the Qur'an itself. There really is no substitute for putting the whole of the scripture into the hands of the student; only by that means will the qualities of the Qur'an become clear. In this book, therefore, we have presented a limited number of Qur'anic extracts which, it is believed, illustrate the various types of material found therein; in no way do we suggest that these pieces are a sufficient introduction to the proper appreciation of the power this scripture has in the Muslim world.

In writing the introduction, the student audience for whom the book is primarily intended has been kept in mind. The introduction attempts to place the segments of the book in an over-all perspective and to provide, in cases where it seemed desirable, a general summary of the major tendencies of the literature. No attempt has been made to provide a full interpretation of any passage; that we conceive to be the task of the instructor, although the bibliography appended at the end of this book has been designed to provide the independent student with ideas for places to which to turn for further information. Likewise, the introduction does not attempt to provide an overview of the entire Islamic phenomenon; that is a task which must be left to another book.

Unless otherwise indicated in the bibliography, the material presented here has been translated especially for this book. Once again keeping in mind the audience for which the series is designed, certain liberties have been taken with the passages in the attempt to make them readable and understandable; while we would like to consider the passages here translated as contributions to scholarship, we recognise at the same time that in certain instances we have left the literal rendering of texts, employing abbreviation and paraphrase for what we consider good pedagogical reasons. We have, however, in all cases attempted to be true to the message, tone, and style of the original. We have tried to maintain a consistent system of transliteration throughout the book, including the pieces reprinted from other sources; for some words (surah, for example) we have preferred to use what seems to be the most recognisable form for most students rather than what is technically required to maintain the transliteration system.

A number of people must be thanked for their assistance in the preparation of this book: Floyd MacKay and Vi Lake of Calgary for much labour; T. Lawson of Montreal for valuable assistance with the Baha'i passages, although we take full responsibility for the ultimate selection of the material comprising this section; C. E. Bosworth and Norman Calder of Manchester for providing helpful editorial assistance at various stages in the preparation of the manuscript, for which we are indebted; our editor, John R. Hinnells, for providing crucial guidance in order to bring the book into its final shape.

We would like to express our thanks to the following publishers and authors for permission to reprint extracts from the below-mentioned books held under their copyright; their co-operation has been greatly appreciated. (Specific page references are to be found in the bibliography.) Baha'i World Centre, Haifa, for *Selections from the Writings of the Bab*, translated by Habib Taherzadeh (1978), and *Basharat (Glad Tidings): Tablets of Baha'u'llah revealed after Kitab-i-Aqdas*, translated by Habib Taherzadeh (1978); E. J. Brill, Leiden, for M. Brandel-Syrier, *The Religious Duties of Islam as taught and explained by Abu Bakr Effendi* (1971), and J. Knappert, *Swahili Islamic Poetry* (1971); Frank Cass, London, for E. H. Palmer, *Oriental Mysticism: a Treatise on Sufiistic and Unitarian Theosophy of the Persians* (1867/1969); Islamic Research Academy, Karachi, for A. A. Maududi, *Birth Control: its Social, Political, Economic, Moral, and Religious Aspects* (1968); Longman Group Ltd., Harlow, for Salem Azzam (ed.), *Islam and Contemporary Society* (1982); National Spiritual Assembly of Baha'is of the United States for 'Abdu'l-Baha, *Some Answered Questions* (copyright 1930, 1954, 1964, 1981), and Shoghi Effendi, *The World Order of Baha'u'llah: Selected Letters* (copyright 1939, 1955, 1974); A. M. Rashed, the London Mosque, London, for Mirza Ghulam Ahmad, *The Philosophy of the Teachings of Islam* (1979); Christian Troll, New Delhi, for his *Sayyid Ahmad Khan: a Reinterpretation of Muslim Theology* (1978).

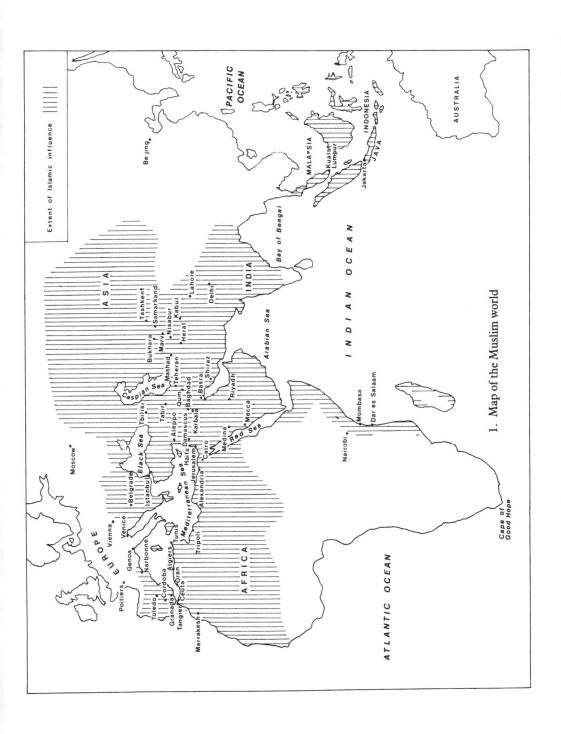

1. Map of the Muslim world

MONTHS OF THE MUSLIM YEAR

Muharram
Safar
Rabi' I
Rabi' II
Jumada I
Jamada II
Rajab
Sha'ban
Ramadan (the month of the fast, *sawm*)
Shawwal
Dhu'l-Qa'da
Dhu'l-Hijja (the month of the pilgrimage, *hajj*)

The Muslim year is based on the lunar cycles with no correction to align it with the solar year. Starting with Muharram, every other month has thirty days, the rest twenty-nine. In order to keep to the lunar cycle, an extra day is added to Dhu'l-Hijja (called *yawm al-kabs*) eleven times in thirty years.

1 INTRODUCTION

1.1 SCRIPTURE, ITS VALUE AND INTERPRETATION

While the picture many people have of Islam is of a Middle Eastern or even Arabian religion – and that is the way the faith presents itself sometimes – the phenomenon of the Muslim religion has, in fact, spread throughout much of the world. The far reaches of South East Asia, most especially Indonesia, and vast portions of Africa are important modern centres of the faith, along with much of the area between these two extremes, traditionally seen as Islamic. Today, Arabs account for only fifteen per cent of the world Muslim population.

Tying all these regions together is the Qur'an, written and recited in Arabic. The Qur'an provides the basis of all Muslim religious speculation, is a constant touchstone in virtually every religious text, and plays a vital role in the day-to-day life of the individual believer.

The Qur'an – a word taken to mean 'recitation' – is the collection of the religious utterances of Muhammad, son of 'Abd Allah, who was born around the year 570. Muhammad, a native of the Arabian cultic centre of Mecca, portrayed himself as a prophet in the line of Israelite prophets, understood to start with Adam and trace a line up through Moses, Abraham, and Jesus up to Muhammad as the final prophet. Muhammad's utterances take on the characteristics of much of the Biblical material but, at times, appear to show influences of the Arabian context as well, especially in their rhythmic emphases. Surahs 112 (2.1.2) and 100 (2.1.3) especially display this Arabian oracular quality of parts of the Qur'an while surah 81 (2.1.4), with its emphasis on the coming end of the world and the judgement day, conjures up pictures of a forceful preacher giving his message to his irreligious, immoral fellow-Arabians. The moral message conveyed through the use of Biblical characters in passages such as surah 29 (2.1.5) is intriguing in the way in which the Biblical stories are retold, often in a brief and referential style, and then emerge in a stereotyped narrative: a prophet is commissioned, his people reject him, the people are punished but the prophet survives. The practicalities of ruling a religious community also make themselves felt in the text of Muhammad's utterances as displayed in the opening verses of surah 5 (2.1.6), where a vast number of legal topics are broached, although they could hardly be said to be treated in any depth. Surah 17, verses 22–39 (2.1.7), is often seen to be a thematic parallel to the ten commandments of the Bible (Exodus 20:1–17, Deuteronomy 5:6–21). Muslim law, as displayed in the Qur'an, clearly follows the trends of its Jewish predecessor in its scope and, in some cases, its specifics as well.

The Qur'an is traditionally said to have been collected into book form some thirty years after the death of Muhammad in 632 and it was at that time that it adopted the form in which we see it today, with the long surahs arranged at the beginning, the shorter ones at the end. The major exception to this arrangement is surah 1 (2.1.1), the opening chapter, which functions as a liturgical introduction to the entire book as well as functioning as a vital and essential piece of the daily prayer ritual in which it must be recited in Arabic by every Muslim (see 1.3, 3.2.3.2, 4.2.1).

As the Arabs expanded out of their original geographical and cultural context, taking with them their new-found faith, the desire to spread their religion was ever-present. The Qur'an, as the major document of the faith, was strangely opaque to its new audiences once it was removed from its original setting. The Biblical references seemed to presuppose knowledge of the Jewish and Christian scriptural and exegetical tradition; customs were referred to which held little meaning for those outside the immediate context of their origin. Moreover, with the new circumstances and the desire to make scripture appealing to the masses, the need for interpretation was overwhelming. Outstanding in the early centuries for bringing together vast quantities of material bearing upon how the Qur'an was to be understood was Abu Ja'far Muhammad ibn Jarir al-Tabari and his book *Jami' al-bayan 'an ta'wil ay al-Qur'an*.

Al-Tabari, who was probably born in 839 and died in 923, started his life in Amul in Tabaristan, northern Persia. He studied and eventually settled in Baghdad, although he embarked on a number of sojourns in Syria, Egypt, and his birthplace. He devoted his life to scholarly activities, collecting Muslim traditions from preceding generations. While fairly traditional in his theological outlook, al-Tabari attempted to strike out on his own in the juristic field, forming his own school of law; it quickly fell into obscurity. That fate was not to befall his major written works, however. Part of his great reputation rests upon his book of world history, *Ta'rikh al-rusul wa'l-muluk* (see 1.2, 3.1.2), which covers the era of the Biblical prophets, details some early rulers, and then moves on to Sasanian history. The text becomes far more detailed after this portion, being organised by the years of the life of Muhammad, the first four caliphs, the Umayyad dynasty, and the 'Abbasid rulers up to the year 915.

Al-Tabari's other major work, his commentary on the Qur'an, is a compendium of earlier opinions of interpretations of the scripture, with his own opinion interspersed. It has been a valued commentary throughout the Muslim world, although it did not become as widely circulated as some other exegetical texts, probably because of its bulk (the printed edition runs to thirty volumes). Al-Tabari's self-conscious approach to the interpretative task, while not showing any particular sophistication by modern standards, is seen in his interpretation of what has become the focal point for Muslim discussion of Qur'an 3:7 (2.2.1), where the Qur'an divides itself into 'clear' and 'unclear' verses, leading the way for scholars to debate over the distinction between the two and how to determine it.

Al-Tabari was by no means the first Qur'anic exegete, although the importance he placed upon the chain of transmitters (*isnad*) in the citation of his interpretations guaranteed his acceptance by later generations (see 1.2). Early writers who lived before these *isnad* demands, often did not have their works treated so kindly by those who came after.

Muqatil ibn Sulayman was born in Balkh in Persia, lived in Marv and, during the civil war in Khurasan after the 'Abbasid revolution, moved to Basra and then Baghdad, returning to Basra a bit later to die there in 767. There is a great deal of uncertainty in Muslim sources concerning the person of Muqatil, his theological position, and the reason that Islamic tradition generally looks so unfavourably upon his work. While various anathemic doctrines are cited as being held by him, no such point of view is upheld by any of his works to which we have access. It is more likely that Muqatil's work, coming before the stringent requirements for the *isnad* as mentioned, simply did not meet the criteria of later generations and thus was ignored.

Regardless of the official position on Muqatil, his *Tafsir*, which is probably the earliest such text in existence (although its present form suggests that it has been subjected to a great deal of editing in the generations after his death) is full of fascinating material. It is a work full of narrative embellishments of the Qur'an, especially as his commentary on surah 1 (2.2.2) reveals. Note should be taken of his style of presentation of the material, with the abrupt division between text and commentary and the use of the Qur'an itself to interpret a given passage of scripture. The work is still primarily available in manuscript with only a small portion of it available in print.

Exegetical activity by no means ceased with al-Tabari, either. The following centuries saw the emergence of philological, philosophical, rational, and traditionalist commentaries. 'Imad al-Din Isma'il ibn 'Umar ibn Kathir was born in Basra in 1300 and moved to Damascus when he was six, where he studied with some of the most famous scholars of his time including the Hanbalite theologian, jurist, and reformer Taqi al-Din Ahmad ibn Taymiyya (d. 1328) (see 1.8). Ibn Kathir became known as a scholar of law and a teacher of *hadith* as well as being praised as one of the most respected preachers and lecturers in Damascus. He died in 1373. His major work, a commentary on the Qur'an, entitled simply *Tafsir al-Qur'an* (2.2.3), provides a synopsis of earlier material in a readily accessible form, a factor which gave the work much popularity in subsequent generations. His reliance is totally upon *hadith* material; the era of Ibn Kathir, in fact, marks the final submersion of rationalism under the powers of traditionalism. No longer did even the measure of personal opinion displayed in the work of al-Tabari have any substantial place in the understanding of the Qur'an.

The Qur'an plays many roles in Muslim life and thought. One of its important theological values is seen in its standing as the proof of Muhammad's prophethood: this book is Muhammad's miracle *par excellence* which validates his status as a prophet sent by God. Probably in response to Christian polemical pressures, Muslims from early times on found it necessary to formulate an argument which would demonstrate the status of the Qur'an as a miracle. A book by 'Ali ibn 'Isa al-Rummani, born in Iraq in 908 and dying in 996, is one of the earliest complete texts to put forth a literary argument for the inimitability *(i'jaz)* of the Qur'an. Prior to al-Rummani, this doctrine had been asserted primarily in one of three ways. The argument of *sarfa*, the turning away of people by God from imitating the Qur'an, was associated with the important Mu'tazilite thinker (see 1.5) al-Nazzam (d. *c.* 835) and was an important doctrine right up to the time of al-Rummani, also a Mu'tazilite. The second argument, found succinctly in the works of al-Jahiz (d. 864), suggests that it is the contents of the Qur'an which make it inimitable, especially when this facet is combined with the dogma of Muhammad as illiterate. Third is the argument which displays the greatest evolution in substance and upon which the burden of proof of inimitability ultimately falls. An early form of the argument was expressed by al-Maturidi (d. 944), who notes that the challenge put forth to the unbelievers in the Qur'an (e.g. surah 17:88) to produce something 'like' the Qur'an – and essentially this is the underlying basis of all of the discussions of inimitability – is based upon three notions: the content of the scripture (as with al-Jahiz), the peculiarity of the nature of the scripture, and the language of the text. From these primitive beginnings al-Rummani develops in his *al-Nukat fi i'jaz al-Qur'an* (2.3) a systematic but tentative argument for the inimitability of the Qur'an based primarily upon this latter argument, summed up for him in the term *balagha*, a word perhaps best defined, if somewhat awkwardly, as 'the aesthetic effectiveness of the Qur'an on a verbal level'. This forms just one, although certainly the most important, of seven elements which he cites in support of the over-all doctrine of the inimitability of the Qur'an.

1.2 RELIGIOUS HISTORY

As Islam is conceived as governing all facets of the individual Muslim's life, so too Islam provides a total understanding of the world around the individual. Islamic accounts of history, always tied in their origin to the Qur'an, provide a narrative about the world from its beginning to its end to supplement the brief statements found in scripture. Naturally, the bulk of this material deals with Muhammad and the Islamic period, but the earlier periods have gathered a great deal of popular attention as well.

3.1.1 is taken from one of the numerous popular books describing the marvels of creation, this one written by Muhammad ibn Ahmad ibn Iyas who died in 1524, having been the governor of Tripoli, Aleppo, and Damascus. All such works treating these matters assure their readers that the ultimate source of this material is to be found in the *hadith*, the traditions which are ultimately seen to derive from Muhammad. The Qur'an also plays a role here, but even then, the interpretation of those scriptural passages will always be understood in the light of what Muhammad said about them. This care concerning sources is reflected in the attention paid to the citing of sources, understood to have been transmitted from Muhammad; 'Abd Allah ibn 'Abbas and Ka'b al-Ahbar are two prominent names found in this text.

The story of creation begins with the obvious question (asked, naturally, of Muhammad himself) of where God was before He created even His own throne. Even there, however, there is disagreement over the first thing created.[1] The precedence of the pen in the myth of creation is based upon the philosophic concept of destiny. Since all events in this universe have been predestined by God, it is assumed that He wanted to write them down before He began His creation so that He would have a record for the future. Muslims generally believe that whatever happens to them, whether good luck or disaster, has been written by the pen especially for them at God's order. The pen, it is believed, has written down everything that will ever happen to anybody, past, present, and future.

Following the discussion of the pen are questions which reflect concerns over Islamic cosmology: is the earth flat or round and what does it rest on? All these notions were clearly developed in a time before the concepts of magnetism and gravitation had been enunciated; a pre-Copernican world-view prevails in this concept of the universe. At the same time, there is a noticeable dissatisfaction; a need to place creation in the context of logical sequences of cause and effect is displayed. The earth must be heavy, so what is strong enough to support it so that it does not fall down into the bottomless abyss of space? The earth may be thought of as resting on the horns of a bull, which in turn stands on the back of a fish; both animals are fed regularly for only if alive will they be strong enough to carry the earth. The fish has to swim, so it needs water. But what is at the bottom of that? In the end the story can only conclude that God alone knows the answers. The fact that the carriers of the earth are alive explains things such as earthquakes: they are simply caused by the bull shaking its horns. The same sense of causality applies ultimately to the problem of water circulation on earth as well.

Islamic prehistory follows the line of the Biblical prophets, incorporating the Jewish and Christian elaborations of these stories along with adding special elements relevant to Islam. Al-Tabari, in his major world history (see 1.1), provides an elaboration of the famous story of Abraham and the demand of God that he sacrifice his son (3.1.2). Here we see the way in which stories are creatively retold. Especially important is the role of Abraham in the origin of the pilgrimage ritual of Islam; Abraham's actions in this sacrifice scenario are the prototype for Muslim actions in the *hajj*. A special emphasis, therefore, falls on these elements of the story, one of the factors which makes this a different story from its Biblical counterpart. The repetitiousness of the material displays al-Tabari's style as a historian in his concern to record as much detail as possible.

The *Sira* ('life story') is the official Islamic biography of Muhammad as prophet which recounts his various exploits in life and documents the growth of the early Muslim community. The *Sira* of Abu 'Abd Allah Muhammad ibn Ishaq, who lived his life in Medina, Egypt, and Baghdad and died in 767, is the most famous of its kind and provides the basic information for all classical and modern biographical accounts of Muhammad. This sort of work is supplemented, however, by a number of sub-genres, one of which is entitled *mawlid* or nativity, a richly embellished life of Muhammad which concentrates on the many miracles which God made him perform, especially those in the early part of his life.

The many *mawlid* texts that are extant in Arabic, Turkish, Malay, Swahili, and other languages are partly didactic and partly liturgical. They teach the common people (as opposed to the educated classes) what everybody is supposed to know about Muhammad's birth and youth. This narrative is usually interrupted by hymns to Muhammad which are sung by Qur'anic schoolboys with the whole audience singing only some of the refrains. A *mawlid* text is recited on the eve of the nativity of Muhammad, 12 Rabi' I, and sometimes on seven consecutive nights thereafter. Recitation of the favourite chapters of the Qur'an and singing of hymns to Muhammad and frequent prayers to God for good health, to ward off evil, and for admission into paradise are inserted. The listeners are blessed, it is believed, by simply hearing these devout recitations which they could not perform themselves since the majority of the population is not educated in classical Arabic. The *mawlid* recitation and festival is the most popular occasion in the Muslim calendar.

The contents of the *mawlid* are conventional. It begins with the conception of Muhammad by his mother Amina which is announced by angels and animals and accompanied by miracles. The prophets of the past appear in her dreams to offer comfort and encouragement. When Muhammad is born he recites his prayers immediately, by divine inspiration. He grows up as an orphan, for his mother dies when he is six; his father had died when he was not yet born. His uncle, Abu Talib, takes him on trips to Damascus for trade, and the young Muhammad becomes a trader and camel driver. A rich young widow named Khadija watches him riding at the head of a caravan and falls in love with him. Their marriage was, of course, arranged in heaven. The version of the *mawlid* presented here in 3.2.1 is that of Ja'far ibn Hasan al-Barzanji who was born in Medina and died in 1766. His work, *Mawlid al-nabi*, is well known throughout the Muslim world and has been translated into numerous languages.

Another part of the popular biography of Muhammad conventionally begins with the purification often referred to as the breast-washing. Muhammad is suddenly seized by two angels who lay him on the floor and open his breast. They take out his heart and squeeze out a black clot which is put in all human hearts by Satan. Having thus purified his heart, they put it back again and no one can see a scar. Now Muhammad is free of deceit and mendacity, so he is ready to become the messenger of God's word on earth. For this purpose God invites him to come and sit before His exalted presence, to see Him with his own eyes, for who would believe a prophet who had not seen God Himself, as did Moses? In order to tell his nation about the perils of hell and the pleasures of paradise, Muhammad is given a conducted tour through the seven heavens and hell to see for himself how the souls suffer who did not keep God's commandments and how those who did enjoy eternal happiness. In addition, he meets seven prophets of the past including Moses and Aaron, who pay him homage as a prophet greater than they. Even Jesus admits Muhammad is greater. In this way, the excellence of Islam above all other religions is instilled in the minds of the people who listen. This story, known as the *mi'raj*, owes its name to the Arabic word for the ladder which Muhammad climbed to heaven. As a text, it is read or chanted as a story or a poem relating all the miraculous things that Muhammad saw in hell and heaven on the night of 27 Rajab, called *laylat al-Mi'raj*. The text provided here in 3.2.2 already has Muhammad in Jerusalem, ready to ascend to heaven; it is taken from a Swahili version which itself is a translation by Al-Amin ibn 'Ali, a modern scholar of Mombasa, of the Arabic work written by Najm al-Din Muhammad ibn Ahmad al-Ghayti. Al-Ghayti, born between 1494 and 1504, was a religious scholar in Cairo and died in 1573. The work entitled *Qissat mi'raj al-nabi* has attracted a great number of commentaries and translations throughout the Muslim world.

Apart from the narrative form of the biography of Muhammad as found in the *Sira* and the popular literature which supplements it, there is also the large body of material consisting of what are called the *hadith* reports which relate events, statements, and decisions of Muhammad (see 3.2.3.1 through 3.2.3.3). This material was recorded for a specific purpose: it was to act as a source of law of the Muslim community after the death of its founder. Exactly when this material was written down and how it came into being is a vexed question much discussed by both traditional Muslims and modern scholars. Regardless of this problem (which is discussed further below in 1.4), the basic point is clear: Muhammad serves as an example to individual Muslims for the proper life of a believer. Whatever Muhammad did is worthy of emulation. It is therefore important that what each individual does should have the backing of the example of Muhammad; thus, the *hadith* reports provide this 'biographical' material to support the practices of the community, regardless of the judgement scholars may make on its historical value.

The *hadith* material was gathered into large books in the third Muslim century (ninth–tenth century) and gained a certain semi-canonical status within the Sunni community at least as reflecting the true practice of Muhammad. Six books are generally accepted: those written by al-Bukhari (d. 870), Muslim (d. 875), Ibn Maja (d. 886), Abu Dawud (d. 888), al-Tirmidhi (d. 892), and al-Nasa'i (d. 915). These books are organised according to legal topic, with some seventy chapters in al-Bukhari's collection for example. Al-Bukhari transmits a total of 7,397 traditions in his work.

As well as providing the narrative account of an event connected with the life of Muhammad, that is, the section of a *hadith* known as the *matn* or text, each tradition also has with it an *isnad*, or chain of authorities. This *isnad* provides the names of those who transmitted the report from generation to generation down to the compiler of the book in question. Ultimately, for the report to be considered totally reliable, the report must stem from Muhammad himself and be transmitted through one of his close followers or companions. The importance of the *isnad* in traditional Muslim thought is virtually equal to the text itself. Without a fault-free chain of transmitters, a *hadith* cannot be considered trustworthy. A great deal of energy was spent in establishing the reliability of individual transmitters of *hadith*, when they lived, whether they could possibly have heard the *hadith* from the person the *isnad* claimed they heard it from, and how dependable each individual was to begin with. The science of *hadith* criticism became largely a science of *isnad* criticism in classical Islamic times. The presence of all the names of the transmitters of the traditions is, therefore, an essential part of the material and, while it may seem redundant, it must be viewed as an intrinsic part of the *hadith*. An example of the full use of the *isnad* is provided in 3.2.3.1 below, but in the interests of brevity, such material has been omitted in the other passages.

The examples of *hadith* material found in 3.2.3.1–3.2.3.3 demonstrate the range of the material and display its value for the community. The legal aspects of the first two sections are obvious. Al-Bukhari's section on drink broaches a large number of questions concerning what can be drunk and how and when and by whom; note that the Qur'anic prohibition of wine is certainly a matter which receives a great deal of attention, with the *hadith* material having to provide the authoritative interpretation of what the Qur'an really means by 'wine'. *Hadith* reports also reflect what were probably real disputes in the early Muslim community over just what was permissible; different people's views became embodied in the form of a *hadith*, attributed to the opinion of Muhammad ultimately. Similarly, the section from Muslim on reciting the first surah of the Qur'an in prayer (see 2.1.1 and 4.2.1) reveals the function of the *hadith* in preserving the practice of the community on a matter that the Qur'an left apparently unstated.

Although the Qur'an states that Muhammad is 'just a man', popular imagination vested Muhammad with many special qualities, as has been seen in the legendary portions of his biography already treated. This aspect is found in the *hadith* as well, as reflected in 3.2.3.3 from Abu Dawud which gathers together Muhammad's medical insights; these statements are, of course, of legal import also, legitimising various medical practices, but they also reflect a view of Muhammad as fully imbued with knowledge of everything in the world.

While the Qur'an displays the status of Muhammad as a prophet, bringing a religious message, and the *hadith* emphasizes his value as an exemplar for the community, the *Sira* or life story of Muhammad does both of these things as well as displaying the political side of his activities in the way in which he fought battles and strove to make alliances in his efforts to unite Arabia under his control. Perhaps few other documents contained in the *Sira* of Ibn Ishaq demonstrate this aspect of Muhammad's endeavours as well as the so-called Constitution of Medina (3.2.4) as recorded in his work. A difficult document to understand and one which has attracted the attention of scholars for years now, this 'constitution' is generally interpreted to be the agreement which Muhammad established in Medina (or Yathrib as it was then called) when he emigrated there on his *hijra*. It establishes what the responsibilites of each group who live in the town will be towards each other and the measure of support which they will give to Muhammad, whose authority is seen ultimately to derive from God.

Wafat al-nabi is the title of a common collection of legends around the death of Muhammad. Even prophets must die but God grants His beloved prophet many favours. Numerous tales have clustered around this central theme, describing in detail how all his friends and followers wept at hearing that their great leader was dying but how the angels rejoiced that he was coming to join them in heaven. Central issues addressed in the passage are how Muhammad can guarantee paradise to his devoted followers and, most important of all, whether he asked 'Ali or Abu Bakr to take over the leadership from him, thereby setting in motion the two separate lines of succession, the Sunni and the Shi'i. The text presented in section 3.2.5 is taken from that of al-Qadi ibn Musa ibn 'Iyad ibn 'Amrun al-Yahsubi who was born in Ceuta in 1088. He occupied the position of judge there and subsequently in Granada. He died an exile in Marrakesh in 1149.

As salvation history, the Islamic account looks forward to the hereafter; at that time, the proper recompense and reward will be meted out as is deserved. Numerous manuals have been written purporting to provide the crucial pictures of the apocalyptic events and the subsequent time. There is general agreement on the following predictions. Gradually the world will become increasingly sinful. Honest people will be few and most people will be morally corrupted. Disease will spread and kill many; earthquakes and volcanic eruptions will be followed by terrible dust storms. Mountains, cities, palaces, and tombstones will be blown apart. The sun and stars will go out so that the earth will be totally in the dark. All the rivers and seas will disappear so that no living thing will remain. God, displeased with all the human vice, will give a sign to Israfil, who will blow the trumpet, resulting in the miserable death of the last people still alive, blinded by the duststorms. At the sound of the second trumpet, the storm will blow the sand away from all the graves so that bodies, suddenly reunited with their souls, will rise and stand, lamenting their sinfulness and praying to God for forgiveness. After the third trumpet blast, Muhammad will rise and, mounted on his faithful Burak (used in the night journey), ride to the scales which have become visible in front of God's throne. Each person's sins will be weighed on the left scale, good deeds on the right scale. After individual judgement, Muhammad will lead the faithful into paradise along the bridge over the fires of hell. The pressure of the crowds will be tremendous, causing all the sinners to fall into the fire, but the righteous will be saved. The text provided here in 3.3 is an extract from a typical example of the genre written in Swahali verse by the contemporary Zanzibari poet and scholar, Hajji Chum (*c.* 1890–*c.* 1960).

1.3 RITUAL

Islam has a full body of law governing every aspect of a Muslim's life; part of that body of law are the religious devotions commonly known as the 'Five Pillars of Islam'. These five pillars are by no means the only ceremonial aspect for Muslims nor are they even the central piece of the entire legal structure but they have become isolated within Muslim thought as a significant summary of Muslim life.

Abu Muslim 'Abd al-Qahir al-Baghdadi was a Shafi'ite jurist and Ash'arite theologian who died in 1037. Born in Baghdad, he was taken to Nisabur by his father at an early age and was educated there under the tutelage of Sufi scholars. He became a prominent teacher in the area, gathering around himself many students. His talents stretched to many subjects including mathematics, Sufism, and theology.

Al-Baghdadi has gained a great deal of his fame for a book on heresiography, documenting the theological sects of Islam. But other works of his are just as significant. His work on abrogation in the Qur'an is a unique legal treatise which uses the Qur'an as a pretext for a detailed discussion of variation between the various schools of law (see 1.4, 5.1). His main work on theology, *Kitab usul al-din*, 'On the Roots of Religion', provides a theological summary of the major aspects of Islam as al-Baghdadi saw it. It is a work constructed in traditional fashion, consisting of 15 chapters. He starts with the sources of knowledge and then moves to the creation of the world, the characteristics of the Creator, the external attributes of God, the names of God and their qualities, and an explanation of God's justice and wisdom. From there he goes to the prophets, miracles, the pillars of Islam, the imposition of duties on Muslims, rules for humanity, the roots of faith, the role of the leader of the community, the role of the learned class, and sums up with a treatise on disbelievers. The work takes its reader, therefore, from what is known by the human, through all of the logical consequences which follow from human existence from the Muslim point of view, those being the responsibilities of being a Muslim. It is there that this notion and explanation of the Five Pillars of Islam fits in, as is found in section 4.1.

The five pillars as al-Baghdadi explains them are witnessing to faith, prayer, charity, fasting, and pilgrimage. The second of these is often seen to be the crucial element in Islam, with much of life focusing around the five periods of the day devoted to prayer. The ritual prayer, known as *salat*, is a fully structured activity that does not vary anywhere throughout the Muslim world. The elements of the prayer (4.2.1) are always to be recited in Arabic and follow a regular pattern in the repetitions and in the actions which accompany the recitations, regardless of the day of the week; only the number of times a given set of rituals will be performed will vary, according to the time of day.

The language of Islam in East Africa is, and has been since the tenth century, Swahili. In that language, as in Arabic, numerous prayers have been written for daily use. These prayers are called *du'a*, distinct from *salat*, the five daily ritual prayers which must be recited in Arabic. These personal (as opposed to ritual) prayers are not made up by individuals on the spur of the moment but are written down and, in Arabic, printed for the believers to memorise.[2]

In Swahili, as in Malay, Urdu, and Persian, numerous prayers have been, and still are, composed by poets in verse. There is a very extensive Islamic devotional literature in Swahili, comparable to Christian books of hymns and prayers. This Swahili Islamic worship literature is unpublished and thus virtually unknown outside of East Africa. Yet these sung prayers possess great beauty and deserve to be better appreciated. The poets write these prayers down and teach them to their communities; often the poets are themselves Islamic scholars. These prayers can be sung in the mosque as hymns or at private prayer sessions. Weddings are frequent occasions for new poems to be composed, often by order of the host. The contents of such poems are usually conventional. For example, after every wedding there is a farewell song sung to the bridal couple. These songs, though freshly written for the occasion contain certain set phrases like: 'Live together in harmony like a garment with its hem' (i.e. sewn tightly together) or 'like water in a cup'. There are numerous other religious prayer-songs in Swahili, for example, mourning songs to be sung after a funeral, songs of good-bye to the pilgrims on their way to Mecca and songs of welcome when they come back. There are also songs to pray for the fishermen while they are sailing out, so that God may speed them home in safety after a rich catch, prayer poems to ask God for rain in times of drought, and even a prayer for a woman to sing when she wants to conceive. Examples of these types of popular prayers are to be found in 4.2.2 and 4.2.3.

Sharaf al-Din Muhammad ibn Sa'id al-Busiri was born in Egypt in 1212 and died there in 1294. He was a famous scholar, calligrapher, religious teacher, and poet. Tradition relates that one day when he was gravely ill, he had a dream in which Muhammad appeared to him and threw his robe over his shivering body so that the fever ceased. When he woke, he composed a poem of 162 couplets which made him famous. Its title is *al-Burda*, 'The Robe', and it praises Muhammad in such extreme terms as to make him semi-divine. Seven hundred years later, the poem is still so popular that it is recited frequently in Egypt, Morocco, Nigeria, East Africa, Malaysia, and Indonesia. Poetic translations of it have been made into Malay and Swahili. Its popularity rests on the fact that it provides a summary of the legend of the figure of Muhammad as he was imagined in the thirteenth century, a popular picture which sees a definite move in the notion of Muhammad closer towards the Christian vision of Jesus as the miracle-worker. In his opening verses, the poet begins, as was the tradition in his day, by lamenting an unhappy love affair until, in verse 19, he turns away from such foolish emotions and that is where the passage in 4.2.4 begins.

Another greatly valued ritual activity which lies outside the Five Pillars but which continues to command great respect among devout Muslims is the ability to recite the Qur'an. Abu Zakariya' Yahya ibn Sharaf al Din al-Nawawi, was a famed Shafi'ite jurist who lived from 1233 to 1278. He wrote a manual on the etiquette of Qur'an recitation entitled *al-Tibyan fi adab hamalat al-Qur'an*, 'The explanation of the correct procedures for handling the Qur'an', a text for all those who came in contact with the Qur'an. The book is intended to provide the guidelines for individuals to devote themselves to a life in the service of God. While some of the concern in this regard was with the details of Qur'an recitation as such and thus some of his manual covers those matters, he was also concerned with the general attitude to and use of the Qur'an by all Muslims.[3] The section translated here (4.3) provides an example of the range of the author's concerns as to how much of the Qur'an should be recited at a given time; emphasis is always on the practices of esteemed persons in the past.

1.4 LAW

An articulated body of law developed as a result of an involved process in the early Muslim community. While Muhammad was alive, he was understood to be the source of law for all Muslims; there was no need to develop or establish an abstract system of law to govern the community. The early period of Islamic expansion, perhaps the first 100 years after the death of Muhammad, saw a concern not with building up an elaborate system of universal law but rather with a pragmatic programme of trying to meet the needs of individual situations as they arose throughout the empire. What apparently happened was that, as the empire expanded, the law of the land that was found in each conquered district tended to remain the basis of law for that area; such an approach was the sensible one on the part of the conquerers, for it certainly led to fewer problems with the conquered populations. However, as a result of this, each individual district developed its own distinctive law pattern. The differences should not be exaggerated here, for some sense of uniformity is likely in religious ritual and the like from an early stage, but the responses to new situations would have varied to a fair degree in different areas. This variation would not have created any problems in the first century but the demands for unification of the empire after the period of the conquests would have had their effect upon the legal situation as well.

As has been discussed in 1.3, the demands for legal authority created a large growth of *hadith* literature as each area attempted to support its own legal stance with the example of Muhammad. But this process in itself was one which created much discussion and controversy concerning precisely what the bases of law should be. It was al-Shafi'i (d. 819) whose position finally dominated; it was he who argued that it was the example of Muhammad which must be taken as a legal source second only to the Qur'an. Eventually, a full system of jurisprudence emerged in which the Qur'an and the *sunna*, the word used to refer to the example set by Muhammad as embodied in the *hadith*, were joined by *qiyas* (analogy) and *ijma'* (consensus of the community) to produce the body of law known as the *shari'a*, the way of life; even here variation was possible and, in fact, manifested itself in the emergence of four schools of law named after four major figures in early legal teaching: Abu Hanifa (d. 767) whose school dominates India and Pakistan today; Malik ibn Anas (d. 795) represented especially in North Africa; al-Shafi'i, found in Indonesia; and Ahmad ibn Hanbal (d. 855), the law school of present-day Saudi Arabia.

What jurisprudence developed was the *shari'a*, a path which becomes a guide to action for the individual Muslim. The concept is based upon the idea of God as the ruler of the world whose orders must be obeyed; it is generally seen as a system of law imposed from the outside upon the believers. Actions are categorised into five levels: obligatory – actions which are rewarded for performance and punished for being omitted; recommended – actions which carry only reward but no punishment for omission; indifferent – a vast majority of actions for which God grants permission for their performance but no reward or punishment is involved; reprehensible – actions whose performance brings punishment but the avoidance of which brings no reward; and forbidden – actions which will be punished and for which avoidance will be rewarded. These categories therefore include all that was to be done – the positive law – along with what was not to be done.

Illustrative of the variation between the schools of law over small points of detail is that found in the book by 'Abd al-Qahir al-Baghdadi (see 1.3) on abrogation in the Qur'an, *al-Nasikh wa'l-mansukh* in 5.1. The notion of abrogation of the law was championed by some jurists to explain cases where a law that was present in the Qur'an had been replaced by another law. The classic example was found in the prohibition of wine, where the total outlawing of the substance was a gradual procedure, still reconstructible in the text of the Qur'an. But the question remained of how to know which verses were abrogated and which were still in force. Al-Baghdadi's book is an encyclopedic approach to the topic. The pretext for the passage provided here is the debate over the exact status in the law in Qur'an 6:145, which provides a shorter list of forbidden foods than other Qur'anic passages. However, al-Baghdadi quickly moves into a discussion of the exact ramifications of the law itself, outlining various contentious issues and different opinions on them.

The fame of Abu Hamid Muhammad ibn Muhammad al-Ghazzali comes from his crucial role in the development of Islamic mysticism (Sufism – see 1.7) and its acceptance in orthodox Islam. Born in 1059 in Khurasan, northern

Persia, al-Ghazzali was trained as an orthodox theologian and lawyer and established himself as a leading scholar by the time he was appointed as a teacher in Baghdad in 1091. By 1095, however, he became dissatisfied with his career and decided to devote himself to the mystical quest for personal experience of God. Until his death in 1111, al-Ghazzali lived the life of an ascetic but he did manage to write a number of books as well, all with the aim of elucidating the moral, metaphysical, and mystical aspects of Islam so as to reconcile Sufism with orthodoxy and to prove that the Sufi way of life was necessary for the true Muslim. His massive *Ihya' 'ulum al-din*, 'The Revival of the Religious Sciences', is his most famous and most important work; in it he makes the attempt to bring out the relationship between orthodox theology and religious law, as well as the relationship between practical and speculative mysticism. The work is divided into four major sections: worship, concentrating on the 'inner meaning' of the rituals of Islam; personal behaviour, which sees the progression from religious law to mystical training as intimately linked; the deadly sins, which details the discipline needed for the mystic quest; and the way to salvation, concentrating on the interpretation of spiritual experience. The passage presented here in 5.2 on birth control comes from the second section of his book and illustrates well the depth of al-Ghazzali's legal training and acumen; the over-all context, however, makes it clear that the ultimate purpose of these types of excursus in his book is so that individuals may bring their persons under full disciplined control in preparation for the mystic quest. This control will, of course, have to be one founded upon the law of Islam.

Abu Bakr Effendi (5.3) lived in the nineteenth century and died in 1880. He was trained as a religious scholar in Istanbul and Baghdad and went to South Africa as an emissary of the Ottoman government to help solve disputes over matters of law among the Malay Muslims living in the Cape. Abu Bakr spent much of his time lecturing and arranging for a mosque to be built, but he also wrote a work entitled *Bayan al-din*, 'The explication of the Religion', a part of which is provided here in translation. The work is distinctive because it is written in Afrikaans but printed in the Arabic script. As a legal text, however, it is a close copy of a sixteenth-century Ottoman element law text of the Hanafi school of law, entitled *Multaqa al-abhur* written by Muhammad ibn Ibrahim al-Halabi. This illustrates the essentially conservative nature of official Islamic law, even when it is transplanted from one part of the world to another. The fact that most of the South African Malays were members of the Shafi'ite rite of Islamic law resulted in the influence of Abu Bakr's work continuing after his death in only part of the Cape Muslim community.

Marriage and divorce are, of course, of central concern to Islamic law; a great deal of attention is paid in every legal manual to the precise details governing the conduct of these institutions. A small taste of that material is provided in 5.4, a passage taken from the work entitled *al-Hidaya* by 'Ali ibn Abi Bakr ibn 'Abd al-Jalil al-Farghani al-Marghinani who died in 1197. The work itself is one of the most important texts outlining the Hanafi school of law and has gathered around itself a large number of commentaries, explaining the more difficult passages and expanding the detail even further.

1.5 THEOLOGY

The development of theology in Islam stems, once again, from the contemplation of the twin sources of authority: the Qur'an and *hadith*. The process of arriving at some sense of religious self-definition involved a systematic explanation of what it meant to be a Muslim and, while that process may be seen to start within the Qur'an itself, it is only really in the later centuries, when political and social problems of the Islamic community come to the fore, that theology as such begins to emerge.

The common adage in Islamic theory that there is no separation between religion and politics is seen fully in action in the most commonly accepted theory of the rise of Islamic theology. After the death of Muhammad in 632, a series of four men took over the leadership of the community, these four considered to have been selected by the elders of the community as suitable leaders. These men were Abu Bakr, who ruled for only two years; 'Umar, who ruled for ten years and under whom a large part of the Islamic conquests were undertaken; 'Uthman, who ruled from 644 to 656; and 'Ali who died in 661.

'Uthman managed to create a degree of ill-will among certain portions of his community; he was accused of favouring his own family above everyone else in making political appointments to positions of power in the ever-expanding empire. Apparently more ill-feeling was created by his act of collecting the Qur'an and then sending his copy out while ordering that all other versions be destroyed. A group of malcontents gathered in Medina in 656 and assassinated him.

'Ali was appointed as the fourth ruler over the Muslims. He, however, did not pursue the matter of the death of 'Uthman by searching out the guilty parties and prosecuting them. Rather, he left the matter unresolved. Mu'awiya, a member of 'Uthman's family who had been appointed governor of Syria by 'Uthman, took up the case of his kinsman and claimed that it was his duty to avenge his death. 'Ali and Mu'awiya met in battle at a place called Siffin and fought until an agreement was made to submit the matter to arbitration. The issue to be decided was basically one of whether or not 'Uthman had been justly killed: were his errors acts which breached divine law and thus made him an apostate and therefore liable to be killed?

One portion of 'Ali's supporters disagreed with this entire procedure, saying that there could be no judgement except by God and thus that the battle between the parties should continue so that God could decide who was correct by deciding the outcome of the battle. As a result, this group, which became known as the Kharijites, withdrew all support from 'Ali; not only did they feel that 'Uthman was a grave sinner and deserving of death (they had, after all, been fighting on the side of 'Ali), they reached the conclusion that 'Ali, too, had sinned by virtue of his decision to submit to arbitration and thus that he too must be fought to the end. Their platform became one which required that people must rebel against an unjust ruler. 'Ali was eventually assassinated by a Kharijite rebel in the year 661 and Mu'awiya was able to gain full control of the empire in the disruption that followed those events. Mu'awiya set up a ruling family – giving rule to his son and so on down the line – that was called the Umayyad dynasty which survived until the 'Abbasid revolution in the year 750.

Such are the events as they are generally sketched out in early Islamic history. The use of military force in these disputes indicates that there was probably a lot more at stake than simply the matter of the justness of 'Uthman's murder; these disputes were as much over power and the question of who was to rule the community as anything else, if not even more so. But the events are read by Muslim historians and by many Islamicists as reflecting theological disputes taking place early on in the community. Whether this is historically accurate is certainly under debate, but the theological reading of the early history of the community reveals, at the very least, the dimensions of the various groups and the questions which plagued them in the early centuries.

The Kharijites are a group who theologically represent the position that all actions can be judged by comparison with the prescriptions of the Qur'an and the *sunna*. Those who fall short can be declared to be grave sinners or unbelievers and are thus to be excluded from membership in the community. This is a strident position; it forces action on the part of the Kharijites against all who do not agree with their stance. A group whose origins are certainly unclear emerges with a position which urges more of a preservation of the *status quo*. Known as the Murji'a, this group argued that decisions regarding the status in the community of people who appeared not to be complying with the divine law must be left to God. A profession of faith was all that was necessary for someone to be judged a member of the community, while the external actions of a person cannot be judged as an indication of the person's interior faith – only God can actually judge in such matters. Classically, in the case of 'Ali and 'Uthman, neither should have been killed for both claimed to be Muslims. A further dispute within this camp took place over the question of whether actions ever affected the status of a believer in Islam. Some argued that one either had faith or one did not and that actions were something simply added to that but which had no bearing on one's status; the reward for good actions would come in the hereafter. This is a position generally associated with the jurist Abu Hanifa, who argued that since people were considered fully Muslim before the revelation and the formation of the body of law in Islam, one's status as a Muslim could not be affected by one's actions at all. The other position, adopted by the group commonly referred to as the traditionalists (and one which comes the closest to later orthodoxy) and often identified with the jurist Ibn Hanbal (see 1.4 and 1.7) argued that there could be degrees of faith. That is, one could be a better Muslim than someone else depending upon one's actions; this position therefore does not put off all recognition of one's good works until the hereafter but rather sees some reward for them in the here and now.

The basic dispute, therefore, was one of who is and who is not a Muslim. How was this concept 'Muslim' to be defined? The rights and privileges of community membership were at stake. But this was not the only theological matter at issue. The question of free will versus predestination also became a major topic for dispute and factionalisation. The origins of this dispute are frequently traced once again to political positions; whether or not this is historically valid is debatable but the dimensions of the question once again become clear when viewed in such a light. Another possible explanation of the origins of this dispute is suggested to be found in contemplation of the Qur'an, where contradictory statements would, at least on the surface, appear to be found. Politically, it is suggested that the Umayyads encouraged a position of predestination in order to bolster their claims to leadership and the legitimacy of their rule. The Umayyad caliphs were presented as God's appointed rulers on earth and the entire matter had been predestined; it could not have turned out any other way than it did. As such, of course, armed rebellion against the ruler was rebellion against God and such rebellion put one outside the Muslim community and liable to death. It is suggested, however, that many pious Muslims simply could not go along with that. Were they supposed simply to sit back and let the ruler do as he liked even if it was fully against Islamic principles? Surely those deeds which the rulers did which were wrong could not have been predestined by God. Surely people must have free will. The earliest group to adopt this stance was known as the Qadarite party, meaning those who argue concerning *qadar*, God's decree. The earliest position was that good acts of humans come from God and that evil acts must originate in the individual; God, being just and merciful, could not be the author of evil. The position becomes most fully elaborated in what is likely to be one of the earliest theological treatises in Islam, the *Risala* or 'letter' ascribed to al-Hasan al-Basri, who was born in 642 and died in 728 and lived in the city of Basra, presented here in 6.1. The author was a distinguished religious teacher in early Islam who became an important symbolic figure for many different groups, including the mystics especially, as a legitimiser of any given position. He is, therefore, a figure clouded in some mystery and the ascription of this letter to him may well be suspected as fraudulent. Regardless of that, however, in this short work the author argues on the basis of the Qur'an that humans have a free will; he argues against interpreting the Qur'an as predestinatory, taking any phrase in the scripture which would suggest otherwise (e.g. 'God sends astray whom He will') as only appropriately interpreted in the light of other statements (e.g. 'God sends astray the evil-doers'), that is, that people are already evildoers by their own free choice and God merely sends them away after their decision.

It is from this early Qadarite party that the origins of the speculative theological group known as the Mu'tazilites arise. Developing what is known as the *kalam*, the Mu'tazilites are generally seen as the group responsible for the incorporation of Greek philosophical thought into the Islamic theological milieu. A number of paths would have produced this blending. The Greek philosophical tradition had been preserved by various Christian groups in the Near Eastern area; Muslim contact with these groups, especially in the context of inter-religious dispute, is likely to have been a major factor in Muslims being forced to defend themselves in the terms of the Christian philosophical presuppositions. Conversion of Christians to Islam would also have led to the infusion of Greek ideas.

Around the time of the rise of the 'Abbasids in 750, the Mu'tazilites started to gain prominence. Their platform centred on five principles which united the group amidst some lack of uniformity in doctrine over-all. The group championed the idea of the unity of God and all the implications of that idea. God is one and nothing can be allowed to impinge upon that; not only does the Qur'an state this but logic demands it as well, they argued. The second element of Mu'tazilite thinking centred on the idea of God being just; in fact, the Mu'tazilites were often known as the 'People of Unity and Justice'. This was especially connected to the doctrine of free will. God would be neither just nor good if He punished people for acts for which they were not responsible; humans must be free.

One implication of the notion of the justice of God and free will also relates to the doctrine of the unity of God and the exact status of the Qur'an. The Qur'an seems to say of itself that it is the Word of God and is recorded in heaven on the heavenly tablet and that it was 'brought down' on a single night. Does not the notion of the Qur'an as the Word of God imply that the words of the text are eternal alongside God, God's attributes definitely having to be eternal alongside Him? If the Qur'an as a finite book is eternal alongside God, then have we not denied the unity of God?

The Mu'tazilites denied that the Qur'an was pre-existent before its revelation and asserted that it, like any other finite object, was created but remained the speech of God without being fully identical to an attribute of the divine.

The Mu'tazilite's stance may be summed up with three further principles. The promise and the threat states that God has promised, and thus must, reward good and punish evil. The grave sinner will be punished eternally in hell and, for most of the Mu'tazilites at least, would never escape from there. This is contrary to most later orthodox thought and was at the time a counter-argument to the Murji'a who held that even the known grave sinner was to be treated as a believer, an attitude which could encourage moral laxity, the Mu'tazilites believed, and was to be countered by the threat of hell. Directly related to this is the fourth principle, that one cannot judge the grave sinner and must leave the question to God. This position is usually connected to al-Hasan al-Basri; while the Kharijites said that one should kill the grave sinner and the Murji'ites said that such a person should be treated as a believer, Hasan held to the intermediate position, that such a person could be declared neither a believer nor an unbeliever but rather a hypocrite. Practically, this position is no different from that of the Murji'a and was politically neutral, but it was a moral position that was seen to be more stringent.

Finally, the Mu'tazilites held to the principle of commanding the right and forbidding the wrong, a common Qur'anic phrase which in this context probably arose from political situations, that armed rebellion against a criminal ruler was justified, at least, many added, when there was a likely chance of success.

The Mu'tazilite's position is that revelation is to be understood in the light of reason. God's actions which can be observed – that is, in the way in which the world operates – can be seen as rational; for God to be consistent, all His actions must be rational. Thus reason/rationality must interpret revelation. Now, this led to the charge by anti-rationalists that God was being made subject to human reason. This kind of objection to Mu'tazilite procedures led to a reaction against them, a reaction that was most significantly based upon the use of rational tools just as for the Mu'tazilites but with a bit less audacity perhaps. It is in that reaction that the foundations of Muslim orthodoxy are to be found.

It would be wrong to assume that the entire Muslim population or even a major proportion of it ever got caught up in the Mu'tazilite movement during the 'Abbasid period. More likely is that 'traditional' thought predominated, clinging to the notion of predestination and a 'literal' interpretation of the Qur'an. Early in the tenth century, this type of traditional thought received a sound basis through rational argumentation especially in the work of al-Ash'ari (d. 942). This author's method was to use extensively the basic Muslim source materials – the Qur'an and the *sunna* – on which to base his rational arguments. He fully supported the position of predestination: God is all-powerful and all-knowing; He creates the power for individuals to act yet those people are responsible for their own actions, partially at least because people feel responsible. Al-Ash'ari appears to use the term 'acquisition' in this sense. Likewise, God's attributes are real and, thus, it is meaningful to talk of God's hand and God's throne. Al-Ash'ari argued fully against de-anthropomorphism; the fact is, according to him, that we just do not know how these things are but they are there and they must be accepted on faith *bi-la kayf*, without knowing how.

It is out of the theological position and method of al-Ash'ari, and out of the theological agenda established by the Mu'tazilites, that Muslim orthodoxy is revealed in the creedal statement of Ibn Qudama in 6.2 and the more popular theological statement of 6.3. Ibn Qudama al-Maqdisi was a Hanbalite lawyer and theologian who lived from 1146 to 1223 in Damascus and Baghdad. His creedal statement is hortatory in character, being addressed to a specific group of people in the statement: 'O brothers!' The urging that takes place in the document for its audience to adhere to the Qur'an and the *sunna* and the dire warnings concerning the heretics which come at the end indicate as well that this document probably had its origin as an address to a specific audience. The content of the creed itself can be traced back to earlier Hanbalite sources[4] and thus represents a late distillation of a tradition which probably originated in that form some 200 years prior to Ibn Qudama himself. There are, however, several technical distinctions which have emerged over the centuries which distinguish Ibn Qudama's position from the contemporary position of the Ash'arite school with whom Ibn Qudama had a running dispute. Of concern were matters such as precisely how to define faith and the extent to which reason could be used in determining the nature of God. Ibn Qudama's position was influenced by the mystical heritage of Ibn Hanbal (see 1.7, 8.1) and the rejection of anything considered to be non-traditional which moved people away from the Qur'an and the *sunna*.

To a greater extent than the Christian churches, the Islamic schools of theology teach their students the logical structure of God's qualities. Muhammad al-Fadali al-Shafi'i was rector of al-Azhar in Cairo for many years and died in 1821. His catechism, portions of which are provided in 6.3, was the textbook on the principles of theology at al-Azhar for the most part of the first half of the nineteenth century. Whether his work was an original piece of work or based upon the work of another scholar, as is often the case with such texts, is an issue which still requires investigation. It is certain, though, that his catechism had authority in all parts of the Shafi'ite world; it has been translated into Swahili as well as Malay and Javanese.

The chief satisfying aspect for philosophers in al-Fadali's catechism is its logical simplicity. The qualities of God are all based on and derived from the one fundamental property, namely that God is absolute. From this follows His other basic qualities: uniqueness, otherness, omniscience, omnipresence, and eternity. Step by step we are led to realize that from the simple assumption of the one God, the Islamic concepts of God's absolute power and human predestination are inescapable conclusions.

From this it follows, with equally unavoidable logic, that people owe God complete submission as His slaves. Since nothing exists which God did not create and nothing happens which He does not do, people have no option but to follow the direction of God's will. This is the popular philosophy of Islam; not all Islamic scholars agree with it but a vast majority of the common people in Islamic countries do.

1.6 SECTARIAN MOVEMENTS

To a degree quite distinct from Christianity, Islam has not fractured into numerous sects over the fourteen centuries of its existence. There have, of course, been various splits, especially within the theological field (see 1.5) where Muslim theologians, intent on explicating a statement attributed to Muhammad, but obviously invented after the fact, compiled lists of seventy-odd sects which comprised Islam, only one of which, it was generally understood, would be 'saved'. Many of these sects were, in fact, little more than slightly variant doctrines connected to names of various individual thinkers in early Islam; they did not, in reality, represent true sectarian divisions.

The Shi'a of 'Ali, the son-in-law and cousin of Muhammad, however, would appear to be a different matter. This was not a dispute over theological interpretation so much as a struggle over political power with religious implications, as has been outlined above in 1.5. 'Ali's cause became a rallying point for rebellion against the Umayyad dynasty, only to be crushed or out-manoeuvred by other parties.

The work entitled *Nahj al-balagha*, 'The manner of eloquence', is a collection of sermons, sayings, and letters attributed to 'Ali and edited from earlier sources by al-Sharif al-Radi who lived from 969 to 1016 in Baghdad. The very collecting together of these literary pieces indicates the reverence paid by the Shi'a to the person of 'Ali as the rightful inheritor of the right to rule the Muslim community; just as in the case of Muhammad, every word uttered is worthy of being remembered. More than that, the word of 'Ali is considered to be third only to the word of God and the word of Muhammad in its beauty – a concept here considered to encompass meaning, content, and style. The book itself contains some 245 sermons, 75 letters, and 200 sayings from which four sermons and one letter have been excerpted here in 7.1.1. 'Ali praises the family of Muhammad in his sermons, thereby suggesting a justification for his claim to pre-eminence; also emphasized are his struggles on the side of true Islam against other, spiritually weaker members of the community. 'Ali is also displayed as having knowledge of the return of the twelfth *imam* at the end of time.

One of the central motifs of Shi'ite thought becomes the lamenting over the family of 'Ali, most especially with the understood martyrdom of 'Ali's son Husayn at Karbala in Iraq. The tales of the battles and Husayn's eventual death (7.1.2, 7.1.3) are told throughout the Shi'ite world and cannot fail to produce tears in those who listen and participate. The events surrounding the death of Husayn have become a ceremony celebrated annually during the first ten days of the month of Muharram, culminating in the day of 'Ashura, 10 Muharram, a day of great significance in the Shi'ite world and the day which focuses on this most celebrated of all Islamic legends. Every year, millions of his faithful followers in Iraq, Iran, Pakistan, India, and East Africa commemorate the sad events with rituals of mourning. A replica of the mausoleum at Karbala is carried around and the mourners sing hymns and recite prayers during the procession and the night-long mosque service that follows it. Scenes of self-flagellation are common occurrences during the procession.

The 'sacrifice' of Husayn is compared to Abraham's readiness to sacrifice his son in obedience to God and that sacrifice is celebrated on the same day of

'Ashura with the slaughter of a sheep. This underlies the parallelism with the passion of Jesus in Christianity who is also compared to the lamb slaughtered by Abraham (see 3.1.2). The attachment of the people of the Shi'a to their 'Prince Husayn' is so strong that they will weep and sob on the day commemorating his passion. Naturally, an elaborate literature has grown up around the mysterious person of Husayn, in prose and in verse, historical and legendary, in which the famous martyr is celebrated. Many poets and bards, professionals and amateurs, will recite or chant verses in which the passion of Husayn and his family's sufferings are described in detail and the preachers will admonish their audiences about this irreparable loss, moving them to tears. Songs, eulogies, dirges, and prose works have been composed in Arabic, Persian, Malay, Gujarati, Swahili, Turkish, and Urdu for the purpose of being read or proclaimed on the night of 'Ashura.

Husayn was the most loved scion of the 'house', that is of the 'Alids or the family of Muhammad. The tradition stresses that he was by inclination a scholar, studying scripture and recording law as expounded by his grandfather Muhammad. The text in 7.1.2 comes from a 4,000 line epic in Swahili on the passion of Prince Husayn. It is very similar in content to several epic poems in Persian and Urdu.

In Iran, Iraq, and Pakistan, followers of the Shi'a perform these poetic texts in a kind of theatre called *ta'ziya*, 'mourning' in honour of Husayn. The 'death camp' of 7.1.3 is one of the most popular tragedies belonging to the tradition of the *ta'ziya*; it comes from a Swahili version stemming from an unknown poet who probably originally came from India. Developed in Iran during the last half millennium, the performances connected to the recitation of these poems have become quite elaborate. Yet this tradition cannot really be compared to European drama. A small group of performers, professionals or amateurs, will recite rather than enact the words of the heroes and heroines. The parts are endlessly spun-out and repetitious, as the surviving women lament the fate of the dying men and babies. The details are rather bloody, comparable to some Shakespearean scenes. Invariably the audience will weep sorrowfully while the performance goes on; all that is a part of the tradition of 'Ashura. An oft-repeated phrase is: 'May my soul be a ransom for you'; the virtue of sacrificing oneself as a ransom for one's people is thus constantly inculcated and has resulted in the readiness of the followers of the Shi'a to risk death for their cause.

The Shi'ites themselves have suffered several splits during their history, all stemming from disputes over who precisely had inherited the leadership or position of rightful *imam*; the Zaydis, the Druze, and the Isma'ilis are prominent divisions, separate from the main group who are known as the Ithna 'Ashariyya or 'twelver' division, found today primarily in Iran. The Isma'ilis have likewise themselves suffered splits, with the group known as the Nizaris predominating today, especially those Isma'ilis of East African origin. Led by the Aga Khan, the living *imam* present in the world today (a central item of

Nizari Isma'ili thought, in contrast to all other Shi'ite groups who have seen their lines of *imams* come to an end with the last one generally going into 'occultation'), the group has been deeply influenced by Hinduism and is marked by its utter devotion to its leader. Such aspects are revealed in the Ginans or hymns and prayers (7.2.1), which are sung or intoned in the *jamatkhana* or prayer house. The hymns are old songs composed in a language that is a mixture of Urdu, Sindhi, Gujarati, and Balochi, thought to be of medieval origin. Rather than being truly hymns in praise of God, the Ginans are more comparable to the Islamic texts called *wasiyya* in Arabic, 'exhortation' or 'admonition'. One recurrent theme in them is the payment of the tithe, *dashond*, some twelve per cent of one's income paid to the Aga Khan to be spent as he wishes on projects of communal benefit. Complete trust is vested in the person of the Aga Khan by his followers, for he is the living Qur'an in the community and a manifestation of God in the world; he is the interpreter of God's will for his community and all who accept him. His words (7.2.2) are fully authoritative and unconditionally valid. As this passage implies, he possesses the only correct interpretation of the Qur'an and he shares it with his devoted followers. The mystical tendencies of the commentary are evident, indicating the influence of both Sufism and Hinduism.

A more modern split within the Shi'ite environment, although one which declares its independence from Islam and describes itself as 'an independent world religion' and whose members do not consider themselves Muslims, is the Baha'i faith. The movement takes as its starting-point in history the date of 23 May 1844. It was on this day that a young merchant of Shiraz, Sayyid 'Ali Muhammad, declared himself to be a messenger of God, thereby bringing to an end the dispensation of Muhammad. The work known as the *Bayan*, written in Persian (7.3.1) is his main work, in which a new *shari'a* or way of life, is formulated. For the heresy of declaring himself a prophet, the Bab, as Sayyid 'Ali Muhammad became known, was imprisoned and eventually killed by a firing squad on 9 July 1850 at the age of 31. During those six years, the Bab's literary output in Persian and Arabic was enormous and only a fraction of it has been published.

In the Persian *Bayan* of the Bab, many references are made to *man yuzhiruhu Allah*, he whom God will make manifest: 'At the time of the manifestation of him whom God shall make manifest, everyone should be well trained in the teachings of the *Bayan*, so that none of the followers may outwardly cling to the *Bayan* and thus forfeit their allegiance unto him. If anyone does so, the verdict of 'disbeliever in God' shall be passed upon him. . . . Take good heed of yourselves for the sum total of the religion of God is but to help him, rather than to observe, in the time of his appearance, such deeds as are prescribed in the *Bayan*'.[5] It was Mirza Husayn 'Ali Nuri, born on 12 November 1817, one of the foremost disciples of the Bab, who recognised himself as 'He whom God will make manifest' in 1853 while he was imprisoned in Tehran. Baha'u'llah, as he became known, made his claim public some ten years later in Baghdad. His writings (7.3.2), which are marked by claims to absolute divine authority, comprise well over 100 titles, all of which are considered scripture by the Baha'is. He died in Palestine in 1892.

'Abdu'l-Baha, the oldest son of Baha'u'llah, was born on the same day that the Bab made his declaration – 23 May 1844. He is held by Baha'is to be the 'Centre of the Covenant of Baha'u'llah' and the perfect exemplar of Baha'i life. His extremely active life was marked by visits to Europe and North America in the attempt to spread his father's religion. He was a prolific author and many of his writings, as sampled in 7.3.3, make attempts to distill the so-called twelve Baha'i principles out of his father's writings: oneness of God, oneness of religion, oneness of humanity, independent investigation of the truth (as opposed to blind obedience), world government, universal language, equality of men and women, universal compulsory education, economic problems of the world soluble only through spiritual/moral and ethical means, abolition of all forms of prejudice, harmony of science and religion, and universal peace.

Upon 'Abdu'l-Baha's death on 26 November 1921, his grandson, Shoghi Effendi, assumed the office of the Guardian in accord with the provisions of his grandfather's will. Through his efforts, the Baha'i faith has spread to many countries of the world. Shoghi Effendi's writings (7.3.4), while not considered divine revelations, are considered binding upon Baha'is; it is, in fact, his vision which characterises the central concerns of the Baha'i community today. Upon his death on 4 November, 1957, the affairs of the Faith passed to a group of people known as 'Hands of the Cause' who continued in this capacity until the election of the first House of Justice in 1963. Today the Baha'is of the world look to and depend upon the House of Justice, located in Haifa, Israel, for guidance in subjects not specifically dealt with in the scriptures of their faith.

The Ahmadiyya schism, on the other hand, is totally insistent that its members are Muslims despite the attempts of many people, including the government of Pakistan in recent years, to declare the group non-Islamic. The movement was founded by Mirza Ghulam Ahmad (d. 1908) in Qadian, India, with the proclamation that he was to be the reformer of Islam in the fourteenth century of the religion's existence. This by itself is not an overly contentious claim in the Islamic context; each century was foretold to have its reformer. The Ahmadiyya stress, therefore, the reforming nature of Ghulam Ahmad's career. Crucial to the dispute between the Ahmadiyya and the rest of Islam (Sunni, most especially) was, and continues to be, Ghulam Ahmad's claim to receive divine guidance of a type limited to prophets. His explanation of his revelatory experiences (7.4) is crucial to the debate; at stake was the finality of Muhammad's prophethood. The text itself was presented in Lahore at a conference of the 'Great Religions' held in December 1896. The introduction suggests that the paper itself was not a result of 'human effort' but rather was 'a sign from among the signs of God'. The very aim of the paper was to provide the listener with 'a new faith'. The other groups who were to be represented at the conference would find that their positions paled in comparison to Ghulam Ahmad's.

As a movement today, the Ahmadiyya has spread widely throughout the world, placing special emphasis on missionary activity especially among Muslims in West and East Africa but also among Christians in Europe and North America. Their publication programme is the clearest manifestation of their presence, with translations of the Qur'an being given away in many languages along with many other simple appeals to draw people to a purified Islam in the same manner as many of the modern reformers who stay within the confines of orthodoxy (see 1.8).

1.7 MYSTICISM

Some have seen in the mystical movement in Islam known as Sufism the way in which the Muslim religion was prevented from falling into total legalism and through which there was maintained a value for religious experience and expressions of piety in non-formal ways. That Sufism introduced its own dangers into Islam is apparent from a great deal of modernist polemic which directs itself against the 'evils' of saint worship and the like as well as decrying many of its theological elaborations.

Sufism is a mystical movement and like all such things that go by the term mystical, it is separated from other kinds of religious piety by the ideas that, one, its practitioners believe in the possibility of direct communication with or knowledge of God, and that, two, such communication or knowledge can be achieved through human effort by means of specific practices. Such mystics devote their lives through various means – often renouncing day-to-day worldly existence – to the search for a closer relationship with God.

Such persons are claimed to have existed early on in Islam, rejecting both the political involvement of the theological sects and the very way of life of the politicians themselves. Such people put more store on their personal religious experience than on the developing traditional practices, believing themselves to have come to a better understanding of what the Qur'an means and what its purpose is. Such people looked to the figure of Muhammad for support of their conception of Islam and books were compiled, such as that by Ibn Hanbal, represented in 8.1, which gather together reports about the life of Muhammad which reflect the ascetic ideal.

Ahmad ibn Hanbal was a prominent theologian, jurist, and traditionist who lived from 780 to 855 in Baghdad; he is the eponymous leader of the Hanbalite school of law (see 1.4). He travelled extensively in the Hijaz, the Yemen, and Syria, and throughout Iraq. The major work for which he is famous is his *Musnad*, a vast compendium of *hadith*, classified not by subject as with the famous 'six books' but by the names of the final guarantors of the *isnad*. He was a jurist of the highest ability, using the full extent of his subtle powers of judgement. Ibn Hanbal was also important as a theological figure. He believed in the reality of the attributes of God as described in the Qur'an but yet affirmed, against the anthropomorphists, that God cannot be compared to anything but Himself. His *Kitab al-zuhd*, 'Book of Renunciation', (8.1) is a collection of *hadith* (although for brevity the *isnads* have been omitted in the translation) describing Muhammad's life as it encourages asceticism. Such a book fits into the over-all ethical stance of its author. All action must serve God and faith consists of the combination of inner belief and outer action; faith is total commitment on the part of the individual which requires sincerity before God, renunciation of the world, relinquishing of desires, fear of God, and a discerning mind with regard to the law. The asceticism encouraged in the traditions from Muhammad, therefore, is the basis of practices that should be cultivated by all Muslims, not only those who declare themselves 'Sufis' as such.

Like the figure of Muhammad, the Qur'an too became a source of doctrine as well as a basis upon which to argue for the legitimacy of the mystic quest, as revealed in Ibn 'Ata''s commentary (8.2). Abu'l-'Abbas Ahmad al-Adami, who was known as Ibn 'Ata', was born in *c.* 850 and died as a result of a beating received while defending his compatriot in Sufism al-Hallaj, in 992, some two weeks before the latter's execution for heresy. He lived his entire life in Baghdad, starting out as a Hanbalite traditionist but coming more and more under the influence of Ibn Hanbal's ascetic way of life. He believed, according to Louis Massignon, in the social dimension of the mystical life as being in essence 'fraternal mutual aid, the works of mercy and mystical substitution, all conceived as ways of leading to union with God'.[6] The work of Ibn 'Ata' is preserved in the *tafsir* of Abu 'Abd al-Rahman al-Sulami (941–1021) who incorporated the isolated Qur'anic glosses of the earlier scholar into his own book *Haqa'iq al-tafsir*, 'The Truths in Exegesis'. Ibn 'Ata' goes beyond simply trying to justify the mystic quest in terms of the Qur'an; he has the aim of wanting to bring out the allusions found in the text, so that those who search after mystic experience will understand them.

From the eleventh century, Sufism began to become institutionalised, creating monasteries and rites of initiation and showing an increased tendency towards creating a theological basis from which all of Sufism could be derived. One major figure from the time was al-Ghazzali (d. 1111 – see 1.4, 5.2) whose writings have one over-all point and that is to argue for the legitimacy and even necessity of the mystic quest.

The creation of the Sufi *tariqas* or brotherhoods, usually named after a great Sufi master, created an institutionalised mysticism that has survived down to our own day. The members of such orders generally follow the doctrine and practices associated with the eponym of their order as their way to union with God. One of the obvious things which separates such groups then is the practice – what is chanted, what is used in general to produce ecstatic states: poetry, dancing, music.

'Abd al-Qadir al-Jilani, who was born in 1077 and died in Baghdad in 1166, is probably the best-known saint in Islam and is still the most widely venerated one. His tomb in Baghdad, over which Sultan Sulayman built a fine monument in 1535, is still a goal of many pilgrims; his works (mainly prayers attributed to him) are still being printed in Cairo and he is well known in Pakistan and Muslim India. His veneration is so common in West Africa that the Algerians claim that he was born in their country even though his name suggests he was born in the province of Jilan in northern Persia along the coast of the Caspian Sea. 'Abd al-Qadir is also frequently mentioned in Hausa literature from Nigeria;[7] he is venerated in Kenya and Zaire. In Swahili, there is a printed booklet of tales of his miracles and in Javanese there is a much bigger work on his life and works. He has thus become the most universal of all the Islamic saints. It is often difficult to assess in the numerous tales that are told about him where history ends and legend begins but those who believe in him are, of course, not concerned with such matters.

The legends of 'Abd al-Qadir presented in 8.3 have been taken from collections of tales told about him in North, West, and East Africa, and Indonesia as well as the Middle East. Most of the tales selected here are extremely popular and are retold in many languages. Some can be recognised as being of pre-Islamic origin. The essence of the tales is not in being episodes from the saint's life but in being fables and legends, that is tales with a moral lesson. For instance, the story of the chicken bones suggests that a disciple has to eat dry bread first; then, when he has achieved complete power over all his physical desires by continuous asceticism, he will also have the power to bring dead animals back to life. The tale of the sandals becoming lethal weapons emphasises God's power to use anyone or anything He wishes to punish the wicked and to destroy even a gang of criminals. A saint is a person who understands this and so is able to help God's plans along by working for Him.

The *dhikr* ('remembrance' or 'repetitive prayer') of the *tariqa* connected to the figure of 'Abd al-Qadir, the Qadiriyya, is documented in 8.4. These prayers were selected from texts in Arabic, some written down by scribes belonging to the Qadiriyya by special request, others coming from printed prayer books published by the Qadiriyya for their members' use. The Qadiriyya is one of the oldest Sufi sects and is still very widespread, stretching from West Africa to Indonesia. The members of the Qadiriyya are married, as are most Sufis, and persons who claim descent from 'Abd al-Qadir are still alive and are leaders of the community. They are addressed as 'Our Tijanis' (literally 'Our Crowns') in these prayers. The Qadiriyya is a *tariqa* in the sense that it provides a path (*tariqa*) to paradise according to its followers. This path involves rituals consisting of prayers such as the ones given here which are performed during the night. The (mainly male) members come together and recite these prayers from the time following the evening prayer until dawn. At midnight they pause for a meal. The Qadiri prayers contain repetitions of the same and similar formulae, including items such as the ninety-nine names of

God, and are accompanied by rhythmic movements of the body. Thus the faithful bow and rise up many hundreds of times until some of them go into a trance; this does not appear to be the actual purpose of the exercises, for at least some groups of the Qadiriyya do not encourage the practice. The beatific vision and the mystic union which are the ultimate purpose of every mystic are not the direct result of these religious exercises but may be attained only much later after many years of meditation, concentration, and abstinence. Exercises of this kind are, in fact, organised for the younger members of the group who use the *dhikr* as a way of 'remembering God and repeating His praises'.[8]

The Javanese have always been a very religious people. They have an ancient culture in which Hinduism was blended with the religion of the original Malayo-Polynesian or Austronesian type. Later, during the Middle Ages, Buddhism was introduced and the Javanese learned to worship the Bodhisatt-vas alongside Shiva and Indra. In the late Middle Ages, Islam was introduced by merchants from the western Indian Ocean and began to spread slowly across the island. Compared to the quick Islamisation by conquest of other parts of Asia, in Java the expansion of Islam was peaceful, so that the Javanese retained many features of their ancient culture and so, preserved their unique Javanese identity. As a result, they created a unique island Islamic culture in which mysticism played a much greater role than in the heartlands of Islam. Their Islam still reflects a certain spirit of Buddhist pacifism, not being motivated by the strong mercantilism of those who brought Islam to their country. The Javanese spirit has been raised in the warm valleys of what has been described by many travellers as the most beautiful island on earth. Grace and gentle beauty surround the children of Java so that they imagine a divine world without conflict, a dreamy heaven that could hardly be more colourful than their own island. Their relationship with God is likewise of a gentle and benign character, one which expresses itself in a tolerance for many things. Some people are permitted even now to bring food and flowers to aged statues of gods and Buddhas or to the graves of famous saints and ancestors. Javanese religion is all-embracing rather than proudly exclusivist. Since the Javanese now number about seventy million, they are among the most numerous of all Islamic peoples.

The text 8.5 contains an anthology of admonitions and wise sayings from one of the oldest preserved manuscripts from Indonesia. The manuscript, written in Javanese script on palm-leaf strips, was brought to Holland with one of the first voyages to the Far East from Amsterdam in the late sixteenth century. It contains numerous excerpts from various Islamic scholars, Arabic, Indian, and Indonesian, some Javanese, some Malay; some texts which were originally written in Arabic were translated into Javanese.

The contents of the manuscript are, for a minor part, concerned with law, and, for a more considerable part, theology and dogmatics; the largest part is devoted to *tasawwuf* (becoming a Sufi), passages about unification with God and the disappearance of the self (*fana'*), the practice of *dhikr*, the experience of divine proximity, the visibility of the divine countenance, the three stages on the way to God (staying within the law of Islam, taking the path to God, and witnessing the ultimate reality), the necessity to perform ascetic practices, to make extreme efforts, and to surrender oneself trustingly to God. There is no apparent order in the texts, no sequence from lower to higher, from elementary to advanced. Some free renderings of the most beautiful parts have been given.

Little is known of the life of the author of 8.6, 'Aziz ibn Muhammad al-Nasafi. He was still living after 1281 and was a member of the Kubrawiyya Sufi order, founded by Najmuddin Kubra who was born in 1145 in Central Asia and died in 1220. A mystic path which can lead individual disciples to God's qualities in heaven, who may then incorporate those qualities in themselves is the aim of the quest for the Kubrawiyya. The path requires abstinence from as much food as possible, complete surrender to their *shaykh* ('spiritual guide'), constant ritual purity, fasting, silence and retreat, constant recollection of God, giving up resistance to God's decree, and refraining from prayer for reward in the hereafter. Al-Nasafi's work is entitled *Maksad-i aksa*, 'The Remotest Aim', in its Persian translation, apparently made from a Turkish original; it outlines his understanding of the path and the goal of the mystic quest.

1.8 INTERPRETATIONS OF ISLAM IN THE MODERN WORLD

In looking at the modern situation of any religion, the essential questions are how do people react to change going on around them and what is their attitude towards the authority of the past, especially in matters of law. A threefold division is often suggested as an analysis of major trends separating various attitudes. Different names are given to these groups by different scholars but the divisions are basically the same. The normative or orthodox group sees the past (as they envisage it) as legitimately leading to the present and that the past is sufficient to guide people today. The neo-normative or revivalist group demands a reinterpretation of the present through a re-evaluation and re-creation of the past such that it fits within the modern context. The acculturationists or modernisers tend to legitimise the modern context by reference to the past.

An example from the Islamic context will put this in perspective. Polygamy is a contentious issue in modern Islam, although no one doubts that Muslims in the past saw polygamy as legitimised by their religion. For the normative group, this is sufficient as an explanation of the phenomenon and, as a result, there can be no objection to it; to think otherwise is simply to accept Western standards of morality. For the neo-normativists, the emphasis is on the Qur'an; the Qur'an was aiming at monogamy by its pronouncements and now that fact is recognised, Muslims should live by it. In that argument, the past (i.e. the Qur'an) is re-evaluated in order to legitimise an ideal of the modern world. For the acculturationists, the basic moral point is that men and women are equal and thus monogamy must be right; it is, for this group, an after-the-fact point that the Qur'an will support this position.

The neo-normative position which has gained a great deal of strength and popularity in Islam in recent years, may well be seen to start with Ibn Taymiyya who died in 1328. He rejected contemporary Sufi practices – miracle working, excessive asceticism, worshipping saints, and visiting saints' tombs. If such practices could not be legitimated by reference to true traditions coming from Muhammad then such practices were not acceptable. The appeal was, as it is now, to a re-evaluated purified past of idealised practice.

A similar train of thought arose in the eighteenth century as well, primarily in the Arabian group known as the Wahhabis. Once again, the movement arose primarily against Sufism, both in its practical realm and on an intellectual plane, for example against the Sufi doctrine of God. The worshipping of saints had led to moral laxity on the part of the people, the leader of the movement Ibn 'Abd al-Wahhab (1703–92) said; furthermore, the attitude of reverence to saints and religious personalities in total had led to a blind acceptance of their authority in the interpretation of religious matters. This was wrong, according to the movement, and there must be a return to the Qur'an and *hadith* with all practices based only upon those sources. This was, and continues to be in all neo-normativist movements, a double-edged approach which can lead one of two ways. One, it can lead to an excessive reliance upon texts, leading to literalism and fundamentalism or, two, it can allow the opening up to independent reasoning and eventually even to modernism.

With the rise of the power of Europe in the nineteenth century and the political subjugation of the Islamic world, we enter truly into the 'modern period'. This European control of the Muslim countries has undoubtedly been the biggest factor in the whole contemporary picture of Islam; this has been emphasised by the introduction of Western political structures and Western administrative and juridical systems. As well, the introduction of Western culture – the press, cinema, music, translated works of European authors – has also brought about what appears to many today as a confrontation between the two systems.

One major area where the force of the confrontation is felt is in the area of social institutions. With travel and communications so improved in the modern world, with marriage and divorce serving different social functions within the modern context, the traditional system of Islam has been strained; if the traditional system is to change (and some of course would argue that it should not) then a total re-evaluation may be required. It is to this task that various reformers in the modern world have addressed themselves.

Sir Sayyid Ahmad Khan (1817–98) is often seen as setting the stage for later reformers especially in India where he was active in providing opportunities for modern education. Islam, as it was actually believed and practiced by most of its adherents, would be threatened seriously by modern advances in thought and science. What was to be done? Where was the vital centre of Islam to be located? Khan, as revealed in section 9.1, revived the position of the Mu'tazila with its overriding view of rationality. Like the early reformer in Egypt, Muhammad Abduh (1845–1905), he argued that Islam and reason were totally compatible if Islam was properly understood. His conception of Islam was generally based upon the spiritual and moral elements of the Qur'an alone.

The twentieth century has seen a greater distancing between the neo-normativists and the modernists than revealed in someone such as Khan. Sayyid Qutb (1906–66), the intellectual voice for the Muslim Brotherhood in Egypt, remains, through his writings, one of the prime enunciators of the revivalist strand of thought. His vision of Islam is a 'simple' one, based upon an idealised vision of Islam during the time of Muhammad, an Islam which should be recreated in the present. Islam has the perfect social system for humanity, one which will cure all the ills of modern society. Once a truly Muslim state is established, then Islam will come back into its own, as it was in the time of Muhammad and shortly after. It is not necessary to borrow ideas from the West, for Islam has all that is needed; an application of Islamic principles is all that is needed. In fact, the attempt to fit into the foreign models provided by the West is what has created all the modern problems for Muslims and Islam. The passage in 9.2, describing what Islam is all about, gives a synopsis of Qutb's point of view. It was written while its author was in prison between 1954 and 1964 for having conspired to kill Egyptian president Abdel Nasser. The political persecution which he felt is manifested in this book in its demands that only Islam has the answer to modern problems.

Mawlana Sayyid Abu'l-A'la Mawdudi (1903–79) was the founder of the Jama'at-i-Islami in India and, after the foundation of Pakistan, became a prime religio-political figure in that newly-created country. Educated in both modern and traditional sciences, he spent the initial period of his working life as a journalist, becoming the editor of the leading Muslim newspaper in India, al-Jam'iyat. He resigned from that position in 1928 to devote himself to writing, taking up the editorship of the monthly Tarjuman al-Qur'an in 1933; this magazine remained the major vehicle for the transmission of his ideas. His vision of the revival of Islam was based upon a return to the Qur'an and hadith, his feeling being that the true essence of Islam had been lost over time as people moved further and further away from their textual roots. Mawdudi's emigration to Pakistan in 1947 gave him a opportunity to put some of his ideas into political action in his attempt to urge the establishment of an Islamic state in Pakistan. His writings from that point on concentrated on socio-political issues and he became a major force in the political opposition in the country, as each government was attacked for its failure to institute the proper Islamic state. Mawdudi's statement on birth control (9.3) illustrates his concern with the essential issues of modern life and with his desire to create 'truly Islamic' solutions to those problems posed by the encounter with Western society by reference to the basic Muslim source material.

The Ayatullah Khumayni (1900–89) was given a religious education in Qum in Iran and then taught philosophy, ethics, and law. In the 1960s he began to criticise the Shah during his school sermons in Qum and, in March 1963, state police raided his school, killed several students, and he was arrested; after being released, he once again criticised Iranian policies especially the extent of American domination, and was arrested once again in June 1963. His arrest led to a bloody revolt which was crushed by the Shah's troops. Eventually, Khumayni was exiled and he lived from 1964 until 1979 in Iraq and France, agitating for an overthrow of the Shah and a return to Islamic principles. In February 1979, he returned to Iran to establish the Islamic Republic of Iran. The two segments reprinted here (9.4.1, 9.4.2) stem from the period shortly after that return to Iran and both express the perceived threat of the West (most especially the United States and Israel) to all of Islam; thus the urgency of the united face of Islam against its opponents is emphasised.

The desire to unify Islam is also the underlying motive behind the document produced by the Islamic Council of Europe, entitled the Universal Islamic Declaration, sections of which are reproduced in 9.5. The text was formulated in April 1980 by a number of Muslim scholars; its aim was to provide an explanation of 'the fundamental principles and salient features of the Islamic order' (introduction). The document starts with an affirmation of the traditional theological principles of Islam ('Islam's approach to life') and then provides a critique of 'The crisis of contemporary civilisation'. The excerpted portions on politics, economics, education, social policy, defence, and co-operation all indicate the modern concerns of the Muslim community in the light of the failure of modern social structures, both capitalist and communist, 'to create a balanced society'.

1.9 CHRONOLOGICAL SUMMARY

c. 570	Birth of Muhammad
c. 610	Beginning of Muhammad's Qur'anic utterances
622	Muhammad's move to Medina – the *hijra*
630	Conquest of Mecca
632	Death of Muhammad
634	Death of Abu Bakr, the first caliph
636/7	Conquest by Muslims of Damascus and Jerusalem
639/40	Conquest by Muslims of Egypt and Persia
644	Death of 'Umar, the second caliph
656	Death of 'Uthman, the third caliph
661	Death of 'Ali, the fourth caliph, Muhammad's son-in-law and figurehead of the Shi'a
661–750	Umayyad caliphate
680	Death of Mu'awiya, first caliph of the Umayyads

680	Death of Husayn, son of 'Ali
691	Construction of the Dome of the Rock in Jerusalem
711	Muslims enter Spain
713	Muslims enter India
728	Death of the theologian-mystic al-Hasan al-Basri
750–1258	'Abbasid caliphate
762	Baghdad founded
767	Death of the historian Ibn Ishaq
767	Death of the jurist-theologian Abu Hanifa
767	Death of the exegete Muqatil ibn Sulayman
795	Death of the jurist Malik ibn Anas
820	Death of the jurist al-Shafi'i
c. 835	Death of Mu'tazilite theologian al-Nazzam
855	Death of the jurist-theologian Ahmad ibn Hanbal
869	Death of the author al-Jahiz
870	Death of the traditionist al-Bukhari
875	Death of the traditionist Muslim
874	Twelfth *imam* goes into 'hiding'
886	Death of the traditionist Ibn Maja
888	Death of the traditionist Abu Dawud
892	Death of the traditionist al-Tirmidhi
909	Rise of the Isma'ili Fatimids in North Africa
915	Death of the traditionist al-Nasa'i
922	Death of the mystic Ibn 'Ata'
923	Death of the historian-exegete al-Tabari
935	Death of the theologian al-Ash'ari
944	Death of the theologian al-Maturidi
956	Beginning of conversion of Seljuk Turks to Islam
969	Cairo founded
973	Al-Azhar founded in Cairo
996	Death of the grammarian al-Rummani
1016	Death of Shi'i writer al-Sharif al-Radi
1021	Death of the mystic al-Sulami
1037	Death of the teacher al-Baghdadi
1099	Crusaders capture Jerusalem
1111	Death of the mystic-theologian al-Ghazzali
1149	Death of the judge Ibn Musa ibn 'Iyad
1166	Death of the mystic 'Abd al-Qadir al-Jilani
1187	Saladin retakes Jerusalem for the Muslims
1197	Death of the jurist al-Marghinani
1220	Death of the mystic Najmuddin Kubra
1223	Death of the theologian Ibn Qudama
1229	Jerusalem ceded to Frederick II
1244	Turks take Jerusalem

1258	Baghdad destroyed by Mongols
1277	Death of the jurist al-Nawawi
after 1281	Death of the mystic al-Nasafi
1294	Death of the scholar al-Busiri
1328	Death of the reformer-theologian Ibn Taymiyya
1373	Death of the exegete-historian Ibn Kathir
1453	Ottoman Turks capture Constantinople
1492	Expulsion of Muslims from Spain
1524	Death of the governor Muhammad ibn Iyas
c. 1550	Islam in Cambodia
16th C.	Islam in Borneo
1573	Death of the writer Najm al-Din al-Ghayti
1744	Pact between Ibn 'Abd al-Wahhab and Muhammad ibn Sa'ud
1766	Death of the writer Ja'far ibn Hasan al-Barzanji
1792	Death of the reformer Ibn 'Abd al-Wahhab
1798	Napoleon invades Egypt
1821	Death of Muhammad al-Fadali, rector of al-Azhar
1850	Death of Sayyid 'Ali Muhammad, the Bab
1880	Death of missionary Abu Bakr Effendi
1883	Rise of the Ahmadiyya in India
1892	Death of Baha'u'llah of the Baha'is
1898	Death of the modernist-reformer Sir Sayyid Ahmad Khan
1905	Death of the modernist-reformer Muhammad 'Abduh
1908	Death of Mirza Ghulam Ahmad, Ahmadiyya founder
1921	Death of 'Abdu'l-Baha of the Baha'is
1924	Secularisation of Turkey
1947	Creation of Pakistan
1947	Creation of Israel
1957	Death of Shoghi Effendi of the Baha'is
1966	Death of Egyptian Muslim Brotherhood member Sayyid Qutb
1979	Creation of the Islamic Republic of Iran under Imam Khumayni
1979	Death of Pakistani reformer-politician Mawlana Mawdudi

2 SCRIPTURE, ITS VALUE AND INTERPRETATION

See 1.1. The chapters of the Qur'an represent some of the different varieties of material found therein. The Arabic transcription in 2.1.1, 2.1.2, and 2.1.3 should be used to follow a recording of Qur'an recitation, if possible; the rhythmic structures of the text will then become clear. Interpretations of

2.1.1 are to be found in 2.2.2 and 8.2; on its use in prayer see 3.2.3.2; 2.1.4 presents the vivid imagery of the coming end of the world. In 2.1.5 attention should be paid to the stereotyped presentation of the prophets. Elaborations of parts of the legal passages in 2.1.6 will be found in 4.2 and 5.1; 2.1.7 is sometimes compared to the Biblical 'ten commandments', both in structure and in content. 2.2.1 gives some introduction to the theory of interpretation in early (ninth–tenth century) Islam while 2.2.2 gives an example of very early Muslim exegesis in practice. 2.2.3 reveals the use of hadith *materials in commentary (so compare 3.2.3). 2.3 demonstrates the interaction between theology and exegesis as well as emphasising the central theological notion of the miraculous character of the Qur'an, proved here by a detailed analysis of the literary qualities of the text.*

2.1 THE QUR'AN

2.1.1 *Surat al-Fatiha* (1) – The Chapter of the Opening
bismi-llahi-r-rahmani-r-rahim In the name of God, the Merciful, the Compassionate.

1. *al-hamdu lil-lahi rabb-il-'alamin* Praise belongs to God, Lord of all beings.
2. *ar-rahmani-r-rahim* The Merciful, the Compassionate.
3. *maliki yawm-id-din* Ruler of the judgement day.
4. *iyya-ka na'budu wa iyya-ka nasta'in* Only You do we serve and only from You do we seek aid.
5. *ihdi-na as-sirat al-mustaqim* Guide us along the straight path.
6. *sirat alladhina an'amta 'alayhim* The path of those whom You have blessed.
7. *ghayr-il-maghdubi 'alayhim wa la ad-dallin* Not those against whom You have sent Your wrath nor those who are astray.

2.1.2 *Surat al-Ikhlas* (112) – The Chapter of the Pure Religion
bismi-llahi-r-rahmani-r-rahim In the name of God, the Merciful, the Compassionate.

1. *qul huwa Allahu ahad* Say: He is God, One.
2. *Allahu as-samad* God, the Everlasting One.
3. *lam yalid wa-lam yulad* He has not given birth nor has He been born.
4. *wa-lam yakun lahu kufuwan ahad* And there is no equal to Him.

2.1.3 *Surat al-'Adiyat* (100) – The Chapter of the Swift Mares
bismi-llahi-r-rahmani-r-rahim In the name of God, the Merciful, the Compassionate.

1. *wa'l-'adiyati dabha* By the panting swift mares.
2. *fa'l-muriyati qadha* By the strikers of fire.

3. *fa'l-mughirati subha* By the raiders at dawn
4. *fa atharna bihi naq'a* Raising clouds of dust.
5. *fa wasatna bihi jam'a* Penetrating there into the centre.
6. *inna'l-insana li-rabbihi la-kanud* Indeed man is ungrateful to his Lord
7. *wa innahu 'ala dhalika la-shahid* And indeed he is a witness to that.
8. *wa innahu li-hubbi'l-khayri la-shadid* Indeed he is strong in his love of good things.
9. *a-fa-la-ya'lamu idha bu'thira ma fi'l-qubur* Does he not know that when what is in the graves is overthrown
10. *wa hussila ma fi's-sudur* And what is in the breasts is brought out
11. *inna rabbahum bihim yawma'idhi la-khabir* Indeed their Lord will be aware of them on that day!

2.1.4 The Chapter of the Rolling Up (81)

In the name of God, the Merciful, the Compassionate.
1. When the sun is rolled up, 2. And when the stars are thrown down, 3. And when the mountains are made to move, 4. And when pregnant camels are abandoned, 5. And when savage beasts are brought together, 6. And when the seas heat up, 7. And when people are coupled together, 8. And when the buried infant is asked 9. About the sin for which she was slain, 10. And when the scrolls are unrolled, 11. And when heaven is laid bare, 12. And when hell is set ablaze, 13. And when paradise is brought near, 14. Then a soul will know what it has produced. 15. No! I swear by the retreaters, 16. The runners, the sinkers, 17. And by the night as it passes away, 18. And by the dawn as it breathes, 19. Indeed, this is the word of a noble messenger, 20. Possessor of power, secure with the Lord of the throne, 21. Obeyed and most trustworthy. 22. Your companion is not possessed. 23. Truly he saw him on the clear horizon; 24. He is not stingy with the unseen. 25. And this is not the word of accursed Satan. 26. Where then are you going? 27. It is only a reminder to all beings, 28. To whoever of you wishes to go straight, 29. And you shall not wish without God, Lord of all beings, wishing.

2.1.5 The Chapter of the Spider (29)

In the name of God, the Merciful, the Compassionate.
1. Alif, Lam, Mim[1]
2. Do people think that they will be left alone because they say: 'We believe', and that they will not be tested?
3. We tested those who were before them. Most certainly God knows those who speak truthfully and He most certainly knows the liars.
4. Or do those who commit evil reckon that they will escape Us? Evil is what they judge!
5. Whoever hopes to meet God, God's term is coming; He is the all-Hearing, the all-Knowing.

6. Whoever strives, strives only for his soul; God is above all of the created beings.

7. Those who believe and do good works, We shall most certainly acquit them of their evil deeds and We shall most certainly reward them with the best of that which they have done.

8. We require that people be good to their parents; if someone strives to make you associate with Me something of which you have no knowledge, then do not obey them. To Me is your return and I shall inform you of that which you have done.

9. Those who believe and do good works, We shall most certainly admit them among the righteous.

10. Among the people are some who say: 'We believe in God', but when one of them is hurt in the way of God they regard the persecution of the people as the punishment from God. Then if help comes from your Lord they most certainly say: 'Indeed, we were with you'. Does God not have knowledge of what is in the breasts of the created beings?

11. Most certainly God knows those who believe and He most certainly knows the hypocrites.

12. Those who disbelieve say to those who believe: 'Follow our path and we shall bear your sins'. But they cannot carry anything even of their own sins; they are truly liars.

13. Most certainly they shall carry their loads and other loads along with their loads. On the day of resurrection they shall most certainly be questioned about that which they were inventing.

14. Indeed We sent Noah to his people and he stayed among them for a thousand years less fifty, and the flood seized them and they were evil-doers.

15. But We saved him and the occupants of the ark. We made it a sign for all beings.

16. And Abraham, when he said to his people: 'Serve God and fear Him. That is better for you if only you understood'.

17. 'You serve beside God idols and you create a lie. Those whom you worship beside God do not have power to provide sustenance for you. So seek sustenance with God and worship Him and give thanks to Him. To him you will return.'

18. 'If you utter lies, nations before you cried lies as well. The messenger is only responsible for the clear message.'

19. Have they not seen how God originates creation and then brings it back again? Indeed, that is easy for God.

20. Say: Journey in the world and observe how He originated creation. Then God causes another growth to grow. Indeed God is powerful over all things.

21. He punishes whomever He pleases and is merciful towards whomever He pleases. To Him you will be turned back.

22. You are not able to frustrate (Him) in the world or in the heavens. You do not have a friend nor helper apart from God.

23. Those who disbelieve in God's signs and the meeting with Him, those are the ones who despair of My mercy and they are the ones who shall have a mighty punishment.

24. The only answer of his people was that they said: 'Kill him or burn him', but God saved him from the fire. Indeed in that are signs for a people who believe.

25. And he said: 'You have taken for yourselves idols apart from God, they being tokens of love between you in a worldly life. Then on the day of resurrection you will deny one another and curse one another. Your place shall be the fire and you shall have no helpers'.

26. Lot believed him; and he said: 'I take refuge with my Lord who is the all-Mighty, the all-Wise'.

27. We gave him Isaac and Jacob and placed among his descendants prophecy and the book and We gave him his reward in this world; indeed he shall be among the righteous in the hereafter.

28. And Lot, when he said to his people: 'You are committing indecencies which before you no created being has ever done'.

29. 'Do you come to men and cut off the way and do you bring dishonour to your assembly?' The only answer of his people was to say: 'Bring on us the punishment of God, if you are one of the speakers of truth!'

30. He said: 'My Lord, help me against the people who commit indecencies!'

31. When Our messengers came to Abraham with the good news, they said: 'We are going to destroy the people of this town; indeed its people are wrong-doers'.

32. He said: 'Lot is in it'. They said: 'We know who is in it. We shall most certainly save him and his family except his wife; she is from those left behind'.

33. When it was that Our messengers came to Lot, he was troubled because of them and distressed for them. They said: 'Fear not and do not grieve; we shall save you and your family except your wife – she is from those left behind'.

34. 'We shall most certainly send down on the people of this city a punishment from heaven because they have been ungodly.'

35. Indeed, We have left there a clear sign for a people who understand.

36. To Madyan, their brother Shu'ayb; he said: 'O my people, serve God and await the last day and do not commit mischief on the earth, creating corruption'.

37. They called him a liar. So the earthquake seized them and in their homes they lay fallen.

38. And 'Ad and Thamud; it is clear to you from their dwellings. Satan glorified their deeds for them and turned them from the path although they saw clearly.

39. And Korah and Pharaoh and Haman; Moses came to them with clear proofs but they acted proudly on the earth but they could not outstrip Us.

40. Each one we took for their sin and among them were those against whom

we sent a sandstorm and others the scream took while others we made the earth swallow and others we drowned. God will not wrong them but they have wronged themselves.

41. The likeness of those who take protectors other than God is as the likeness of the spider who takes for itself a house; indeed, the frailest of houses is the house of the spider, if only they knew!

42. Indeed God knows what they call on other than Him. He is the all-Mighty, the all-Wise.

43. These similes – we strike them for the people but only those who know understand them.

44. God created the heavens and the earth with the truth. Indeed, in that is a sign for the believers.

45. Recite what has been revealed to you of the book and perform the prayer. Prayer forbids indecency and dishonour. The remembrance of God is the greatest. God knows what you do.

46. Do not dispute with the people of the book unless it be with what is best except for those of them who do wrong. Say: 'We believe in what has been revealed to us and revealed to you. Our God and your God are one; we have submitted to Him'.

47. Thus We have revealed to you the book; those to whom We have given the book believe in it; among these also are those who believe in it. Only the disbelievers deny Our signs.

48. You did not recite before this from a book nor did you write one with your right hand, for then those who follow falsehood would be the doubters.

49. Rather, it is (a collection of) clear signs in the hearts of those who have been given knowledge. Only the wrongdoers deny Our signs.

50. They say: 'Why are signs not sent down on him from his Lord?' Say: 'The signs are with God and indeed, I am a clear warner'.

51. Is it not enough for them that we reveal to you the book which is recited to them? Indeed, in that is a mercy and a reminder for a people who believe.

52. Say: 'God suffices as a witness between you and me'. He knows what is in the heavens and the earth. Those who believe in falsehood and disbelieve in God, those, they are the losers.

53. They ask you to hasten the punishment. If there had not been a stated term, the punishment surely would have come on them. It shall come on them unexpectedly while they are not aware.

54. They ask you to hasten the punishment. Indeed, hell encompasses the disbelievers!

55. The day when the punishment shall overwhelm them from above them and from below their feet, and He shall say: 'Now taste what you were doing!'

56. O My servants who believe, indeed My earth is vast; so worship Me alone.

57. Every soul shall taste death, then to Us you shall return.

58. Those who believe and do good works, We shall lodge them in the lofty

rooms of paradise, underneath which rivers flow. They shall reside there. Excellent is the reward of those who act,

59. those who are patient and put trust in their Lord.

60. How many animals are there that do not carry their own sustenance? God provides for them and for us. He is the all-Hearing, the all-Knowing.

61. If you ask them: 'Who created the heavens and the earth and subjected the sun and the moon?', they most certainly will say: 'God'. How is it, then, that they are turned away?

62. God spreads out and straightens the sustenance to those of His servants as He wishes. God has knowledge of all things.

63. If you ask them: 'Who sends down water from the heaven and brings life to the earth after it was dead?', they will most certainly say: 'God'. Say: 'Praise be to God'. But most of them do not understand.

64. This life in the world is only a pastime and a sport; indeed, the abode of the hereafter, that is life, if only they knew!

65. When they ride on ships, they call on God, being sincere to Him in the religion. But when He brings them to land, they become polytheists

66. so that they may disbelieve in what We bring them and so that they may enjoy themselves. But they will know soon!

67. Have they not seen that we have given them a secure sanctuary while people all around them are snatched away? Are they believers in falsehood and deniers of the favour of God?

68. Who does greater evil than the person who invents a lie about God or tells lies about the truth when it has come to them? Is there not a lodging in hell for the disbelievers?

69. Those who strive with Us, We shall most certainly guide them in Our ways. Indeed, God is with those who do good.

2.1.6 The Chapter of the Table (5) – excerpts
In the name of God, the Merciful, the Compassionate.
1. O believers, fulfil your agreements. Permitted for you are beasts in flocks, except that which is recited to you, except that you should not consider game to be permitted when you are in the ritual state of pilgrimage. God decrees whatever He wishes. 2. O believers, do not profane God's waymarks or the holy month or the sacrificial offering or the necklaces or those going to the sacred house seeking grace and good pleasure from their Lord. But when you have left your ritual state of pilgrimage then hunt for game. And do not let enmity for a people who hindered you from the sacred mosque make you be aggressive towards them. Help one another in piety and fearing God; do not help each other in sin and enmity. And fear God for surely God is severe in retribution. 3. Forbidden to you are carrion, blood, the flesh of swine, what has been sanctified to other than God, that which has been strangled, beaten to death, killed by a fall, gored or eaten by beasts of prey – except those (animals) you have slaughtered properly – and that which has been sacrificed to idols.

(Also forbidden) is partition by diving arrows, that is ungoldliness. Today those who disbelieve despair of your religion; so do not fear them but fear Me! Today I have perfected your religion for you, and I have completed My favour upon you, and I have chosen Islam for your religion. But whoever is forced by hunger, not purposely committing sin, surely God is all Forgiving, Compassionate. 4. They will ask you about what is permitted to them. Say: The good things are permitted to you. (Also permitted) are hunting animals and dogs that you have taught, teaching them as God has taught you. Eat what they catch for you and pronounce God's name over it. Fear God for God is surely quick at the reckoning. 5. Today the good things are permitted to you and the food of those who were given the book is permitted to you and your food is permitted to them. (Also permitted) are pure, believing women and pure women of those who were given the book before you, if you give them their dowries, keeping them pure by marriage and not taking them in fornication or as secret lovers. Whoever disbelieves in the faith will find that their work comes to nothing and in the hereafter they will be among the losers. 6. O believers, when you rise for prayer, wash your faces, your hands up to the elbows, and wipe your heads and your feet up to the ankles. If you are in a state of impurity, then purify yourselves. If you are sick or on a journey or come from the toilet or have touched women and you cannot find any water, then use pure dust and wipe your faces and hands with it. God does not want to make things difficult for you but rather wishes to purify you and to complete His favour to you; perhaps you will be thankful! 7. And remember God's favour to you and His covenant which He made with you when you said: 'We hear and we obey'. Fear God for surely God is knowing of what is inside the breast.

2.1.7. The Chapter of the Night Journey (17) – excerpts

22. Do not put alongside God another god or you will sit condemned and forsaken. 23. Your Lord has commanded that you shall serve no other but He and to be good to parents. If one of the two of them or both of them grow old with you do not say: 'Fie', to them or reproach them but speak to them in a respectful speech 24. and lower to them the wing of humility out of mercy and say: 'My Lord, have mercy upon them just as they raised me when little'. 25. Your Lord knows best about what is in yourselves if you are righteous; surely God is all-Forgiving to those who repent. 26. And give to the kinsman what is his due and likewise to the needy and the traveller and do not squander. 27. Indeed squanderers are brothers of the satans and Satan is ungrateful to his Lord. 28. If you turn away from them seeking the mercy from your Lord which you are hoping for, then speak to them in a gentle speech. 29. And do not keep your hand chained to your neck nor stretch it out totally or you will sit blamed and uncovered. 30. Indeed your Lord stretches the provision to whomever He wishes; indeed He is informed of and observes His servants. 31. Do not kill your children from fear of poverty. We will provide for them and you. Indeed, killing them is a great sin. 32. Do not

approach fornication. Surely it is an indecency and an evil way. 33. Do not slay the soul which God has forbidden unless it be for a right cause. Whoever is wrongfully killed, we have made their heir an authority but let him not exceed in slaying; there will be help for him. 34. Do not approach the property of orphans unless it be in a fair manner until they are of age. And fulfil the covenant, for surely the covenant shall be questioned about. 35. And give full measure when you measure and weigh with a straight balance; that is best and most commendable in the end. 36. Do not pursue that of which you have no knowledge. Indeed the ear, eye, and heart all shall be questioned. 37. Do not walk on the earth haughtily; certainly you cannot tear open the earth nor can you reach the height of mountains. 38. All of that which is evil is hateful with God. 39. That is the wisdom of that which your Lord has revealed to you; do not put alongside God another god or you will be cast into hell, blamed and rejected.

2.2 COMMENTARIES ON THE QUR'AN

2.2.1 Abu Ja'far al-Tabari on the interpretation of Qur'an 3:7
He it is who revealed the book to you; in it are the clear verses – they are the mother of the book – and the others are the unclear verses.

Abu Ja'far said:

The meaning of God's saying: *He it is who revealed the book to you* is that it is God, from whom nothing is hidden in heaven or earth, who has revealed to you the book, that is, the Qur'an. There has already occurred in what has come before in this commentary the reason on behalf of which the Qur'an is called a book, so we may dispense with the repetition of the explanation here.

As for His saying: *In it are the clear verses*, that means verses from the book, that is *verses* are verses from the Qur'an.

As for the word *clear*, they are the meanings which are strengthened by explication and clarification. They are verified by the indications which are given by them for the categories of the permitted and the forbidden, the promise and the threat, the reward and the punishment, the things commanded and those prevented, the details and the examples, the sermons and the admonitions, and other matters which are similar to all of that.

Then God described these *clear verses* by saying that: *they are the mother of the book*, meaning by that, that they are the source of the book which contains within it the duties of the religion, including the responsibilities and the penalties and the rest of that which creation needs in the law of their religion. Also included are the responsibilities which are assigned in this world and the hereafter.

These are called *the mother of the book* because they are the major portion of the book and they are a place of refuge for the people of the Qur'an when they are in need of such. That is what the Arabs did, in that they named the gathering of a major portion of something its 'mother'. So they named the banner of the people under which they gathered in their fighting groups their 'mother'; also the leader who handled the majority of the matters of the village or district was called its 'mother'. We have already explained that in what has come before so we shall do without a full repetition here.

Mother of the book is in the singular; it is not made plural as in 'They are the mothers of the Book'. *They* is used, however, because all of the *clear verses* are intended by *mother of the book*, but not each verse of them is the *mother of the book*. If the meaning was such that each of the *clear verses* was the *mother of the book*, there would be no doubt in the matter, because then it would have been said: 'They are the mothers of the book'. The analogous statement of God to: *They are the mother of the book* as we have interpreted it in the singular sense of *mother* which is the grammatical complement of *they*, is in Qur'an 23:50: *We made the son of Mary and his mother a sign*, but He did not say: 'two signs' because the meaning is: 'We made the two of them together a sign'. So the meaning is singular because they gave a single warning to humanity. If the intention had been that each one of them independently gave a warning to humanity, then it would have been stated: 'We made the son of Mary and his mother two signs', because then in each one of them there would have been a warning. The signs are that Mary had a child not by a man and that her son spoke from the cradle as a baby. So, in each of those events is a sign for the people. . . .

As for His saying: *unclear verses (mutashabihat)*, the meaning is those unclear in recitation with divergencies in meaning, just as God has said in Qur'an 2:25: *They will be given that which resembles it (mutashabiha)*, that is, things which have a resemblance but which differ in actual substance.[2] This is also similar to what God said in relating what the Children of Israel said in Qur'an 2:70: *Cows are much alike (tashabaha) to us*, by which they meant: 'To us they resemble one another externally although their kinds differ'.

The interpretation of this passage is then as follows. Indeed, He, from whom nothing in the heavens or the earth is hidden, has revealed to you, O Muhammad, the Qur'an, which has verses which are clear with explanation; they are the source or grounding of the book which contain the duties which are incumbent upon you and your community in religion; it is your place of refuge and theirs from whatever frightens you or them of the requirements of Islam. The other verses are the unclear ones in recitation which have differing meanings.

There is, however, disagreement among the interpreters in their treatment of: *In it are the clear verses – they are the mother of the book – and the others are the unclear verses*. Which verses are the clear ones in the Qur'an and which are the unclear?

Some people say that the *clear verses* from the verses of the Qur'an are those which are valid (in legal ruling), that is, the abrogator verses or those whose ruling is firmly established. The *unclear verses* are those whose ruling has been left behind, that is, the abrogated verses. Among those who say that are the following.

Ya'qub ibn Ibrahim told me that Hisham told him that al-'Awwam informed him on the authority of someone from Ibn 'Abbas who said concerning the statement: *In it are the clear verses*, that these are three verses from Qur'an 6:151: *Say: 'Come, I will recite what your Lord has forbidden for you'*, and so on, for three verses, as well as what is in Qur'an 17:23: *Your Lord has commanded that you shall serve no one but Him* and so on to the end of the passage (verse 39).

Al-Muthanna told me that Abu Salih told him that Mu'awiya ibn Salih told him on the authority of 'Ali ibn Abi Talha from Ibn 'Abbas who said concerning: *He it is who revealed the book to you; in it are the clear verses – they are the mother of the book*, that the clear verses are the abrogators and those which set out the permitted and the forbidden, the penalties and the responsibilities, what one believes in and what one does. And he said concerning: *The others are the unclear verses*, that they are the abrogated verses, verses of the category of those which precede and those which come after, parables and stories and what one believes in but does not have to act upon.

Muhammad ibn Sa'd told me that his father told him that his uncle told him that his father had reported on the authority of his father from Ibn 'Abbas who said concerning; *He it is who revealed the book to you* to *The others are the unclear verses*, that the *clear verses* are those which are the mother of the book, that is, the abrogators to which one has an obligation and upon which one must act, whereas the *unclear verses* are those which have no obligation attached. . . .

Others say that the *clear verses* are those in which God has firmly established the explanation of the categories of permitted and forbidden while the *unclear verses* are those which are similar (*ashbaha*) to them in meaning but differ in their wording.[3] Among those who say that are the following.

Muhammad ibn 'Amr told me that Abu 'Asim told him on the authority of 'Isa from Ibn abi Najih from Mujahid concerning the statement of God *In it are the clear verses*, that is what is found of the categories of permitted and forbidden. Those which are equivalent to them are the *unclear verses* which confirm the others. Examples are to be found in Qur'an 2:26: *He does not deem them misguided thereby unless they are disobedient* which is like 6:125: *Therefore God places abomination on those who do not believe* which is like 47:17: *Those who are guided He increases in guidance and gives them their godfearingness.* . . .

Others say that the *clear verses* are those which can bear only one interpretation while the *unclear verses* are those which have many interpretations. Among those who say that are the following.

Abu Hamid told me that Salama told him on the authority of Muhammad ibn Ishaq who said that Muhammad ibn Ja'far ibn al-Zubayr told him concerning: *He it is who revealed the book to you; in it are the clear verses*, that in them is the proof of the Lord and the protection of the believers and the rejection of the particular and the hidden; there is no alteration or distortion in what they describe. *The others are the unclear verses*, that is, in confirming; they can embrace alteration, distortion, and interpretation. God puts the believers to the test with them just as He puts them to the test with the permitted and the forbidden but the clear verses cannot be changed to something hidden nor can they be distorted away from the truth.

Others say that the meaning of *clear verses* is those verses of the Qur'an in which God gives rulings and tells the stories of the communities and their prophets whom God sent to them. They are distinguished by the explanation of that given to Muhammad and his people. The *unclear verses* are those which resemble the stories which are repeated in various surahs, both stories which agree in wording but differ in meaning and those which differ in wording but agree in meaning. Among those who say that are the following.

Yunus told me that Ibn Wahb informed him that Ibn Zayd recited Qur'an 11:1: *Alif Lam Ra'. A book whose verses give clear rulings, then are set forth in detail, from the One, the all-Wise, the all-Aware,* and then mentioned the account of the messenger of God in the next twenty-four verses of this surah, and then the twenty-four verses about Noah. After that he recited from Qur'an 11:49: *This is from the tidings of the unseen.* Then he began again with: *And to 'Ad* (verse 50) and recited until he reached: *And seek forgiveness from your Lord* (verse 90), then he stopped. He had mentioned Salih, Abraham, Lot, and Shu'ayb and had excelled at it. This is the explanation of: *whose verses give clear rulings, then are set forth in detail.* He said: the unclear verses are found in the mention of Moses in many places and they are unclear yet they all have one meaning and resemble one another. Included here are passages such as Qur'an 23:27: *Take into it,* 11:40: *Embark therein,* 28:32: *Insert your hand,* 27:12: *Enter your hand,* 20:20: *A serpent running,* 7:107: *A serpent plainly visible.*[4] Then Hud is mentioned for ten verses, Salih for eight, Abraham for the next eight, Lot for eight, and Shu'ayb for thirteen. Moses has four verses. All this is done for the prophets and their people in this surah. That is finally terminated at verse 100 where it is said: *That is from the tidings of the cities; we tell it to you. Some of them are standing, others are destroyed.* He said concerning the unclear verses of the Qur'an: Whoever God rejects thereby with trials and tribulations will say: 'Why is it that it cannot be so?'

Others say, rather, the *clear verses* are those of which the learned class knows their interpretation and understands their meaning and their explanation, while the *unclear verses* are those which no one can use their knowledge to understand, in that God has exclusive possession of their interpretation to the exclusion of all of creation. Some unclear matters are things such as the time of the return of Jesus son of Mary, the time of the appearance of the sun in the west, the hour of resurrection, the end of the world, and other things like those. No one knows those things. These people say that God called some of the verses of the Qur'an unclear because of the disconnected letters which preceed some of the surahs, like *alif-lam-mim* and *alif-lam-mim-sad, alif-lam-mim-ra'* and *alif-lam-ra'* and others like those, because they are unclear in their wording and coincide with the numerical value of the letters. A group of Jews at the time of Muhammad wished to understand beforehand how long Islam and its people would last and their final fate. God made all their stories false and taught them not to strive after His knowledge about that sort of thing beforehand through the unclear (mysterious) letters. They will not attain that knowledge nor will they know anything else in advance. That is because only God knows.

2.2.2 Muqatil ibn Sylayman on the interpretation of Surah [1]

In the name of God, the Merciful, the Compassionate. *Praise belongs to God:* that is, thanks to God. *Lord of all beings*: that is, the *jinn* and mankind; this is similar to God's saying in Qur'an 25:1: *So that he may be a warner to all beings.* *The Merciful, the Compassionate*: two names of compassion, one of which is more compassionate than the other. *Al-Rahman* (the Compassionate) relates to the sense of being merciful while *al-Rahim* (the Merciful) means to be inclined towards the giving of mercy. *Ruler of the Judgement Day*: that is, the day of reckoning, just as God said in Qur'an 37:53: *Are we the ones to be judged?*, that is, those subject to the reckoning. Concerning this (it is said that) the kings of the world will rule the earth and He will inform them that no one other than Him will rule over the day of resurrection. That is contained in His saying in Qur'an 82:19: *That day the command belongs to God.* The saying of God: *Only You do we serve*: that is, we declare your unity just as in God's saying in Qur'an 66:5: *Those who worship*, that is, those who declare the unity of God. *Only from You do we seek aid*: in Your worship. *Guide us (ihdina) along the straight path*: that is, the religion of Islam because there is no guidance in any religion other than Islam. According to the variant reading of Ibn Mas'ud the text reads *arshudna*, 'guide us'. *The path of those whom You have blessed:* that is, We have indicated the way of those whom We have blessed, that is, the proofs of those whom God has blessed with prophethood, just as in God's saying in Qur'an 19:58: *Those were from among the prophets whom God blessed* among whom was Abraham. *Not those against whom You have sent Your wrath:* that is, a religion other than the Jewish one, against whom God was wrathful. Monkeys and pigs were made from them. *Nor those who are astray*: God is saying: 'And not the religion of the polytheists', that is, the Christians.

He said: 'Ubayd Allah informed me that his father told him on the authority of Hudhayl from Muqatil from 'Alqama from Murtadd from Abu Hurayra that the Messenger of God, may the prayers and peace of God be upon him, said: 'God, Most Exhalted and Most High, said: 'This surah arose between Me and My servant in two halves'. When the servant said: *Praise belongs to God, Lord of all beings*, God said: 'My servant thanks Me'. When he said: *The Compassionate, the Merciful*, God said: 'My servant praises Me'. When he said: *Ruler of the Judgement day*, God said: 'I will praise My servant and the rest of the surah shall be for him'. So when he said: *Only You do we serve*, God said: 'This is for My servant; Me alone he serves, he serves Me. The rest of the *surah* is for My servant'. So when he says: *'Only from You do we seek aid*, this is for My servant who seeks aid only from Me. *Guide us along the straight path*: this is for My servant. *The path of those whom You have blessed.* So this is for My servant and not those who are astray; this is for My servant alone'.[5]

The narrator said: 'Ubayd Allah told me that his father told him that Hudhayl told him on the authority of Muqatil who said: Whenever one of you is reading this surah and reaches its conclusion saying: *Nor those who are astray*, he should say 'Amen'. Indeed the angels are believers and if the saying of 'Amen' by the angels coincides with the saying of it by people, the previously committed sins of the people will be forgiven.

The narrator said: 'Ubayd Allah told me that his father told him on the authority of Hudhayl from Muqatil concerning the words of the Most Exhalted and Most High in Qur'an 15:87: *We have revealed to you the seven mathani* that he said that they are the seven verses of surah 1. *And the great Qur'an*: all of it is great because it is the speech of the Compassionate, the Exalted, the Most High.

The narrator said: 'Ubayd Allah told me that his father told him that Hudhayl told him on the authority of Waqi' from Mansur from Mujahid who said that when surah 1 was revealed the Devil wailed.

The narrator said: 'Ubayd Allah said that his father told him on the authority of Abu Salih from Waqi' from Sufyan al-Thawri from al-Suddi from 'Abd al-Khayr from 'Ali, may God be pleased with him, concerning the words of God in Qur'an 15:87: *The seven mathani*, that he said that they are (the seven verses) of surah 1.

2.2.3 Ibn Kathir on the interpretation of Muhammad as the seal of the prophets, Qur'an 33:40

Muhammad is not the father of any of your men

It is forbidden that one should say after this time: 'Zayd, son of Muhammad', that is, Muhammad is not his father although he did adopt him as a son. Muhammad did not have a male offspring until he attained puberty, at which time al-Qasim, al-Tayyib, and al-Tahir were born to him by Khadija, but they all died when they were young. Mariya, the Copt, bore to Muhammad Ibrahim but he died also while still suckling. Muhammad had four daughters by Khadija: Zaynab, Ruqiyya, Umm Kalthum, and Fatima. Three of them died during the lifetime of Muhammad. Fatima survived until she became ill and died six months after Muhammad.

But the Messenger of God is the seal of the prophets and God is powerful over all things

This is just like the saying of God in Qur'an 6:124: *God knows where he places his messages.* This is the verse which stipulates that there will be no prophet after Muhammad; if no prophets are to come after him, then there will no messengers after him, because the function of being a messenger is a specialised part of the function of prophethood. Every messenger is a prophet but not vice versa. Many sound reports are transmitted on the authority of the messenger of God, as told by the companions of Muhammad in this connection. Imam Ahmad (ibn Hanbal) reports that Abu 'Amir al-Azdi told him that Zuhayr ibn Muhammad told him on the authority of 'Abd Allah ibn Muhammad ibn 'Aqil from al-Tufayl ibn Abi ibn Ka'b from his father that the prophet of God said: 'My likeness among all the prophets is like the likeness of a man building a house. He is proficient at it, he does it well, and he leaves a single brick out. Then the people begin to go around the building, marvelling at it, and say: "It would be complete if not for this brick". Indeed, in the building, I am the place for that brick'. This report is found in al-Tirmidhi on the authority of Bandar from Abu 'Amir al-'Azdi. He declares the report totally sound.

Another report comes from Imam Ahmad ibn Hanbal who said that 'Affan told him that 'Abd al-Wahid ibn Ziyad told him that al-Mukhtar ibn Fulful told him that Anas ibn Malik said that the messenger of God said: 'Messengership and prophethood have ceased. There will be neither a prophet nor a messenger after me'. That grieved the people so he said: 'But there will be good tidings'. They asked: 'O messenger of God, just what are those good tidings?' to which he replied: 'They are the dreams of Muslims and they are part of prophethood'. This is transmitted by al-Tirmidhi on the authority of al-Hasan ibn Muhammad al-Za'farani from 'Affan ibn Muslim; in his opinion this report is sound but more difficult than that transmitted by al-Mukhtar ibn Fulful. . . .

Another report comes from . . . Imam Muslim who said that Yahya ibn Ayyub and Qutayba and 'Ali ibn Hajr said that Isma'il ibn Ja'far told us on the authority of al-'Ala' from his father from Abu Hurayra that the messenger of God said: 'I excelled over the prophets . . . in six ways: I have been given mosques, I have been helped with fear, beasts of the field have been permitted to me, the earth has been given to me as a mosque and a place of purity, I have been sent to humanity as a whole, and prophecy has been sealed with me'. Al-Tirmidhi and Ibn Maja transmit this on the authority of Isma'il ibn Ja'far and al-Tirmidhi says it is totally sound. . . .

The reports on this topic are numerous. It is an expression of the mercy of God to his servants that he sent Muhammad to them. He conferred honour upon them, such that Muhammad was the seal of the prophets and the messengers and He completed the pure (hanif) religion with him. God has said in His book and through His messenger in the reliably transmitted sunna from him, that there will no prophet after him. Thereby everyone may know that anyone who claims this station after Muhammad is a liar, a teller of falsehoods, the anti-Christ, a misguided person, and someone not offering guidance. Should someone violate that and practise magic and come with all sorts of tricks and magic charms and the like, it must be known that all of it is trickery and is misguided. This is just as God has demonstrated in the cases of al-Aswad in the Yaman and Musaylima, the Liar, also in the Yaman with their false positions and inane statements. It is recognised by all those who possess intelligence and discernment that they were two misguided liars. God has cursed them and, therefore, so is anyone who appeals to them until the day of resurrection when they are sealed by the Messiah al-Dajjal. All of these liars God created because of the affairs which the learned ones and the believers witness by the lying of those who come with it. This is the completion of the beneficence of God in His creation. As a consequence of their falling, they do not order the good nor forbid the evil, except by coincidence or when it is the way to some other end. The end result of the lie and immorality in their speech and actions is just as God has said in Qur'an 26:221–2: *Shall I tell you upon whom the satans descend? They descend upon every liar and sinner*, to the end of the passage. This is so even despite the prophets; they are at the extreme of piety, righteousness, goodness, uprightness, and justice in what they say, do, command, and forbid along with what they confirm by way of miracles, clear indications, and demonstrations. May the prayers and peace of God be upon them for as long as the heavens and earth exist.

2.3 THE NATURE OF THE QUR'AN: AL-RUMMANI ON THE IDEA OF INIMITABILITY

Aspects of the inimitability of the Qur'an appear in seven ways which are as follows: (1) the lack of imitation even though there is an abundance of reason and a great need to make the attempt; (2) the challenge put forth to everyone; (3) the prevention from imitation by God; (4) the eloquence of the Qur'an; (5) the true predictions about coming events; (6) the Qur'an being out of the ordinary, contradicting custom; and (7) the analogy of the Qur'an to all other miracles.

The fourth aspect, eloquence, has three levels, the highest, the lowest, and the middle. The highest is the miraculous and that is the eloquence of the Qur'an. This is possible, just as the eloquence of certain learned people is possible, but there is nothing else in this category. Eloquence does not lead to making the meaning understood because there can be meaning between two speakers, one of whom is eloquent and the other of whom is not. Nor is eloquence to be found in precise expression at the expense of meaning, because the wording may still produce a meagre, disgusting, limited, or formal meaning. True eloquence connects the meaning to the heart or emotion in the best form of expression. So, the highest eloquence occurs at that level only in the best of forms which is the eloquence of the Qur'an and the highest level of eloquence belongs to it alone. The highest level of eloquence is impossible for Arabs and foreigners and this is like the impossibility of satirical poetry. The latter is impossible for the poet, whereas the eloquence of the Qur'an is impossible for all.

Eloquence is analysable into ten sections which are as follows: (1) concision; (2) simile; (3) metaphor; (4) harmonious use of words and individual letters; (5) analogous endings of speech divisions; (6) paranomasia; (7) alteration; (8)

implication; (9) hyperbole [including synecdoche]; and (10) pleasing expression.

(1) Concision

Concision is the shortening of a portion of speech without disturbing the meaning. When it is possible either to express a given meaning with many words or to express it with few words, expressing it with fewer words is concision.

Concision is of two types: ellipsis and brevity. Ellipsis is the dropping of a word due to the satisfaction of the sense without it. Brevity is the construction of speech with few words and maximum meaning without omitting any words. So, examples of ellipsis are Qur'an 12:82: *Ask the town,*[6] as well as 2:189, 9:1, and 47:21. Also of this type is the omission of the apodosis of a conditional sentence which is more eloquent than mentioning it; there are many examples of it in the Qur'an as when God said in 13:31: *If only it was a Qur'an that set mountains in motion or caused the earth to break or that spoke to the dead* as if it had been said: 'Indeed, it is this Qur'an!' Another example is found in Qur'an 39:73.

In examples like these, omission becomes more eloquent than mentioning the word because the person must reach to the greatest length to understand it. But if the answer is mentioned, then the person would be confined to the aspect which is its obvious implication. So, omission of the answer when one says: 'If you see 'Ali between the two rows, . . .' is more eloquent than the expression which makes it clear.

As for concision by brevity without ellipsis, it is more obscure than ellipsis. If the ellipsis is obscure, there is simply a need for the knowledge of places where it is valid and of places where it is not valid. Examples of brevity include Qur'an 2:179: *In retaliation there is life for you,* as well as Qur'an 63:4, 48:21, 53:23, 10:23, and 25:43. This type of concision of brevity is common in the Qur'an. People regard as a good example of concision the following proverbial statement: 'Murder is the rejection of murder', but compared to Qur'an 2:179, there is a difference in both its eloquence and its concision. This is apparent in four ways: (1) there is greather usefulness in the Qur'anic statement; (2) there is greater concision in the Qur'anic statement; (3) the Qur'anic statement is not so formal in its repetition of expressions; and (4) the Qur'anic statement is better written with more harmonious letters.

As for greater usefulness, found in the Qur'anic statement is all of what is in their saying: 'Murder is the rejection of murder', and there is additional meaning, which is a merit; contained in it is an elucidation of justice due to the mention of retaliation. There is also elucidation of the desired goal in it due to the mention of life. Also there is the summoning of desire and fear because of the ruling of God about it.

As for concision in expression, if the expression: 'Murder is the rejection of murder', is the most analogous one to the Qur'anic: *In retaliation there is life for you,* the first of these has fourteen letters in Arabic whereas the second has only ten.

As for there being no formality in its repetition of expression, there is repetition of the pattern in the people's saying: 'Murder is the rejection of murder'; if this repetition were absent, it would be more eloquent. When there is repetition like that, it falls short in the area of eloquence of the highest level.

As for the best writing with harmonious letters, that is attained by perception and found in letters. The letters from *fa'* to *lam* are more balanced than the letters from *lam* to *hamza* because of the distance in the writing of the *hamza* from the *lam*. Likewise, the letters from *sad* to *ha'* are more balanced that the letters from *alif* to *lam*. So by bringing together these four factors which we have mentioned, the greater and more beautiful eloquence becomes clear even though the first is eloquent and beautiful.

(2) Simile

A simile is the joining together of two ideas such that one of the two ideas supplies the sense of the other sense-wise or intellectually. It is inevitable that a simile will be either in speech or in itself. As for that which is in speech, it is similar to one saying: 'Zayd is strong like a lion'. The word 'like' joins together the one who bears a resemblance to the one resembled. As for joining by itself, this is the conceptualization in the meaning of this speech. As for the simile of the senses, an example would be 'the two waters' and 'the two gold pieces', one of them occurring in the place of the other and similar things to that. As for the simile in itself, that is found in the example of the comparison of the strength of Zayd to the strength of 'Amr, where the strength is not testified to but it is known by the supplier of the sense of the other; so, a comparison is made.

Similes occur in two ways: comparison of two things harmonious in themselves and comparison of two things which are different which then produce a meaning which joins them together. The first is like the simile of an essence to an essence. The second is the simile of the power of death with the explanation of white magic. The eloquent simile brings to light the most obscure aspects by using the device of the simile along with beauty in writing.

Explanations occur in similes of four kinds: (1) joining of what is not usually sensually perceived to what is – an example is a simile which compares a non-existent entity with an absent person; (2) joining of what customarily does not occur to what does – an example is resurrection after death being compared with awakening from sleep; (3) joining of what is not known by intuition to what is – an example is the comparison of giving back bodies (at the resurrection) with the giving of the book (i.e. the Qur'an) and (4) joining of that which has no descriptive power in it to what does – an example is the light of a lamp being compared with the light of day.

Similes are also of two kinds: eloquent similes and literal similes. Eloquent similes are those such as the acts of the unbelievers being compared with a mirage, while literal similes are similar to statements such as: 'This dinar is like this dinar so take whichever of the two you wish'.

Now we shall mention some of the similes which occur in the Qur'an, calling attention to their explanation as much as possible. One example of this occurs in Qur'an 24:39: *As for the unbelievers, their works are like a mirage in a large plain which a thirsty man mistakes for water until he reaches it and finds none.* The explanation in this verse brings out to the senses what cannot normally be perceived by them. The two elements are joined in an imagined futility resulting from the depth of need and greatness of the want. If it were said concerning the onlooker who believes water can be seen and then it appears that the vision is contrary to what is thought, then, indeed, that expression would be eloquent. Even more eloquent, however, is the expression of the Qur'an, because thirst is greater than the desire for it and the attachment of the heart to it. Then, after this failure, the accounting is obtained, which results in the suffering for eternity in the fire (may we have the protection of God from this condition!) and the simile of the works of the unbelievers with the mirage is among the finest of similes even more so when there is joined with that the beauty of form and sweetness of wording and fullness of usefulness and soundness of guidance contained therein!

Another example is found in God's saying in Qur'an 7:171: *When we shook the mountain above them as if it were a canopy.* This explanation brings out what customarily does not occur, by comparing it to what does customarily occur and the two are joined in the meaning of lifting their respective form. In the simile is the greatest sign for whoever thinks about the extent of the abilities of God in His visible acts. If one does that or he works on it, the victory of his heart will be found along with the attainment of the gain through worship.

Another example is found in God's saying in Qur'an 57:21: *And a garden as wide as the width of heaven and earth.* This is a simile which brings out what is not known by intuition by being compared to what is known by it. In that is a marvellous explanation of what a person may determine of the events; it also conveys the desiring of paradise in the best description along with conveying the heavenly property of spaciousness. Those are brought together powerfully. Other similar examples are to be found.

Another example is to be found in God's saying in Qur'an 55:24: *He has ships sailing in the seas like high mountains.* This is a simile which brings together that which has no descriptive power with that which does; they are joined powerfully except that the mountains are more powerful. In that is a warning in respect of the power which is employed by ships, even given the power of a boat and how useful it is for covering distances between areas.

(3) Metaphor

Metaphor is the attaching of an expression to something other than what is ascribed to it in language, shifting its description in order to provide explication. The difference between metaphor and simile is that the device of comparison is used in a simile as it is expressed and the words are used in a simile in their original sense and are not modified by their employment. A metaphor, on the other hand, is not like that because the explanation provided by the metaphor is an explication of the idiom and the meaning is not ascribed to it in language. Every metaphor requires certain things: something used metaphorically, something for which it is used, and something from which it is borrowed. The metaphorical expression will shift from its origin to a derived sense in order to provide explanation. Every rhetorically effective metaphor is conjoined by a common meaning between the two things which often requires the explanation of the one by means of the other as in a simile; that, however, is done in a metaphor by shifting the meaning of the word whereas with the simile it is done by the device of comparison which thereby suggests the explanation in language itself. Every beautiful metaphor imposes an eloquence of expla-nation for which reality cannot substitute. That is, if reality had taken its place, that would be its primary sense and that cannot occur with a metaphor. However, every metaphor must have some basis in reality; that is the root of the indication of its meaning in language, as in Imru' al-Qays saying of a horse: 'A chain for wild game', while the real meaning is 'an obstacle for wild game'. 'A chain for wild game' is more beautiful and effective. The metaphor is always more beautiful and effective. Every metaphor has need of a basis in reality and also has need of an explantion which cannot be understood literally.

We will now provide an explanation of some examples from the Qur'an of eloquent metaphors. God has said in Qur'an 25:23: *We shall turn to what they did and shall make it dust scattered about.* The real sense of *turn* here is 'go to' but *turn* is more eloquent because it indicates that He treats them in the way of a person arriving from a journey, that is, with utmost deference. Then He turns and sees that they are doing contrary to what He had ordered. In that is a warning about deception along with God's delay. So the meaning which joins the metaphorical meaning and the literal sense is the notion of justice because the action of 'going' to destroy evil is just and *turning* is more eloquent, as we have explained. As for the words: *dust scattered about*, that is a simile which compares what is not normally sensually perceived to what is.

Other examples of metaphor are found in Qur'an 10:94, 69:11, 69:6, 67:7–8, 25:12, 43:4, and 7:152.

(1) Harmony

Harmony is the opposite of having incompatible things together but rather is the balancing of letters in one of three types of writing: (1) incompatible, (2) harmonised at the middle level, and (3) harmonised at the highest level. An example of incompatible writing is found in some poetry which is attributed to the *jinn* because it is not agreeable to anyone who recites it three times without getting muddled. The reason for that is, as we have said, because of the incompatible letters. As for the middle level of harmony, and that is very beautiful, it is found in the best of Arabic poetry. The highest level of harmony is found in all of the Qur'an which is clear to anyone who looks attentively.

The benefit of harmony is found in the beauty of the speech upon its being heard; it is also found in the person's receptivity to the meaning when the beauty of the form and the way of determining it is pointed out. The closest likeness of this is the likeness of reading of a book which is in the finest script and lettering and reading one which is in the ugliest lettering and script. That is a difference of form although it is all one in meaning.

A part of this attribute also comes in the articulation of different letters, some of which come from the deepest part of the pharynx, others from the front of the mouth, and others from the middle.

So, harmony is found in the balancing of extremes such that the text seems easy to the tongue and nice to be heard and one is receptive to its distinctions. When pleasing expressions are added to that, complete with the soundness of exposition of the highest order, inimitability appears because of the excellence of the obvious distinctions in the content of that speech. The challenge includes within it the ability to raise doubts for everyone and it is put forth such that imitation does not occur because of the extent of the inimitability of the Qur'an. As God has said in the challenge verses Qur'an 2:23: *If you have doubts about what We have revealed to Our servant, then produce a surah like it and call on your witnesses other than God, if you are of the truthful*, Qur'an 11:13: *Bring ten surahs like it, forged*, Qur'an 17:88: *Say: 'If people and the jinn got together to produce the likeness of this Qur'an, they could not produce the likeness of it'*, and Qur'an 52:34: *Let them produce a speech like it, if they are truthful*. Proof rose among the Arabs and the foreigners as witnessed by their incapacity to imitate it since it was a clear miracle.

(5) Rhythmisation

Rhythmisation consists of similar letters in syllables of words which impart beauty in the understanding of the meaning. Rhythmisation is eloquence whereas *saj'*, the rhythmic rhymed prose of the pre-Islamic Arabs, is full of faults. That is because rhythmisation follows on the meaning, whereas in *saj'* the meaning follows form. Rhythmisation contains the heart of what wisdom requires of guidance, since its goal is the person who is wise. It is clear from the meaning which is a necessary part of it, that the form must be there. When the similarity of rhythmic endings has a connection to the meaning, then it is eloquent, and when the similarity is contrary to the meaning, then it is faulty and incorrect because it forces meaning to be deduced from another aspect. That is like someone who adores a crown then puts it on a vile African or someone who adores the form of a pearl necklace then puts it on a dog. The baseness and faultiness of that is clear to whoever has some intelligence.

The rhythmisation of all of the Qur'an is eloquent and wise because it provides a path to understand the meaning which argues for it in the best possible form which also indicates the meaning. When the meaning is affected by other than true arguments, it is not to be reckoned with. It comes to that point when there is nothing in the poetry but similar sounds.

Rhythmisation is of two kinds: letters that are the same and letters that are related. Examples of the first kind are found in Surah 20 where *tashqa* ('you are distressed') and *yakhsha* ('he fears') are found at the end of verses 2 and 3 respectively. As for the second kind, that is found where a *mim* is followed by a *nun* as in Qur'an 1:2–3.[7] The best kind of rhythmisation is that with related letters because they surround speech with an explanation of what is intended by the use of rhythmisation and by the syllables themselves when the speech is eloquent and of excellent expression.

Rhyme itself does not allow that effect because it is not the highest level of eloquence; rather, the establishment of metre and the likeness of poetry simply enhances speech. If one of the two ceases, then eloquence leaves that style; as a result, the aural beauty ceases and the speech decreases in meaning. The merit of rhythmisation is found in the syllables and the way it beautifies speech by its similarities and other analogous forms brought out in the verses.

(6) Paranomasia

Eloquent paronomasia occurs in kinds of speech where words from a single root are joined together. Paronomasia is of two kinds: totally resemblant, in that the words have the same meaning, and resemblant, where the words have different meanings. The totally resemblant occur in the statements of reward and punishment as in God's saying in Qur'an 2:194: *Whoever commits aggression against you, commit aggression against them*; that is, they may repay them with what they deserve in a just way, except that God used for the sense of what they deserve the word *commit aggression*, in order to confirm the notion of equality in quantity. This resemblance in speech produces fine expressions. Other examples include Qur'an 3:54 and 4:142.

The second type contains changes in meaning although the words come from a single root. An example is God's saying in Qur'an 9:127: *Then they are turning aside. God has turned their hearts*. There is a relationship between *turning aside* from the mention of God and *turned their hearts* from good; the root of them is the same in that it is 'going away from something': they are going away from the mention of God while from their hearts good goes away. Other examples are found in Qur'an 24:37 and 2:276.

(7) Alteration

Alteration is the alteration of a given meaning into different meanings and into different indications which are joined together in succession. So, alteration of the meaning is like alteration of the root in etymologies in providing different meaning. This is being joined together in alteration. This occurs in the alteration of *malik* where the same meaning is connected to *malik* (with a long 'a') and *malik* (with a long 'i'), *dhu al-malkut* and *malik*, *tamlik*, *tamalik*, *imlak* and *mamluk*.

As for alteration of meaning in different indications, this is found in the Qur'an in various stories, for examples, the stories of Moses mentioned in surahs 7, 20, 26 and others, for the purpose of providing different aspects of wisdom through the repetition of the same story.

(8) Inclusion

Inclusion in speech is the occurrence of a certain meaning without that meaning being explicitly mentioned by name or description, yet it is expressed. It is of two types, one of which comes by indirect indication, the other by analogy.

The first of these occurs when one mentions something such that it is spoken, which then indicates that there is a speaker: that is an indirect indication and inclusion brings both ideas together.

Inclusion is concision which dispenses with a detailed statement since it is indirectly indicated in normal speech. As for analogous indication, that is concision in the speech of God especially because God does not resort to any single aspect of indication; His displaying of it necessitates that every aspect of it which is sound will have been indicated in it.

In the name of God, the Merciful, the Compassionate includes the designation in which matters have no beginning but arise out of the blessedness and the glorifying of God by His name. It is a rule of religion and a sign for Muslims. It is in agreement with worship and is an acknowledgement of the blessing which is from the highest blessing. It is a refuge for the fearful and for support for seekers.

(9) Hyperbole

Hyperbole is the indication of greatness in meaning according to an alteration in the root meaning by means of this explanation. Hyperbole is of several types.

First: a description deviating from the current one by hyperbole; that is, by the rise of the emphatic formation in Arabic – for example, *rahman* (the Merciful) deviates from *rahim* (the Compassionate) by hyperbole. It is not possible to describe anything with it other than God because He indicated in its meaning that it is only for Him and it is the meaning in which His mercy encompasses all things.

Second: hyperbole by having the whole wording in the place of a part of the wording as in God's saying in Qur'an 6:102: *Creator of all things*,[8] or in your saying: 'The people came to me', whereas perhaps only five people came but it seemed like more.

Third: transfer of speech, being the removal of information from the biggest and greatest for its hyperbolic effect; that is, this is understatement through the isolation of the most significant element. This occurs when one says: 'The king came', when a great army belonging to the king in fact came. This also occurs in God's saying in Qur'an 89:22: *Your Lord comes and the angels, row by row*, where the coming of the proofs of the signs are put as His coming in hyperbole. Another example is in Qur'an 16:16: *God came upon their homes at the foundations*; that is, He comes to them in His great strength and so He puts that 'bringing' in a hyperbolic way.

Fourth: transfer of the possible to the impossible for its hyperbolic effect as in God's saying in the Qur'an 7:40: *They will not enter paradise until the camel passes through the eye of the needle*.

Fifth: transfer of speech removing doubt for hyperbolic effect out of a concern for justice. Included in this category in Qur'an 34:24: *Either we or you are being guided or in manifest error*.

Sixth: omission of the response to a conditional sentence for hyperbolic effect as in Qur'an 6:27: *If you could see when they stood in the fire!* This also occurs in 2:165 and 38:1.

(10) Pleasing expressions

Pleasing expressions are manifested when one can appreciate what appears to distinguish something from something else mentally. Pleasing expressions are found in four ways: in speech, condition, allusion, and sign. Pleasing expression in speech is of two kinds: first, speech which appears to distinguish something from something else and is pleasing in expression and second, speech which does not do this, which is confused and impossible as a result, and has no meaning to be understood.

It is not good to connect the name of 'pleasing expressions' to ugly speech because God has praised 'pleasing expressions'. He has said in Qur'an 55:2–5: *The Merciful taught the Qur'an, created people, taught them pleasing expressions,* but this is restricted to that of which He indicated that understanding was possible.

The best expression in speech comes on various levels: the highest of which is the level which joins the reasons for the speech being the best in expression with the alteration of the form which pleases the hearing and is easy to say and the soul accepts it; this alleviates spiritual poverty until sufficient proof arises containing the truth. Pleasing expressions need not stipulate the name or the attribute or writing without the word for the meaning or attribute, as in one's saying: 'The slave Zayd'. This is written indicating property without mentioning the name or the attribute or writing without the name for the meaning or attribute. Examples include Qur'an 44:25–6: *How many gardens, fountains, sown fields, and noble stations have they left behind?* This is a marvellous explanation continuing the warning about delusion with great respite. Other examples include Qur'an 44:51, 43:5, 44:40, and 36:78–9.

Chapter on the explanation of the aspects which were mentioned at the beginning of the book.

The aspects are: the lack of imitation with an abundance of motives, the challenge, prevention of imitation, eloquence, true predictions, being out of the ordinary, and analogy to other miracles.

As for the abundance of motives, the action along with the ability was necessary. There is no doubt that there was the ability in each individual or in the whole community at the time of Muhammad. The proof of that is found in the analogy with people that, if their motives were abundant in drinking water when it was available and they were thirsty and they considered the water good to drink, then they would certainly drink. It is not possible that drinking the water would not occur unless the person died of thirst, because of the abundance of motives for drinking, as we have explained. If they did not drink it while having abundant motives to do so, that is an indication of their failure regarding it. Likewise, since there existed an abundance of motives to imitate the Qur'an and since imitation did not occur, then that indicates their failure.

As for the challenge made to everyone, that becomes clear in the fact that they were unable to abstain from trying to imitate the Qur'an seeing that they had abundant motives, except that it was due to their failure that they were, in fact, unable to do so.

As for the prevention, this is the prevention of the ambitions directed towards imitation; this is according to those learned people who have relied on the argument that the Qur'an is a miracle from the point of view of the prevention of ambitions from imitation.[9] That prevention is outside the norm, just as other miracles which are proof of prophethood are outside of it. This is, according to us, one of the aspects of inimitability which is apparent to intelligent people.

As for true predictions about coming events, this is to be seen where it is not possible that things happened by chance; this, then, is an indication that such predictions are from the world of the invisible. One example is found in Qur'an 8:7: *And when God promised you one of the two groups that it should be yours, and you wished that the powerless one should be yours; but God desires to establish the truth by His words and to cut off the unbelievers totally.* The matter was just as He promised in that there was a victory given to one of the two parties (those being the caravan which carried Abu Sufyan and the group which went out guarding the caravan from Quraysh). God made Muhammad triumph over Quraysh on the day of Badr according to the promise which preceded it. Other examples include Qur'an 30:1, 61:9, 2:94, 2:23, 54:45, 48:27, 48:20, and 48:21.

As for the Qur'an's being out of the ordinary, the customary things occur in certain types of known speech: poetry, *saj'*, address, letters, and the type of prose which is encouraged among the people in *hadith*. The Qur'an presents itself as an isolated literary possibility, away from the customary, because its rank of beauty surpasses every other literary possibility. If it were not that the form was the best possible for poetry, that shortcoming would reduce its rank in beauty greatly.

As for the Qur'an being analogous to all other miracles, indeed its inimitability truly appears from this angle. The crossing of the parted sea and the spirit of the stick being brought alive and other similar occurrences which happened to Moses were single occurrences of an inimitable nature. The miracles were partings from custom and all of creation was prevented from imitating them.

If someone were to say: 'Perhaps it is possible for people to imitate the short surahs of the Qur'an', it should be said in response that is not possible, as can be seen in the evidence of the earlier challenge put forth and the failure to rise to that challenge, as that appears in God's saying in Qur'an 10:38: *Say: bring forth a surah like it.* There is nothing that distinguishes the long and short surahs. If someone were to say: 'It is possible to change the rhyme in the short surahs and to provide a substitute for every word in its proper place. Is this imitation?', say to that person: 'No, because even a hopeless poet is enabled with the rhyme of poetry in that way'.

So if someone were to say: 'You rely in your argumentation on the failure of the Bedouin Arabs, without taking into account the post-classical Arabs; yet, according to you, the Qur'an is a miracle for all. One can find among the post-classical Arabs some excellence in their speech', the following should be said in reply: 'The Bedouin had developed and had full command of the complete grammatical structure of Arabic but among the post-classical Arabs there are none who can use the full structure of the language. The Bedouin Arabs were more powerful in their use of the full language. Since they failed in the imitation of the Qur'an, so the post-classical Arabs must fail to an even greater extent'.

3 RELIGIOUS HISTORY

See 1.2. History here is taken in its widest, traditional religious sense, starting with the legends about creation (3.1.1), going through the ancient prophets – here exemplified in the story of Abraham (3.1.2) – through Muhammad (3.2) to the final end of the world (3.3). The life of Muhammad is important for every Muslim, so the legends surrounding his life (3.2.1, 3.2.2.) and death (3.2.5) are many and are found in all parts of the Islamic world. Muhammad is an exemplar in all of his actions and the hadith *materials (3.2.3) are one of the sources of legal practice for each Muslim. The document translated in 3.2.4 reveals Muhammad as a religio-political figure in the context of seventh century Arabia.*

3.1 STORIES OF THE PAST

3.1.1 The story of creation

Imam Ahmad narrated that the prophet Muhammad was asked: 'Where was our Lord before He had created the Heavens and the Earth?' The prophet spoke: 'He was in a white cloud; above him and below him there was air. Then He created His Throne upon the water'. But al-Tirmidhi said that the first thing God created was the Pen, made from light (others say it was made from white pearls). Its length is the distance between Heaven and Earth. Then He created the Book made from milky pearls. Its pages were made from red rubies; its length was likewise the distance from Heaven to earth and its width was the distance from the East to the West. Malik ibn Anas has said that one side of the Book was made of rubies and the other side of emeralds. While God was seated on His Throne (according to some), He saw the beauty of the Pen; He split it at the tip and created ink to flow through it. This ink will be sufficient until the Day of Judgement. Then God spoke to His Pen: 'Write!'

The Pen spoke: 'Oh Lord, what shall I write?' God spoke: 'Write My knowledge about My creation, as it will exist until the Day of Resurrection'. From that hour the Pen brings forth what He has destined concerning good and evil, happiness and suffering, as it is written: *We have written what they did previously and the effects of that. And we have put it all together in a clear guide* (Qur'an 36:12). God looks into the Book every day and every glance is a creation. He gives food to some, He kills, He gives life, He appoints and withdraws, He does what He likes. Is not the creation and the commandment His? *No female becomes pregnant nor will she give birth without His knowledge; nor will any life be lengthened or shortened unless it is in the Book. For God that is easy* (Qur'an 35:11).

God created the Canopy from light, and the Throne was fixed to it; around the Canopy there are four rivers, one river of scintillating light, one of burning fire, one of dazzling white snow, and one of water. Angels are constantly swimming in these rivers. But Ibn Abi Hatim reports that God created the Canopy from green emeralds and He created four posts for it from red rubies, and the distance from one post to another is 80,000 years of travelling. The posts are carried by eight angels. The Canopy is like a dome over the angels and over the world, and above the waters. The seven heavens were later created beneath it. And He made the clouds like a sieve for the rain, for, if they were not there the earth would be flooded. It is said that the clouds are elevated twelve miles above the earth. 'Ikrima relates that God sends down the rain from the sky in drops, like camels dunging; otherwise there would be floods and the grass would be spoilt wherever it grows and the cattle likewise. *He it is who sends the winds as glad tidings before His mercy, then they carry a heavy cloud. We drive it to a dead country and cause the water to descend from it and with it We make all the fruits come out* (Qur'an 7:57). Ibn 'Abbas says that God has placed angels in charge of the rain and they will drop it where He wants it, on land or in the sea, and, if it is on land, then God will make the fields grow grass and green plants. *He it is who causes water to descend from heaven and with it We have caused plants to come out in all kinds, and green foliage and grains closely packed, and from the date-palm's sheath thick clusters, and orchards full of vines and olives and pomegranates, some similar, others not similar. Watch the fruiting and the ripeness. Therein are signs for the believers* (Qur'an 6:99). And if the rain falls in the sea, God creates tiny pearls and big ones. Aristotle has said that if rain falls in the ocean and at that time the north wind is blowing and a great downpour falls and the sea is agitated then it will bring up oyster shells to the surface, which will open their mouths and swallow the raindrops the way a vagina swallows a drop of sperm. The shells will attach themselves to certain places in the ocean and the raindrops will become pearls.

Ibn 'Abbas has said that God created mountains of snow and hail in Heaven just as on earth there are mountains of stone. *He sends down from heaven mountains of hail and hits whom He wishes with it!* (Qur'an 24:43). Some writers say that God has created angels half of whose bodies is snow and the other half is fire. So if God wishes snow to descend on a place he will order those angels to flap their wings; snow only falls on earth as a result of the flapping of angels' wings. Sometimes hailstones are so big that people and cattle are killed by them. According to Ka'b ibn al-Ahbar, between heaven and earth there is a thin cloud and above that there are white-headed birds with horses' heads, with tufts like women, and they have long wings. They have no refuge, no place to perch, neither in heaven nor on earth. They lay eggs and have chicks on the cloud in the air and they can sit on a cloud the way other birds sit on the water. Among the wonders of India there is, near a town called Dakkin, a mountain which seems to be totally on fire though there is no one to light it. On that mountain there lives a bird called Samandal which nests on that mountain in the fire quite happily because of its sympathy with fire, so that its feathers are not burnt.

The Qur'an says that God created the heavens and the earth in seven days. Some scholars say these were seven earth days but Ka'b ibn al-Ahbar and Ibn Jarir al-Tabari say that these were heavenly days and each day was as much as a thousand years. Ibn 'Abbas said that when God wished to create the earth He ordered the winds all together to whirl round, and they whirled until the waters were agitated and the waves whirled round and beat each other and this did not finish until some butter had formed, first as a skin, then as a hill; the butter waxed while the water receded by God's power. The water surrounded the land and it was like a round object resting in the water; He then split it up into seven strata just as there are seven strata in the heavens. Between two strata there is a distance of 500 years travelling. So it says in the Qur'an 21:30: *We split both open and made from water every living thing.* The name of the first stratum of the earth is Adima, the second is Basita, the third Thaqila, the fourth Batiha, the fifth Hina, the sixth Masika, and the seventh Tharay.

Al-Tha'labi says that on the second earth live some tribes called Iltamas, whose food is each other's flesh and whose beverage is each other's blood. On the third stratum live some tribes whose faces are like the sons of Adam but their mouths are like the mouths of dogs; their hands are like human hands but their feet are like cows' feet, and their ears are like cows' ears and they have fur on their bodies like sheep's wool which is to them like clothes. Their day is our night and their night is our day. On the fourth earth-floor live tribes called al-Hallam; they have neither eyes nor feet, but they have wings like partridges. On the fifth earth-floor live tribes called al-Khashan who are like a type of mule with tails which are 300 cubits long. On that earth grow tall palm-trees; camels live there also. On the sixth earth-floor live tribes called al-Huthum who have black bodies and claws as big as lions' claws. It is said that God will give them power over Gog and Magog at the time when these will swarm out, and they will destroy them. The seventh stratum is the domicile of the devil, the accursed Iblis and his hosts, his rebellious satans.

Some scholars say that the earth is flat while others maintain that it is globular standing in the sky with the heavens revolving around it equally on all sides. The reason why it is standing in the middle is the speed of the rotation of the firmament and its repulsion of it from all directions towards the centre, just like dust placed in a jar; if the jar is spun round with force, the dust will stay in the centre.

The earth is surrounded by the world ocean which is 24,000 pharsangs across (132,000 km.); it sits like a ring around a finger encircling the earth totally. Ibn 'Abbas says that outside the earth there is darkness and behind that darkness there is the mountain of Qaf. It is related that when God created the earth, it was suspended in the air. Then a storm wind came and beat it so the earth became confused and unsteady. It called out: 'O Lord, now the food (that I must grow) is perishing because that wind is shaking me!' God hid the wind and revealed to the Earth: 'I supported you by means of those mountains'. Then it settled down and all trembling calmed. Wahb ibn Munabbih has said that the mountains were created from the waves of the sea. *He raised (the sky) as a roof and made it level. He made the night dark, then made dawn come out. Then He spread out the earth. He made water come out of it, and pastures. He anchored the mountains, for your use, and your cattle* (Qur'an 79:28–33). This passage proves that God created the heavens long before the earth. Al-Tha'labi said that when God had created the earth He sent an angel to it from beneath His throne. The angel entered the space under the seven earths, stretched out one hand towards the east and the other to the west, and so held the earth on both sides, but there was no support for the angel's feet. So God caused a bull to descend from paradise; its name was Nun. It has 40,000 horns; the distance from horn to horn is 500 years. The angel's feet settled on that bull. But now the bull's feet had no support. So God caused a green ruby from among the rubies of Paradise to descend; its circumference is 500 years, and the legs of that bull steadied themselves on that single ruby of green hue. Then God Almighty created a rock as big as heaven and earth together and the name of this rock is Saykhur. It is said that there are in this rock 9,000 hollows and in each hollow there is an ocean and only God knows its size. God had fixed the green ruby on that rock. God Almighty caused the fish whose name is Behemot to descend from the seventh sea which is under the Throne and it is said that that rock was settled on the back of the fish. It is also said that no one can look at that fish because of the glare in its eyes, and if the seas of the earth were all placed in one of its nostrils, they would be together like a mustard-seed on the earth. The fish was standing on the water without moving and it spoke: 'Oh God, praise be to You! By Your power I am capable of carrying what You have given me to carry. Permit me to thank you!' God permitted it and the fish put its head in the water, then took it out again, performing the prostration, which it will continue to do until the Day of Resurrection. Then God created air, under the water and under the air, darkness, and beyond that all knowledge is cut off.

It is narrated that God entrusted the care of the fish to the angels who will arrive with its breakfast every day, as much as it needs; every morning they bring it a thousand fish, each fish being a day's and a night's journey long. For the bull likewise God appointed angels to prepare its breakfast; every day a thousand trees from the Parks of Power, each tree being a day's and night's journey long. Praise be to God Almighty.

It is reported that the accursed devil never stopped trying to penetrate the seven earths until he at last arrived at the fish called Behemot and he talked seductively to the fish and also to the bull which was standing on the fish's back. He said to the fish that the bull was too heavy and its feet too sharp, but God made a carpet which He laid on the fish's back.

Ibn 'Abbas has said that God created the earth on a Saturday, the mountains on a Sunday, and the trees on Monday. On Tuesday He created the vines. On Wednesday He created darkness and light, and on Thursday the dumb animals. Friday, finally, He created Adam. The learned authors differ about the first day of creation; some say it was a Sunday, others that it was a Monday. On Friday he also created the sun, the moon, and the stars. He created Adam only in late afternoon on Friday when the sun was declining. It is called Friday (Day of Joining in Arabic) because on that day Adam's clay was joined. In the extreme north, the region of Capricorn, there are six months of winter when the sun does not shine and all the water is frozen all the time so that no animals can live there. In the extreme south, however, the region of Canopus, there are six months of daylight and summer heat so that no grass grows there either and no animals can live there because of the hot wind. No person can live in that nightless region.

3.1.2 Al-Tabari's account of Abraham and his son whom he was commanded to sacrifice

The reason lying behind God ordering Abraham to sacrifice his son, according to what is related, is as follows. When Abraham left his people, becoming a fugitive on account of his religion and an emigrant for his Lord, he went towards al-Sham and left Iraq. He called unto God, asking that He give him a righteous son by Sarah. He said: *O my Lord, give to me one of the righteous* (Qur'an 37:100), that is, a child who is one of the righteous, just as God mentioned about him in Qur'an 37:99–100: *He said: I am going to my Lord; He will guide me. Oh my Lord give to me one of the righteous.* When the angelic visitors who were sent to those sinners, the community of Lot, came to him, they gave him the good news of a gentle boy as they had been ordered by God with His blessing. When Abraham was told this he said: 'He will be a sacrifice for God!' When the boy was born and reached puberty, it was said to him: 'Keep your vow which you made to God!'

The accounts of those who report that are as follows.

Gabriel said to Sarah: 'I bring you good news of a son whose name is Isaac and after him Jacob'. She struck her brow out of wonderment as God said in Qur'an 51:29: *She struck her forehead* and she said: *Shall I give birth when I am old and this my husband is old? Indeed this is something most strange! They said: 'Do you marvel at God's command? The mercy and blessings of God are on you, o people of the house. Indeed He is praiseworthy and glorious'*. Sarah then said to Gabriel: 'What is the sign of that?' He took a dry stick in his hand, bent it between his fingers such that it shook and turned green. Abraham said: 'He will be a sacrifice for God!'

When Isaac was grown, someone appeared to Abraham in a dream and said to him: 'Keep your vow which you made! God bestowed upon you a boy by Sarah so that you may sacrifice him'. So he said to Isaac: 'Let us go offer a sacrifice to God!' So he took a knife and some rope and went with him until they reached a place in the mountains. The boy said to him: 'O father! Where is your sacrifice?' He replied: 'O my son, I saw in a dream that I will slaughter you. So pay attention to what you see'. He said: 'O my father, do what you have been commanded; you will find me, if God wills, one of the patient'. Isaac then said to him: 'Make tight my bonds so that I will not struggle to pull back your clothes so that none of my blood will be shed on them for Sarah will see it and be grieved. Hurry! Pass the knife over my throat so that death will be easy for me. When you come to Sarah, greet her'. Abraham began to approach him and, while crying, tied him up. Isaac too was crying such that the tears gathered by the cheek of Isaac. He then drew the knife along his throat but the knife did not cut, for God had placed a sheet of copper on the throat of Isaac. When he saw that, he turned him on his forehead and nicked him on the back of the head just as God has said in Qur'an 37:103: *When they had both submitted and he flung him on his forehead*, that is they had submitted the affair to God. A voice called out: 'O Abraham, you have fulfilled the vision!' He turned around and behold, there was a ram. He took it and released his son and he bent over his son saying: 'O my son, today you have been given to me'. That comes in God's saying in Qur'an 37:107: *We ransomed him with a great sacrifice*. He returned to Sarah and told her the news. Sarah became anxious and said: 'O Abraham, you set out to sacrifice my son, and you did not inform me!' . . .

When Abraham was ordered to slaughter his son he said to him: 'O my son, take the rope and the butcher's knife and come with me to the mountains so that your family may gather firewood there'. This he said before mentioning anything about that which he had been ordered to do. When he headed off towards the mountains, he was obstructed in his path by that enemy of God, Iblis, who was trying to prevent him from fulfilling the command of God. Iblis, who had taken on the form of a man, said: 'Where are you going, O Shaykh?' He replied: 'I am going to these mountains because I must do something there'. Iblis said: 'By God, I have seen that Shaytan has come to you in a dream and ordered you to slaughter this little son of yours. And you intend to do that slaughtering!' Thereupon Abraham recognised him and said: 'Get away from me, enemy of God! By God, I will most certainly continue to do what my Lord has commanded'. Iblis, the enemy of God, gave up on Abraham but then he encountered Ishmael, who was behind Abraham carrying the wood and the large knife. He said to him: 'O young man, do you realise where your father is taking you?' He said: 'To gather wood for our family from the mountains'. He replied: 'By God, his actual intention is to sacrifice you!' He said: 'Why?!' Iblis replied: 'He claims that his Lord has ordered him to do so!' Ishmael replied: 'He must do what his Lord commands, absolutely!' When the young man had rebuffed him, Iblis went to Hagar, the mother of Ishmael who was still at home. Iblis said to her: 'O mother of Ishmael! Do you realise where Abraham is going with Ishmael?' She replied: 'They have gone to gather wood for us in the mountains'. He said: 'He has actually gone in order to sacrifice him!' She replied: 'It cannot be! He is too kind and too loving towards him to do that!' Iblis said: 'He claims that God has ordered him to do that!' Hagar said: 'If his Lord has ordered him to do that then he must submit to the command of God!' So the enemy of God returned exasperated at not being able to influence the family of Abraham as he wished. Abraham and his family had rebuffed him with the help of God and they agreed upon the command of God absolutely. When Abraham and his son reached the mountains (which are claimed to be the Thabir mountains), he said: 'O my son! I saw in a dream that I should slaughter you!' Ishmael replied: 'O my father! Do as you have been commanded! You will find me, if God wills, one of the patient'.

Ibn Hamid said that Salama said that Muhammad ibn Ishaq said on the authority of people who know that Ishmael said to his father about that: 'O my father! I welcome my being sacrificed. Fasten my bonds securely so that you will not be harmed by me and so that my recompense will not be diminished. Death is difficult. I do not believe that I will waver at that moment when I sense death's touch. Whet your knife so that you may finish me off and thereby release me. When you lay me down to slaughter me, turn me over on my face. Do not lay me down on my side for I fear that if you gaze into my face, weakness will overtake you and that will come between you and the command of God concerning me. Indeed, I think that you should take my shirt to my mother for it may be that this will be a comfort to her from me. So do it!' Abraham said: 'How wonderful a help you are, O my son, in fulfilling the command of God!' So he bound him just as Ishmael had asked, whetted his knife and flung him on his forehead, making sure that he did not look in his face. He put the knife up to his throat but God turned it around in Abraham's hand. Abraham grasped it again in order to be finished with Ishmael but a voice cried out: 'O Abraham, you have fulfilled the vision! This is your sacrificial victim, a ransom for your son. So sacrifice it, not him!' This is as God said in Qur'an 37:103: *When the two of them submitted and he flung him on his forehead.* Instead he flung the sacrificial victims on their sides. This report is, according to us, truthful in the matter of Ishmael in his indications to his father in accordance with what was indicated when he said: 'Turn me over on my face', in God's saying in Qur'an 37:103–7: *And he flung him on his forehead and we called to him 'O Abraham! You have fulfilled the vision'. In this way we recompense the good-doers. Indeed this certainly is the clear trial. And We ransomed him with a great sacrifice.*

'Abd Allah ibn 'Abbas said that a ram was driven out for him from paradise;

it had grazed there for forty years prior to that. Abraham sent his son and he captured the ram. He took it to the first pile of stones at Mina and pelted it with seven rocks and he set it free. It went to the middle pile of stones. He extracted it from there and pelted it with seven more rocks and then set it free. He caught up with it at the greatest pile of stones and threw seven more rocks at it and took it out of there. Then he took it and brought it to the place of slaughter at Mina and there sacrificed it. By He who holds the soul of Ibn 'Abbas in His midst, this was the beginning of Islam and the head of the ram was hung by its horns to the gutter of the Ka'ba.

Ibn 'Abbas said that when Abraham was ordered concerning the rituals, Satan came to him at al-Sa'y (in Mecca) and tried to defeat him. But Abraham arrived first with Gabriel, on whom may there be peace, accompanying him, to the Jamrat al-'Aqaba. Satan came to him so Abraham pelted him with seven rocks until Satan left. But he met him again at the middle pile of stones so he pelted him again with seven rocks until Satan left. Then he threw Ishmael on his forehead, while he was wearing a white shirt. He said to him: 'Oh my father! I do not have anything for a burial shroud except for this shirt. So take it off me and use it as my burial shroud!' So Abraham turned around and behold there was a choice, white, horned ram. So he sacrificed it.[1]

[Swahili]

d.1766

3.2 MUHAMMAD

3.2.1 *Mawlid al-Barzanji* – the birth story of Muhammad

When God willed the appearance of His truth, the lore of Muhammad, and its manifestation in a body and in a soul, in a form and in a content, He transferred it to its fixed abode, from the peaceful colourful shell. And He, the Near One, the Answerer, selected her to be the mother of the Purified One. And it was proclaimed in the Heavens and on Earth that she, Amina, had become pregnant of one of the Lights of the Essence. And every zephyr blew gently to make a soft breeze freshly fanning the earth which was dressed, after her long period of barrenness, with vegetation with green silken robes. The fruits began to ripen, and the trees approached the picker that he might pick the ripe fruits. And every domestic animal of the Quraysh spoke of his being expected with eloquence in the Arabic tongue.

The thrones of royalty were overturned and the idols of heathendom fell on their faces. The wild animals of East and West prophesied the good tidings, as well as the creatures of the sea. The worlds drank joy from the cup of juvenile strength. The spirits received the glad tiding of the imminence of his time. The value of heathen priesthood diminished and the Christian monks began to be afraid. But every learned scholar was overjoyed with the news and proud with the beauty of this ornament. His mother was visited in her sleep and was told: 'Lo! You have become pregnant of the lord of the worlds, the best of men. When you have given birth to him, call him Muhammad, because his final reward will be praised'.

When she had completed two months of her pregnancy of him whose words were to become famous for their aromatic sweetness, his father 'Abd Allah died in the enlightened city of Medina, while he was staying with his maternal uncles, the Banu Adiy, carpenters of Ta'if. He remained ill for a month. They tended him in his sickness, trying to relieve all his pains.

When nine lunar months of the heavy pregnancy had passed, the time approached that his voice should manifest itself. In the night of the birth there were present with his mother, Asiya and Mary among the women from Paradise.[2] The pains of labour seized her and she gave birth to him – Peace be upon him – and light pearled around his glory, his face shining like the sun, illuminating the night; the night of the nativity which is a joy for religion; the night in which Amina, the daughter of Wahb, received honour which He has never given to any woman. To her family came someone better than the Virgin Mary had borne before her. The consequences of Muhammad's birth held nothing but ill health and pestilence in the horoscopes of the infidels. Voices in the air[3] spread the glad message continually that the Purified one was born and joy had come true.

Muhammad appeared and placed his hands on the earth, raising his head to the high heavens, signifying with this his ultimate rise to power and high authority, and pointing toward the elevation of his power over all other people; and that he was the beloved whose character and nature were good.

His mother called 'Abd al-Muttalib who was around; he appeared, looked at him, and felt great joy overwhelm him. He introduced him to the Ka'ba; he stood there praying with sincere intention and thanked God Almighty for what He had given him. He was born pure, circumcised; his umbilical cord was cut by the hand of Divine Power. He was born fragrant and endued with pomade, his eyes coloured with kohl of divine care.

It is also said that his grandfather circumcised him after seven days.[4] At the occasion he gave a feast and a big meal; he called his grandson Muhammad, and regaled all the residents of his dwelling place.

At the time of his birth there occurred many strange and miraculous things, as signs that God would raise the prophethood to a place of prominence, make it prosper, and that Muhammad was His chosen favourite. Heaven's protection was increased and the audacity of the satanic spirits was removed from it. And the fiery projectiles chased all the accursed spirits from their positions on the ladder to heaven. And for him the glowing stars became more brilliant and with their light the depth and height of the sacred and of forbidden things became illuminated. With him light came forth which shone for him over the castles of imperial Syria. And whoever had the valley of Mecca for his home, could see it and its significance. The palaces in the cities of the Persian kings began to crack, those palaces for which Anushirwan[5] had raised the roofs and made them symmetric. And fourteen of the highest pinnacles came crashing down. The Persian empire was broken because of terror of what would befall it and despoil it. The adored sacred fires in all the realms of the Persians were extinguished. All this happened when the full moon rose brightly and Muhammad's face appeared. A lake, Sawa, which was just between Hamadan and Qumma (two cities in Persia) diminished in size; it dried up entirely when the flow of abundant waves was withdrawn from the springs of these waters. Wadi Samawa filled up with water, and it became a refuge for people in the desert. Previously there had been no water in it that was of any use to the thirst of uvulas. His birth took place a little before dawn on Monday 12 Rabi' al-Awwal in the year of the elephant which God turned away from Mecca, protecting the city (A.D. 570).

His mother suckled him during the first few days, afterwards Thuwayba of the Aslam clan suckled him; she was a freed slave of Abu Lahab. She arrived about the time of his birth, when it was being announced. She suckled him together with her son Masruh, and she welcomed him very much. Before him, she had suckled Hamza, who was later praised for his help to religion. Muhammad later sent her gifts and clothes; she was worth it. He even offered her a monument, as he was always anxious to reward the good things he had received, and he placed it over her grave. It was said against the religion of her tribe that it was a relic of the time of ignorance. It is said that she became a Muslim; Ibn Manda confirms the difference of opinion and relates this version.

Afterwards the young woman Halima suckled him; she was a Sa'diyya, a daughter of the Banu Sa'ada. Every member of her tribe had already rejected her milk because of her poverty. But she had plenty of food for supper after the period of dearth which they had had. Her bosom began to flow abundantly in pearls of milk; her right breast gave milk to one of the two, the other one to his milk-brother. After the time of meagreness and of poverty, she found herself soon rich. And the Noble one grew fat with her, and so did the sheep. And every misfortune and ill luck vanished from her side. The clan of the Sa'ada used to embroider striped cloths and dye them, which provided them with a good living.

Swahili 3.2.2 The night journey and ascension of Muhammad

When they reached the blessed mosque, they saw light radiating from two directions, one from the niche of David with the window, and the other one was a light ray from the grave of Mary. They went inside and prayed a *salat* of two prostrations. They saw the prophets meet in the mosque. Gabriel then went up and called the prayer-call. He performed the prayer but they did not know who would be the leader of the prayer. Gabriel said: 'You must be leader of the prayer, you are the *imam*; the prophets are behind you, you step forward and stand in line. Yours is the salvation and the honour and the glorification. You are the chosen intercessor for all people of good will'. When they finished praying every man pronounced God's names, the qualities of the Lord, and was grateful for the bliss. They congratulated themselves with the gifts of the Forgiver. The qualities of the prophet surpass those of other prophets. Thirst seized the confessor, and cups arrived, filled with milk, water, honey, and sweet palm wine. The intercessor chose the milk and he obtained his request, the prayer for faith and guidance from God. Finally a ladder descended from heaven, decorated with silver and gold and corallite; the prophet and his faithful friend ascended to heaven. They knocked on the gate and the celestial beings answered. They said: 'Who is the owner of the Light that spreads through heaven?' Gabriel answered: 'The intercessor of the good and the evil'. They opened it with haste and hurry, and met him with respect, paying him homage. The prophet saw our forefather, the prophet Adam. He was shown the souls of his progeny and he recognised them; where there was a happy and good soul, he smiled, (but he) wept when it was a bad soul for Hell.[6] He began his greeting to the confessor saying: 'Welcome noble son, messenger, prophet. The guidance is yours, having the star of fortune, you are the leader, going at the head and all the prophets go behind you'. After that they passed on and arrived at the second heaven; knocking as before and being answered as the first time. He saw Jesus and St. John, both of them, their appearance was identical like children of one mother. He greeted them, and they rose to stand for him, to honour him with respect and call him by name. When they had parted, they passed on and arrived at the third heaven, and they knocked with reverence. They were answered: 'Welcome, honourable one'. He saw the sincere Joseph with his fine appearance. He began greeting the confessor with respect. He welcomed him and put him in a good place. After that they arrived at the fourth heaven rapidly. Gabriel said: 'Open ye, the good messenger is here'. He said: 'Welcome, come through with him without delay. The divine assistance is with the intercessor, the good creature'. When he arrived he was met by Idris. The fourth heaven was his post, his seat. He said: 'Welcome, be at ease and rest awhile. Divine assistance is yours, you have good fortune without end'. After that they passed on and arrived in the fifth heaven. They went in and met the Prophet Aaron. He welcomed them with the highest respect; they prayed to God and parted with a good prayer. Then they passed on, the intercessor and Gabriel, in the sixth heaven they arrived, both of them. They knocked on the gate with respect and reverence. It was opened for them and they saw Moses, the one to whom God spoke. They saw the army of Moses, in a state of readiness, and the Prophet was told: 'Raise your head and look!' He saw the army, he could not see where it ended. He was told: 'The army you are seeing is yours, prophet'. He saw Moses, his shape was like that of an animal, he had many hairs standing upright, in spikes. The intercessor greeted him first. Moses answered: 'Welcome to my good brother. You are the good brother, the intercessor for the whole flock, and your community is the best of all communities. When you go to God, you will be given His Generosity, then remember us too, that He may grant us to be your servants'. Finally they passed on and arrived at the seventh heaven. Gabriel said: 'I have come with the beloved. Open the gate that the prophet of the Lord may pass'. So they opened up and God's prophet passed. He saw a person of high rank and great state. The prophet asked: 'Which man is it?' He said: 'Khalil, the friend of God, he is your grandfather and origin'. He gave greetings to his forefather Abraham. Abraham welcomed him and said: 'Yours is the honour. O, intercessor, announce to your community, that they must climb the rungs into Paradise and pay homage, and (then climb) the rungs of the ladder of glorification to the highest Lord'. And where they were, there were many white people, as white as paper, and others mixed; they went into the fire, then joined those who were similar; the prophet said: 'What sort of people are those dignified ones?' Gabriel said: 'These people are like paper, they are the good people, they commit no ignoble deeds; and these others, they became entangled in temptation. They are the ones who committed bad deeds and then repented and became good'. Then they passed on and saw there, where they were, a crowded house, built right under paradise. They went inside and prayed. They saw there 700,000 angels, good creatures. And this number entered the house every day, others and again others in the past and in the present time. They visit the crowded house, it is their glory. Everyone who visits it and comes out, will not return there. And their announcer of prayer is the faithful Gabriel. Their leader of the prayer is Michael, who is in charge, on Fridays, to lead the prayers of two prostrations. They prayed a ritual prayer, and then a personal prayer to the Lord Most Generous. They pray for the prayers of the faithful which they hear, and Michael intercedes in prayers as the *imam*. And the whole communion of the guided is together pleading for them, saying accepted prayers which rise straight up to heaven. Finally they passed on, heading for the throne, the eighth step of the stairway of prophethood, where there is the jujube-tree[7] of the end of all things. They saw many wonderful things, without ending. They saw under it four rivers all flowing, water and milk and honey, and wine the fourth; and its jujube fruits are very sweet, like sugar; one leaf of it covers all nations. There is nobody who can be praised, indeed there is not, except our Lord Almighty, what pleases Him is only an order: 'Be!' And it is! He alters it and they cannot keep looking at the tree. Finally, the bringer of good tidings saw his own river, a present from God, its name is Abundance. They followed it and went along its bed, until they arrived at the good house of beatitude. They saw many creatures they had never seen, nor heard by reports from tellers of tales; and you did not yet think of it in your heart at all. They saw written on the door a good tradition: 'One is the alm and tenfold is its reward; and eighteenfold is promised to him who lends to a person who asks for a loan having suffered a loss. He who created the sacrifice to be asked for, He has also bliss to give'. He saw Paradise, he had never seen its likeness. It was adorned with silver and gold and corallite, and with emeralds and rubies full of colour, and many kinds of silk, good and pleasant. Then they went out and were shown a fierce fire, and he saw terrors of punishment, he could not bear it. He lost consciousness, his senses left him. Gabriel embraced him thereupon and he regained consciousness. The messenger passed on to the eight rung of the ladder. Gabriel could not go and stayed behind. He said: 'I cannot go one span further. Here is my place'. The intercessor went on. There came the cloud of grace of the Majesty, and covered the prophet. The prophet said to him: 'What is your need, friend? What you wish is only an order for God'. Gabriel said: 'My desire, that which I wish: That on the day of the bridge I may be a shield for your community. That I may stretch out my wings to be a protection for their footsteps, lest the hot fire of hell gets them'. Finally he sat down on the palanquin and it went with him. He passed all veils and finally saw Him, my Holy Lord, without physical appearance, with his eyes and there was nowhere to stand, no standing place.[8] He saw the Lord with his two eyes. He began his greeting and his reverential greetings to the Majesty. God answered him: 'Peace be upon you, prophet. You are the chosen one who was placed in a good position'. When he saw Him, his Lord without equal, he could not utter a word with his voice; he went down on his knees. The Majesty spoke to him: 'Ask whatever you want and you will receive it all complete'. He said: 'My Lord, Your servant Abraham is your friend, and I, what is my share?' The Lord spoke to him: 'You are my prophet, remember. My beloved is better than all prophets'. He said: 'We have given David his psalms; and you are the best of prophets, you are the final one. And Solomon the power over demons and birds. When I am mentioned by Name, your name will be mentioned after. And as Jesus has been healing every lame man, and as his word resuscitated those who had died, I have given you to resuscitate many as well. Yours is the treasure of the throne which has no end. And your community is better than all the others. On the Day of Resurrection you will come to witness. When all the unbelievers deny, I tell you, they did not follow the words of those who were sent. O prophet of the first and the last, who will intercede for your community on the heavy day of rally. On the day of the narrow bridge, that will be stretched over the fire, you will that day pray for the bad and the good. These things that you have been given, there is no other person who received them. Praise God for them, give thanks for My gifts. I have made compulsory fifty prayers for you to carry out. You and your community, pray them completely every day'. The veil of light was raised and he went back, and arrived where the faithful Gabriel was. They both descended and saw the prophet Moses, and Muhammad told him the story unto its end. Moses told him: 'Your community will not bear it. Fifty prayers every day is too heavy for them. Turn back to the Lord, beg Him a favour, let Him reduce it for you; your people are weak'. The Prophet went back to the place of meeting with his generous Lord. He begged for alleviation in favour of his people, and he got a reduction of five prayers and remembered them. He arrived at Moses' place, and he told him: 'Go back prophet. Ask for alleviation from your God, the lenient Lord'. And it was a going and returning, he took charge of this task until He reduced it to five prayers as an alleviation God told him: 'My favours have now come to an end. For do not say that five prayers are the original number. They will be given a requital, so take ten prayers, to be certain. This is the number of five prayers out of fifty'. The

Eternal God did not change His word. 'Whoever intends to do a good work, receives clemency for his good acts from God. When a person does so, that person will be rewarded with a good reward. For one act of charity is rewarded with ten rewards in total. Whoever intends to do a bad deed but does not commit it, will not be noted as having had the intention; and whoever did it will be noted one for one, by the favour of our Lord who is Merciful.' Finally they descended and reached the heaven below; they saw dust and heard voices and smoke was inside. The prophet asked Gabriel: 'What sort of people are they?' He said: 'The satans are prevented from seeing Heaven'. After that they descended and arrived in the night, in the holy temple, the house of eternal boon. They saw Burak, she was on the same place as originally. The prophet mounted her in the name of God.

3.2.3 Traditions (*hadith*) concerning Muhammad

3.2.3.1 Al-Bukhari on drink

Chapter: God has said in Qur'an 5:90: *Wine, gambling, idols, and divining arrows are an abomination* and so on to the end of the verse.

'Abd Allah ibn Yusuf told us that Malik informed him on the authority of Nafi' from Ibn 'Umar, may God be pleased with him, that the Messenger of God, may the prayers and peace of God be upon him, said: 'Whoever drinks wine in this world and does not repent of it will find it forbidden in the hereafter'.

Abu Yaman told us that Shu'ayb informed him on the authority of al-Zuhri (who said) that Sa'id ibn al-Musayyab informed him that he heard Abu Hurayra, may God be pleased with him, say that when the Messenger of God went on his night journey (to Jerusalem) he was given two cups, one containing wine, the other milk. He looked at them both and took the milk. Gabriel said: 'Praise be to God who has guided you to the true state of humanity. If you had taken the wine, your nation would have gone astray'.

Muslim ibn Ibrahim told us that Hisham told him that Qatada informed him on the authority of Anas, may God be pleased with him, who said: 'I heard from the messenger of God a *hadith* which no one but me shall tell you. He said: "Among the signs of the final hour are that ignorance shall become rampant and knowledge will decrease; fornication will increase and wine will be drunk. The number of men will decrease while the number of women will increase such that there will be fifty women to each man" '.

Ahmad ibn Salih told us that Ibn Wahb told him that Yunus informed him on the authority of Ibn Shihab who said that he heard both Abu Salama ibn 'Abd al-Rahman and Ibn al-Musayyab saying that Abu Hurayra said that the prophet said: 'A person cannot commit fornication at the same time as being a believer, nor can that person drink wine and be a believer at the same time. Nor is a thief a believer when he is stealing'. Ibn Shihab said 'Abd al-Malik ibn abi

Bakr ibn 'Abd al-Rahman ibn al-Harith ibn Hisham informed me that Abu Bakr would transmit the report from Abu Hurayra and then add to the list: 'Whoever robs violently while people are looking on is not a believer at the same time'.

Chapter: Wine prepared from grapes and other substances

Al-Hasan ibn Sabbah told me that Muhammad ibn Sabiq told him that Malik, that is Ibn Mighwal, on the authority of Nafi' from Ibn Umar, may God be pleased with both of them, who said: 'Wine was forbidden although there was none in Medina at that time'.

Ahmad ibn Yunus told us that Abu Shihab 'Abd Rabbih ibn Nafi' on the authority of Yunus from Thabit al-Bunani from Anas who said: 'Wine was forbidden for us although at that time, that is in Medina, we could find very little grape wine; our normal wine was made from ripe and unripe dates'.

Musaddad told us that Yahya told him on the authority of Abu Hayyan who was told by 'Amir on the authority of Ibn 'Umar, may God be pleased with both of them, who said that 'Umar ascended the *minbar* and said: 'The prohibition of wine has been revealed and this is of five kinds: (wine prepared from) grapes, dates, honey, wheat, or barley. Wine is what overcomes the mind'.

Chapter: The prohibition of wine prepared from unripe and ripe dates

Isma'il ibn 'Abd Allah told us that Malik ibn Anas told him on the authority of Ishaq ibn 'Abd Allah ibn Abi Talha from Anas ibn Malik, may God be pleased with him, who said: 'I was serving Abu 'Ubayda, Abu Talha, and Ubayy ibn Ka'b with a drink prepared from unripe and ripe dates. Then somebody came to them and said: "Wine has been forbidden!" Abu Talha said: "Get up, Anas, let us pour it out!" So I poured it out'.

Musaddad told us that Mu'tamar told him on the authority of his father who said: 'While I was serving something to drink to my uncles – I was the youngest of those present – someone said: "Wine has been forbidden". So they said to me: "Throw it away!" So I threw it away. I asked Anas what they were drinking and he said that it was wine made from unripe and ripe dates. Abu Bakr ibn Anas said that it was the uncles' wine and that Anas knew nothing about it. Some of my companions have told me that they heard Anas ibn Malik say that it was the uncles' wine on that day'.

Chapter: Wine prepared from honey called *al-bit'*

Ma'n said that he asked Malik ibn Anas about an unfermented honey or grape drink and he said that if it does not make one drunk there is no harm in it. Ibn al-Darawardi said that he asked about it and was told that it does not cause drunkenness so there is no harm in it.

'Abd Allah ibn Yusuf told us that Malik informed him on the authority of Ibn Shihab from Abu Salama ibn 'Abd al-Rahman that 'A'isha said that the messenger of God was asked about *al-bit'* and he said: 'All drinks which cause drunkenness are forbidden'.

Abu al-Yaman told us that Shu'ayb informed him on the authority of al-Zuhri who said that Abu Salama ibn 'Abd al-Rahman informed him that 'A'isha, may God be pleased with her, said that the messenger of God was asked about *al-bit'* which is a drink made from honey which the Yemenites used to drink. He said: 'All drinks which cause drunkenness are forbidden'.

The same people report on the authority of al-Zuhri who said that he was told by Anas that the messenger of God said: 'Do not prepare wine in empty gourds or special bowls'. Abu Hurayra used to add to those two a kind of jar and a container made from the trunk of a date-palm.

Chapter: What has been reported concerning the statement that wine is that which overcomes the mind

Ahmad ibn Abi Raja' told us that Yahya told him on the authority of Abu Hayyan al-Taymi from al-Sha'bi from Ibn 'Umar, may God be pleased with both of them, that he said that 'Umar was delivering a sermon from the pulpit of the messenger of God saying: 'The prohibition of wine made from five things, grapes, dates, wheat, barley, and honey, has been revealed. Wine is that which overcomes the mind. I wish that the messenger of God had not left us before deciding for us (the inheritance of) the grandfather, the person with no male heir and the various types of usury'. I said: 'O Abu 'Amr, what of something made from rice?' He said: 'That was not stipulated at the time of the prophet of God', or he said: 'in the statement of 'Umar'. Hajjaj, according to Hammad on the authority of Abu Habban, said (that this tradition should say) 'raisins' in the place of 'grapes'.

Hafs ibn 'Umar told us that Shu'ba told him on the authority of 'Abd Allah ibn Abi al-Safar from al-Sha'bi from Ibn 'Umar from 'Umar who said: 'Wine is made from five things: raisins, dates, wheat, barley, and honey'.

Chapter: What is reported concerning the one who regards wine as lawful when it is called by another name

Hisham ibn 'Ummar said that Sadaqa ibn Khalid told him that 'Abd al-Rahman ibn Yazid told him that 'Atiya ibn Qays al-Kilabi told him that 'Abd al-Rahman ibn Ghanm al-Ash'ari told him that Abu 'Amir or Abu Malik al-Ash'ari who, by God, did not lie to him, said that he heard the prophet saying: 'Among my people there will be some who will consider illicit sex, wearing silk, drinking wine, and playing musical instruments as permitted. There will also be some people who will dwell near the side of a hill. Someone will deliver their roving animals to them, coming to them out of a need. They will say to him to come back tomorrow. God will plot against them at night and will let the hill crush them and He will change the rest of them into monkeys and pigs leaving them like that until the day of resurrection'.

Chapter: Drinking while standing

Abu Nu'aym told us that Ma'mar told him on the authority of 'Abd al-Malik ibn Maysara from al-Nazzal who said that 'Ali, may God be pleased with him, came to the gate of the courtyard and had a drink while standing and said: 'Some people do not like anybody to drink while they are standing but I saw the prophet do just what you saw me do'.

Adam told us that Shu'ba told him that 'Abd al-Malik ibn Maysara told him that he heard al-Nazzal ibn Sabra reporting on the authority of 'Ali, may God be pleased with him, that after he prayed at noon he sat down in the courtyard of the mosque in Kufa to attend to the needs of the people until the time of the afternoon prayer. Water was brought to him and he drank some and ritually washed his face, hands, head, and feet. He then stood up and drank the rest while standing. He then said: 'Some people do not like drinking while standing but the prophet used to do just as I have done'.

Abu Nu'aym told us that Sufyan told him on the authority of 'Asim al-Ahwal from al-Sha'bi from Ibn 'Abbas that he said that the prophet drank from the well of Zamzam while standing.

Chapter: Drinking from golden vessels

Hafs ibn 'Umar told us that Sha'ba told him on the authority of al-Hakam from Ibn Abi Layla who said that while Hudhayfa was at al-Mada'in, he asked for some water. The chief came with a silver vessel so Hudhayfa threw it away saying: 'I have thrown it away because I forbade him to use it but he did not stop. The prophet forbade us from wearing silk or silk brocade and from drinking from gold or silver vessels saying: "They are for them in this world but for you in the hereafter" '.

Chapter: Silver vessels

Muhammad ibn al-Muthanna told us that Ibn Abi 'Adi told him on the authority of Ibn 'Awn from Mujahid from Ibn Abi Layla who said that they went out with Hudhayfa and he mentioned that the prophet had said: 'Do not drink from gold or silver vessels, do not wear silk or silk brocade. These things are from them in this world but are for you in the hereafter'.

Isma'il told us that Malik ibn Anas told him on the authority of Nafi' from Zayd ibn 'Abd Allah ibn 'Umar from 'Abd Allah ibn 'Abd al-Rahman ibn Abi Bakr al-Siddiq from Umm Salama, wife of the prophet, that the messenger of God said: 'Those who drink from silver vessels are dragging their bellies through the fire of hell'.

Musa ibn Isma'il told us that Abu 'Awana told him on the authority of al-Ash'ath ibn Sulaym from Mu'awiya ibn Suwayd ibn Muqarran from al-Barra' ibn 'Azib who said: 'The messenger of God ordered us to do seven things and forbade seven things. He ordered us to visit the sick, to follow funeral processions, to bless someone who sneezes, to accept invitations, to greet everyone, to help the oppressed, and to help those who swear oaths. He forbade us to wear gold rings, to drink from silver vessels, to use silk coverings on saddles, to wear two kinds of silk or two kinds of silk brocade'.

3.2.3.2 Muslim on reciting surah 1 in prayer

The reciting of surah 1 in every *rak'a* of prayer is obligatory

'Ubada ibn al-Samit said that it reached him that the prophet said: 'Whoever does not recite surah 1 is not credited with having observed prayer'.

'Ubada ibn al-Samit said: The messenger of God said: 'Whoever does not recite the mother of the Qur'an (i.e. surah 1) is not credited with having observed prayer'.

Mahmud ibn al-Rabi', on whose face the messenger of God squirted water from their well, said that 'Ubada ibn al-Samit informed him that the messenger of God said: 'Whoever does not recite the mother of the Qur'an is not credited with having observed prayer'.

Abu Hurayra reported that the prophet said: 'If anyone observes a prayer in which they do not recite the mother of the Qur'an, it is deficient'. He said this three times without finishing. It was said to Abu Hurayra: '(This is required even when) we are behind the prayer leader?' He said: 'Recite it inwardly. I heard the messenger of God saying that God had said: "I have divided the prayer into two halves between Me and My servant and My servant will receive what is requested. When the servant says: *Praise belongs to God, Lord of all beings*, God says: My servant has praised Me. When the servant says: *The Merciful, the Compassionate*, God says: My servant has lauded Me. When the servant says: *Ruler of the judgement day*, He says: My servant has glorified Me, and sometimes He says: My servant has entrusted himself to Me. When the servant says: *Only you do we serve and only from You do we seek aid*, He says: This is between Me and My servant and My servant will receive what is asked for. When the servant says: *Guide us along the straight path, the path of those whom You have blessed, not those against whom You have sent your wrath nor those who are astray*, He says: This is My servant and My servant will receive what is asked for'.[9] Sufyan said that al-'Ala' ibn 'Abd al-Rahman ibn Ya'qub told him (this report). He visited him while he was sick and he asked him about it.

Abu al-Samit, *mawla* of the tribe of 'Abd Allah ibn Hisham ibn Zuhra, said that he heard Abu Hurayra saying that the messenger of God said: 'If anyone observes a prayer in which they do not recite the mother of the Qur'an' and then it continues as in the report of Sufyan although in this report it says that God said: 'The prayer is divided into two halves between Me and My servant. One half is for Me, the other half is for My servant'.

Abu Hurayra said that the messenger of God said: 'Whoever has said a prayer and has not recited the opening chapter of the book, that prayer is deficient'. He said it three times the same way.

Abu Hurayra said that the messenger of God said: 'There is no prayer without a recitation'. So Abu Hurayra said: 'What the messenger of God recited in a loud voice, we recite in a loud voice for you and what he recited inwardly, we also recite inwardly for you'.

Abu Hurayra said: 'One must recite in every prayer. That which the messenger of God made us hear, we make you hear. That which he recited inwardly to us, we recite inwardly to you'. A man asked: 'What if we do not add to the recitation of the mother of the Qur'an?' He replied: 'If you add to it, that is good and if you stop with it, that will be enough for you'.

Abu Hurayra said: 'One must recite in every prayer. That which the messenger of God made us hear, we make you hear. That which he recited inwardly to us, we recite inwardly to you. Whoever recites the mother of the Qur'an, that is enough; whoever adds to it, that is better'.

Abu Hurayra said that the messenger of God entered the mosque and someone else entered also and prayed. That person then came and greeted the messenger of God. The messenger of God returned the greeting and said: 'Go back and pray for you have not prayed'. He again prayed as he had prayed previously and then came to the prophet and greeted him. The messenger of God returned the greeting and said: 'Go back and pray for you have not prayed'. This happened three times. Then the man said: 'By He who has sent you with the truth, Whatever I can do better than that, teach me!' So (Muhammad) said: 'When you get up to pray, say the *takbir* ("God is great!") and then recite whatever is easy for you from the Qur'an. Bow down and become quiet. Then rise up so that you are erect. Then prostrate yourself and become quiet. Then rise up and become quiet in a sitting position. Do that throughout all of your prayers'.

Abu Hurayra said that a man entered the mosque and prayed while the messenger of God was sitting in a corner. The rest of the report is the same as the preceding one but they add to it (that Muhammad said): 'When you get up to pray, complete the ablution. Then turn towards the *qibla* and say the *takbir*'.

3.2.3.3 Abu Dawud on medicine
Chapter: concerning the person who seeks a cure

Asama ibn Sharik said that he and Muhammad's companions flocked around Muhammad, greeted him, and sat down. Some bedouins from somewhere came and said: 'O messenger of God, will we receive cures?' He replied: 'There are already cures available. God has not created a disease without providing a cure for it with one exception and that is old age'.

Umm al-Mudhir bint Qays al-Ansariyya said: 'Ali, upon whom may there be peace, who was convalescing, came to Muhammad. At that time we had some dates hanging up to dry. The messenger of God began to eat from them and 'Ali got up in order to do likewise. Suddenly the messenger of God said to 'Ali: "Stop! You are convalescing!" So 'Ali refrained. I then made some barley with cooked vegetables and brought them to him. The messenger of God said: "Oh 'Ali! Eat this, for it is better for you!" '

Chapter: concerning the practice of cupping

Abu Hurayra said that the messenger of God said: 'If there is good in one thing which cures you, it is cupping'.

'Ubayd Allah ibn 'Ali ibn Abi Rafi' said on the authority of his grandmother Salma, servant of the messenger of God, that she said that any time someone complained of a pain in the head to the messenger of God he would say: 'Cup it!' or if it was a pain in the leg he would say: 'Dye it green!'

Chapter: concerning the place of cupping

Abu Kabsha al-Anmari said that the prophet had performed a cupping on his head and between his shoulders saying: 'Whoever sheds some of this blood will experience no pain in not being treated for a certain (disease) with a certain (cure)'.

Anas said that the prophet performed the cupping in three places: in the two veins of the neck and on the upper part of the back. Ma'mar said: 'I performed a cupping and lost my mind as a result until I managed to whisper the opening surah of the Qur'an in my prayer'. He had been cupped on his head.

Chapter: concerning the desirable time to perform the cupping

Abu Hurayra said that the messenger of God said: 'Whoever is cupped on the seventeenth, nineteenth, or twenty-first (of the month) will be healed of every disease'.

Kabsha bint Abi Bakra, or others say Kayyisa bint Abi Bakra, said that her father had forbidden his family to perform cupping on Tuesdays. He claimed on the authority of the messenger of God that Tuesday was the day of blood and that there was a certain hour during the day when blood would not cease to flow.

Jabir said that the prophet performed a cupping on his hip because of a pain there.

Chapter: concerning the cutting of veins and the place of cupping

Jabir said that the prophet sent a doctor to Ubayy and he cut one of his veins.

Chapter: concerning cauterisation

'Amran ibn Husayn said that the prophet prohibited cauterisation even though we had performed it. We were not lucky with it nor did we have success with it. Abu Dawud said that he (Muhammad) had heard the greetings of the angels but when he performed cauterisation he no longer heard them; but when he did not do that, he would hear them once again.

Chapter: concerning snuff

Ibn 'Abbas said that the messenger of God used to snuff (i.e. inhale substances as medicine).

Chapter: concerning spells

Jabir ibn 'Abd Allah said that the messenger of God was asked about spells (used against madness) and he said: 'They are some of the acts of Satan'.

Chapter: concerning antidotes

'Abd Allah ibn 'Amr said that he heard the messenger of God saying: 'I would not be concerned with that which I bring (i.e. the Qur'an) if I drank antidotes, put on amulets, or recited poetry on my own accord'. Abu Dawud said that this was for the prophet alone and that the people were allowed to use antidotes.

Chapter: concerning disapproved remedies

Abu Hurayra said that the messenger of God forbade harmful remedies.

'Abd al-Rahman ibn 'Uthman said that a doctor asked the prophet about frogs being put into remedies. The prophet forbade him from killing the frogs.

Abu Hurayra said that the messenger of God said: 'Whoever drinks a poison, poisoning himself by his own hand, drinks himself into the eternal fire of hell forever, remaining there for eternity'.

'Alqama ibn Wa'il said on the authority of his father (mentioning Tariq ibn Suwayd or Suwayd ibn Tariq) that he asked the prophet about wine which he then forbade. So he asked him again and he was refused again. We said to him: 'O prophet of God, it is a remedy!' The prophet replied: 'No, it is a disease'.

Abu'l-Darda' said that the messenger of God said: 'God has sent down diseases and remedies, and has provided a remedy for every disease. So treat yourselves but do not treat yourselves with forbidden substances'.

Chapter: concerning pressed dates

Sa'd said: 'I was sick and the messenger of God came to visit me. He placed his hands across my chest such that I found it cold on my heart. Then he said: "You have a faint heart. Bring al-Harith ibn Kalada, brother of Thaqif; he practises medicine. Let him take seven pressed Medinan dates and crush them complete with their pits. Then he should administer them to you" '.

'Amir ibn Sa'd ibn Abi Waqqas said on the authority of his father from the prophet who said: 'Whoever greets the morning with seven pressed dates will find that neither poison nor magic will cause harm on that day'.

Chapter: concerning treatment for sore throats

Umm Qays bint Muhsin said: 'I went to the messenger with one of my sons whom I had treated for a sore throat. He said: "Why do you employ this treatment on your children? Use this piece of Indian wood on them for it is a cure for seven things including pleurisy. One may snuff it for sore throats and administer it through the mouth for pleurisy" '. Abu Dawud explained that this is the wood of the costus plant, an aromatic plant.

Chapter: concerning the matter of kohl

Ibn 'Abbas said that the messenger of God said: 'Wear white clothes; they are your best ones. You should be shrouded in them when you are dead. Kohl of antimony is also good for you; it clears the vision and causes hair to grow'.

Ibn Ishaq

3.2.4 Muhammad as a statesman: the constitution of Medina

Ibn Ishaq said: The messenger of God wrote a document concerning the emigrants and the helpers in which he made a friendly agreement with the Jews and established them in their religion and their property, and stated the conditions, as follows.

In the name of God, the Merciful, the Compassionate. This is a writing from Muhammad the prophet, may the prayers and peace of God be upon him, governing the relations between the believers and Muslims of Quraysh and Yathrib, and those who follow them and join with them and strive with them. They are one community separate from other people. The Quraysh emigrants are responsible for their affairs and shall pay the blood-money among themselves and shall redeem their prisoners according to the custom and sense of justice common among the believers.

The tribe of 'Awf are responsible for their affairs and shall first pay the blood-money among themselves; every group shall redeem its prisoners according to the custom and sense of justice among the believers. The same is true of the tribes of Sa'ida, al-Harith, Jusham, al-Najjar, 'Amr ibn 'Awf, al-Nabit, and al-Aws.

Believers shall not leave anyone destitute among them without paying their redemption money or blood-money as is customary.

A believer shall not make an alliance with a freedman of a believer against that believer. The God-fearing believers shall oppose those who are rebellious and those who seek to spread injustice, sin, enmity, or corruption among the believers; the hand of everyone shall be against such a person even if he should be the son of one of them.

A believer shall not slay a believer for the sake of an unbeliever, nor support an unbeliever against a believer. God's protection is one; the least of them may give protection on behalf of them. Believers are allies to each other to the exclusion of other people. Help and equality shall be given to the Jews who follow us. They shall not suffer injustice nor shall their enemies be aided. The peace of the believers is indivisible; no separate peace shall be made when believers are fighting in the way of God unless the conditions are fair and equitable to all. For each raiding party raiding with us, there shall be one following the other. The believers must avenge on behalf of another for whatever harms their blood in the way of God. The God-fearing believers have the best and most upright guidance.

No polytheist shall protect the property or person of the unbelievers of Quraysh nor shall they intervene against a believer. Whoever kills a believer without good reason shall be killed in retaliation unless the next of kin of the deceased is satisfied with blood-money, and the believers shall be against that person altogether, and they are obligated to take action against such a person.

It shall not be lawful for a believer who agrees to what is in this document and who believes in God and the last day, to help or shelter an evil-doer. The curse of God and His wrath on the day of resurrection will be upon whoever does that, and neither repentance nor ransom will be accepted from that person. Whenever you differ about a matter it must be referred to God and to Muhammad.

The Jews shall pay taxes, while they are fighting, alongside the believers. The Jews of the tribe of 'Awf are one community with the believers, the Jews having their religion and the Muslims having theirs, their clients and themselves, except those who act wrongfully and sinfully, for they harm only themselves and their families. The same applies to the Jews of the tribes of al-Najjar, al-Harith, Sa'ida, Jusham, al-Aws, Tha'laba, Jafna (a clan of the Tha'laba), and al-Shutayba. Loyalty is a protection against treachery. The clients of Tha'laba are to be considered as a group. Those associated with the Jews are likewise to be considered as a group. None of them shall go out to war without the permission of Muhammad, but none shall be prevented from taking revenge for a wound. Whoever kills someone kills themselves and their household, unless the one killed has wronged them, for God will accept this.

The Jews must pay their own taxes and the Muslims their own taxes. There will be help between them against anyone who attacks the people of this document. Between them there will be goodwill and sincerity. Loyalty is a protection against treachery. No one shall violate their ally's pledge. Help is due to the wronged. The Jews must pay the tax with the believers so long as war lasts.

Yathrib shall be a sanctuary for the people of this document. A stranger under protection is like oneself; they shall not be harmed nor shall they commit crime. A woman shall only be given protection with the permission of her family. Whenever a dispute or controversy likely to cause trouble arises among the people of this document it shall be referred to God and to Muhammad, the apostle of God. God is the guarantor of the pious observance of what is in this document.

Unbelievers of Quraysh and whoever helps them shall not be given protection. There shall be help between the people of this document against any attack on Yathrib. If they are called to make peace and keep it, they shall make that peace and keep it; if they are called upon to do something similar to that, the believers are obliged to those who do so to go along with it except in the case of fighting for religion. Everyone shall be responsible for the side of the city in front of them; the Jews of al-Aws, their clients and themselves have the same rights as the people of this document with pure loyalty from the people of this document. Loyalty is a protection against treachery; whoever breaches a treaty only does so against themselves. God is the guarantor of the truth and the observance of what is in this document. This does not protect the unjust nor the sinner. Whoever goes forth to fight is safe and whoever stays at home in Yathrib is safe unless they have been unjust or sinned. God is the protector of the pious and the God-fearing and Muhammad is the messenger of God.[10]

Yahsubi   1088-1149

3.2.5 Muhammad's end

One night, the angel Gabriel descended from Heaven with a glad countenance. When the prophet asked him what joyful tidings he had to announce, Gabriel spoke: 'My brother Muhammad, I am happy to tell you that you will soon join me in Heave, for it has pleased my Master to decide that you will die tonight. Welcome to Heaven!' Thus spoke the angel to God's messenger: 'My brother, wise apostle of the Lord! / Please listen to these last words you will hear / from me while you are still alive on earth: / Come with me to my Paradise: it's home! / The birds are singing divine melodies. / The trees are all in bloom and full of flowers / of every colour that the rainbow shows. / I have adorned the gardens and the paths. / The prophets of the past wait eagerly / to welcome you as soon as you arrive. / Your parents and your grandparents are there. / Your first wife waits for you to join her soon, / devout and longing for her husband's love. / I have prepared your palace on a hill, / it overlooks the rivers where they join. / The fruit trees waving in the gentle breeze, / the foliage shading you from Eden's sun, / I put it all in place for you to see, / to live in and enjoy eternally, / for you will be near me for all the time. / Come with your loving brother Gabriel'.

There was a knock on the door of the prophet's house. His daughter Fatima went to open the door and there stood a tall stranger, who addressed her very politely in perfect Arabic, saying that he had to speak to Muhammad ibn 'Abd Allah on urgent business. He looked so serious, his face was so stern and lean, his eyes so large and dark, that Fatima became very frightened and refused to admit him. She shut the door in his face and ran to her father who was lying in bed, already mortally ill. 'Father, there is a man who must be very rude to disturb you so late in the evening. He speaks like an Arab nobleman, but I think he has come from a far country. I did not let him in, he made my heart skip a beat, so frightened was I.' Muhammad smiled and spoke gentle words to his daughter, describing the visitor he had not yet seen. 'My daughter, he that knocks on our door / is neither man nor woman but a slave / of God who sent him to me as a friend. / Yet many people fear him like a scourge, / although he never does a wicked thing. / Yet he makes widows weep when he arrives / to take their husbands from their loving arms, / he changes a child's life to orphanhood / and renders childless many parents' lives. / He is not stopped by doors nor held by walls, / no bolts or locks can shut him out, or in. / He comes when time has come without respite, / he tears the souls away from busy lives. / He goes where go he must and flies away / on noiseless wings as silent as an owl. / When he arrives all human labour ends. / House, wealth, and business is left behind, / for loved ones there is but a quick good-bye. / My child, the caller at the door is Death, / the angel who is sent by God to me, / because my time has come, my end is near, / so let him in for none can shut the door for him.'

Trembling, Fatima went back to open the door because her father said so. The tall stranger was still there, but now he came in, walked quietly up to Muhammad who greeted him warmly calling him 'My brother'. Then Azrail, the angel of death, – for it was he, God's final messenger – spoke solemnly: 'Prophet of God! It has pleased our Master to call you to Heaven. He – praised be His name – told me to respect your wishes to withdraw if you were not ready for me. You are the only one of his creatures to whom He has ever commanded me to grant respite'.

The prophet answered: 'Thank you, Lord of Death, I shall be ready in one hour. May I ask you to come back in an hour's time?' The angel of Death vanished from sight. The prophet bent down his loving head and wept.

Gabriel, the friendly angel, became visible again and asked: 'My brother, what makes you weep? Do you desire more days to live or are you afraid of dying?' 'No,' spoke Muhammad, 'I am neither desirous for a longer life nor afraid to end it. It is God's decree. His name be praised. I weep not for my friends and followers whose faith will lead them to heaven, nor for Fatima who will follow me after six months. I weep for those of my people who will disobey the Lord's commandments after I shall have died. Some will be rich but will pay no alms to the poor for a place in Paradise. Those who deny the word of God will be utterly lost. They will pay no attention to the law of Islam and neglect the prayers. I cannot redeem those who rebel against Him.'

When Fatima saw that her father was weeping she fell at his feet sobbing with grief, fearing the unknown. He said to her: 'My daughter do not weep too much, for death is an experience that awaits us all; it is merely fate fulfilled. Every mortal will taste death, infidels and Muslims too, each of us has his day to follow the road. Do not cry, my darling daughter, none of us can escape His decree'. Fatima asked her father, the possessor of true knowledge: 'When shall we meet again, and where will it be?' Spoke the prophet: 'We shall meet in a beautiful garden where there is plenty of shade and where all our friends will be, and your mother too, will be there to greet you. And my friend Gabriel will be there to help you. I will pray for your safety. God, the Merciful, will say: "All those who believe in the words of My prophet Muhammad, who keep the commandments of the Holy Qur'an, will be saved, if My name is on their tongues I will remove their sins". And I shall be in the garden to welcome you with sweet, scented drinks under green foliage'. 'And my mother?' asked sweet Fatima anxiously, 'where will she be?' 'Your mother Khadija', answered the prophet, 'has gone to live in a palace, sitting on a silken sofa, on an upper balcony she sits overlooking lovely gardens. The walls of her rooms are made of silver, inlaid with pearls. The sand in her garden is fragrant and she has colourful flowers.' Fatima was thankful and praised the Lord for all this.

At that moment the faithful Bilal was heard, calling all true believers to prayer. Muhammad sent for him and when he had come, the prophet told him: 'My friend, today I cannot pray, I cannot rise, nor kneel nor stand. Ask Abu

Bakr to take my place, let him lead the prayers. My heart is full of worry and sorrow. My body feels limp, my soul is confused, but I know that my last hour has come'. When Bilal heard these words from the Trustworthy Friend, he burst into tears, crying aloud: 'Alas! The best of men is going from us! If only I could die with you! Why was I born to suffer this! God's messenger on earth is dying! Misfortune has come to Medina!' He left the room with his hands on his head, weeping as he went. He stopped in the doorway of the mosque and called out aloud: 'You companions of the prophet, he told me that he cannot come today. Let Abu Bakr lead the prayers, he will suffice as a prayer leader. Our trustworthy one cannot stand up, his heart is troubled by the approach of death. His spirit has no rest because of the feeling of imminent death so that he has nowhere to take refuge. He implores all of you, Meccans and Medinans, to follow Abu Bakr'. When Bilal had finished speaking, Abu Bakr mounted the *minbar* to speak to the congregation but he could not speak a word. He bent his head as the tears flowed down his face. Upon seeing him overcome with grief all the Muslims in the mosque realised the disaster that was about to happen and they all started wailing.

The prophet called 'Ali and his brother Fadhili and asked them to help him up. With his arms around their shoulders he was able to walk to the mosque. As soon as Abu Bakr saw him he came down from the *minbar* and invited the prophet to take his rightful place, but the latter raised his hand, indicating that he was to stay. Then he spoke to the faithful followers of his lore: 'My friends, listen, these are my last words. No one can escape God's decree and today is my last day on earth. It has pleased God to take your leader away from you. I pray that you will look after my family who will be without a father. Do not neglect to pray at the appointed hours and do not forget to fast during Ramadan, these things I press upon your hearts. Do not forget to wash before the prayers and make the pilgrimage to Mecca once in your lives. Remember that telling lies is a great shame; on the Day of Reckoning you will be cursed if you do. Do not take the property of others, for doing so would send you to the Fire. Remember that the hypocrites are in the lowest depths of Hell. Remember that slandering your neighbour is wicked, and secret meetings (i.e. conspiracy) and *fitna*, sedition. This is the day of saying farewell, the last day of seeing each other until the day when the angel calls us from our graves'. The prophet laid again his hands on the shoulders of the two brothers who led him back to his room where 'A'isha had newly made the bed. To the men, the prophet said: 'My brethren, leave me here; I am grateful for your help in my last hour'. He lay down while Hasan and Husayn who had come in quietly, watched their grandfather while tears were running down their faces. Then they saw a gentleman coming who greeted them politely saying: 'I beg leave to enter, I want leave to see Muhammad, son of Abd Allah'. Fatima answered firmly: 'Just now it is not convenient, the prophet is very ill'. But the stranger insisted, though politely, that his business was urgent, so Fatima permitted him to see her father. She said to him: 'Why do you want to see my father now, while he is so ill?' But her father said from his bed: 'Fatima, show him in. This is no ordinary visitor, it is no man, no earth-born human being, this is Azrail, he is the carrier of souls. He is coming to fetch me, his business is urgent, let him in without delay, he is sent by the Almighty. . . . He is sent by God Omniscient / who bids him to take the spirits. / he conveys the souls departed, / he pulls out the human spirits / when the time has come for dying / when their term on earth has ended'.

Azrail came in and spoke: 'Peace be upon you. Are you ready?' The prophet Muhammad spoke: 'Please wait for my friend Gabriel to come and see me for the last time. I want a word with him before I go'. And the Angel of Death waited patiently, something he had never done and would not do for anyone else. Soon, Gabriel arrived and with him a host of angels, 70,000 of them. They were singing in unison the verses from the Holy Book. Then it was that Muhammad knew his last moment was there. There was no more life to live for him and no more days of sunshine on earth. His troubles and pains were all past. Michael too, came down with verses from the Holy Book. They greeted each other and while Fatima and her sons wept, he said: 'I give you peace, Fatima, after six months you will follow me, we shall not be separated for long'. He said good-bye to his beloved grandsons and to 'A'isha. Then he closed his eyes and could speak no more. His countenance changed. His limbs became stiff but a pleasant fragrance from Paradise was perceived by all those present. A caller was heard from Heaven, announcing: 'O mortal men on earth, know that God's beloved prophet has departed from this world. God has left us bereft, consider what you have lost'. Here are the verses which the angels recited: *Blessed be the One in whose hand the Kingdom rests. He has power over all things. He has created death and life to try you whether your deeds are perfect. He is great and forgiving* (Qur'an 67:1–2).

3.3 THE FUTURE: SIGNS OF THE END

The holy prophet explained to his followers what would happen at the end of the times and how one was to foresee this.

In those days people will no longer study the Qur'an nor keep the law; everybody will be interested only in satisfying his own greed and lust. There will be an epidemic in Jedda and famine in Medina, the plague in Mecca. There will be earthquakes everywhere in North Africa, thunderstorms in Turkey and all over Europe so terrible that entire regions will be laid waste. Iran and Iraq will be destroyed by murderers and vandals in great numbers. Floods will cause the rivers to rise and sweep away thousands while disease will exterminate the Asians of the East. There will be no more morality or discipline. Then God will cause a monster to appear created from people's bestiality. It will be ugly and horrifying to see. Its name is Dajjal, whom the Europeans call the Anti-Christ. He will ride on a giant ass and subject all the peoples of earth to his will, causing even more filthy behaviour than is already there. He will rule for only forty days with terror and force. Then God will send Jesus down from Heaven on a white horse with a lance in his hand. His throne too, will descend from above and he will seat himself on it, so that the faithful believers will rejoice. From them Jesus will recruit an army and ride out against Dajjal who will be defeated but escape and run for his life. Then God will intervene and command the earth to hold the monster. Suddenly, Dajjal's feet will be glued to the ground so that Jesus can approach and kill him with God's lance. The army of sinners and godless men will be annihilated by the followers of Jesus, who will become king at last and rule with justice for forty years. Each year, however, will be as long as two years and two months are at the present time, so that there will be a long period of peace and righteousness, following the second coming of Jesus. At the end of his period of reigning for eighty-four years, Jesus will return to Jerusalem and pray to God in the Dome of the Rock to surrender his soul again to God, and die there. Seven days later Gog and Magog will finally break through the brass wall that Alexander built to contain them (Qur'an 18:96–9). Waves upon waves of barbarians will come tumbling down from the mountains of the east where they breed in their millions and destroy civilisation, especially all the waterworks, so that the people will perish of thirst. The earth will become dry and dusty except for the filth of the barbarians.

When He created life, He created death also. Azrail is the name of one of God's servants who takes the lives of the children of Adam. He is God's most obedient angel who will even take the lives of hardworking parents, leaving their children orphans without food or support. The Lord will provide for those He wants to live, as a sign for wise people with minds to understand. His decree cannot be changed. To a wicked sinner Azrail appears like a terrifying black monster, menacing the evil-doer with doom and eternal pain. He will forthwith take the soul and tear it out of the body, disgusted by the foul smell of corruption. He will quickly hand it over to the torturers, who will accompany the soul until the end of time. To a righteous person Azrail will appear like a luminous angel in a white robe. All righteous persons spend a large part of their time praying, reading the Holy Book, or meditating upon God's glory. Almost apologetic, the angel of death will approach, announcing himself quietly and asking if it is convenient for the soul to depart now, since God is calling. The good soul has been ready to die for a long time. There are no debts to pay, no scores to settle. Eagerly, the good soul has been waiting for this moment and leaves the body and this life with relief, longing to be near the light of Eternity. The angel of death will carefully hand over this fragrant soul to the angel of reward, who will be a pleasant companion in the grave during the long centuries until Resurrection. For that purpose too, God has created a special angel, called Israfil, who is standing ready now to sound the Trumpet of Doom. That doom will be deserved by the people who then live on earth. There will be no more righteous people, no more preachers of God's word, no one will read the Qur'an, there will be no more compassion nor kindness, no more honour nor propriety, no truth or honesty. Tired of the wicked world and its godless inhabitants, the Lord will give a sign to Israfil who will blow at once. The sound of the trumpet is so terrifying that many living people will die of fright at once. Mountains will shake and fall down on cities, oceans will rise and flood whole countries. Clouds of dust will submerge people. For forty years the earth will be dark and empty, mighty monarchies will be dust. A second blowing will allow the souls to go and search for their bodies. Revived, the bodies will rise from the dust and stand on the dusty earth in the windy night. For forty years they will have to stand there, praying and repenting.

The holy prophet continued to explain. The first trumpet: that fateful day, the day of doom and destruction, the sun will go out like a candle. There will be no trace left of human endeavour, no palaces or cities will stand up. A stormwind will blow dust in the eyes of the dying. The second trumpet: the wind will blow away the sand from all the graves and God will restore the skeletons to complete bodies again, recognisable for the souls that will be hovering overhead looking in all directions. For there will be no tombstones, no mausoleums, no rock inscriptions left. All the dead will be equal, but some will be distinguished by the light on their foreheads which is caused by incessant prostrations before God. For forty years they will stand waiting on the dark plain in the cold wind and the pouring rain, which will gradually wash away much of the filth from bodies and souls. There will be millions and millions of people, like worshippers waiting for the *imam* to lead the prayers. Finally at the sounding of the third trumpet Muhammad will arrive, on Burak, his white horse with a woman's head, led by the angel Gabriel, light radiating from his face and a golden crown on his head. Suddenly, for all to see there will be the pair of scales, called *mizan*, and behind it the Throne of God, of gigantic size will become visible, for this is Apocalypse, the revelation of the last day: there will be no more hidden things. Every soul will be worried over his or her own past secret sins. They will all be revealed and will be seen on the left one of the pair of scales. All the good words and acts will be there too, even the smallest coin you ever gave to a beggar boy will be there in the right one of the pair of scales. There will be no more darkness. In the dazzling light of the divine presence those who have lied to their neighbours, cheated their customers, oppressed the weak, and forgotten the needy will be clearly visible by the dirt on their faces. Those who worked for their loved ones in secret modesty and shared what they had will be clearly visible by their shining faces, by the beauty of their kindness. What if the scales balance? What if your evil is as heavy as your good works? Pray to God. He may remember and send a sheet of paper fluttering down with the words: 'This soul is one of My servants. Once, his mouth pronounced with honest conviction: There is no god but God!' As soon as this note in God's own handwriting settles in the right-hand scale it will tip the balance and that soul will be saved for Paradise.

Judgement for every soul will be over in one hour. The last ordeal will not last longer for anyone, no matter how many sins that person committed during his life.

But then, how do the good souls find their way to the promised Garden? They will have to travel across the *sirat*, a mysterious structure spanning the long distance between the precipice below which is the seething crater of hell-fire and pitch black smoke, and on the other side, visible only faintly for the true believers, there is a bank of bliss, the shore of salvation, the hills of happiness. The distance is one of 3,000 years. Some very profound scholars have written that this abyss is the mouth of a gigantic serpent called Ghashiya in whose stomach God has placed the fires of hell, in order to protect his many delicate angels against its pestiferous fumes. When the serpent breathes, hot winds blow in Arabia. One hair of this monster lies across its mouth from lip to lip: that single hair is the *sirat*, the bridge across the abyss of hell-fire. For those whose sins are heavy, it will take 50,000 years to cross the hair-bridge and by the time they arrive they will be scorched black by the mountain-high flames sent up to torture them and to purify them. The souls of people who have given away all their wealth to the poor will find a white horse or a camel waiting for them, each with its owner's name written on its face. God created those shining animals out of the money which those kind souls gave to poor widows and orphans during their lives. The wise person who never sinned at all but prayed constantly will find a huge white bird that will take that individual across on its back in the time it takes to milk a cow. Whoever arrives on the other bank on the edge of the escarpment, is safe. Walking along, the saved souls will soon see the first tree, large with green foliage. In its shade lush, green grass will grow, inviting the pilgrims to rest. This they will do, thanking God for their salvation. Now they have no more desires, and so, God will allow them to enter paradise. Some will still have a long while to walk upwards to the white gate of paradise, for others the going is light and quick. The slow souls are ashamed to receive all this bliss for the few good deeds they have done during their lives. Those who arrive at the gate will find a boy or girl waiting for them, each one with a key, ready to lead each of the faithful to his own palace in Heaven.

God created paradise with many gates, some say seven, some say eight, or ten, but only God has true knowledge. These gates have names like the Gate of Repentance, the Gate of Prayer, the Gate of Service, the Gate of Patience, the Gate of Truthfulness, the Gate of Purity, and the Gate of Abstinence. Each name signifies a virtue or a good work which will ensure the soul who has practised it while living on earth, a safe entry into paradise through that gate. Some scholars however, maintain that the names are different, but only God knows. It is certain, of course, that these gates have names and that the names have meanings and that the souls of the faithful (and only those) will enter paradise through one of those gates. Furthermore we know that the souls can enter paradise only after they have been virtuous, that is without sins, or have performed good works for the eradication of their sins, or finally by faith and grace, but those things are in God's hand.

As soon as the souls of those who are worthy of paradise are within sight of its gates, they will be allowed to rest from the long journey. Some may have walked for many hours or days, some may have had to climb all the way out of the unclean depth of their sinfulness. With patience and perseverance, after many years, they will arrive at a gate, with God's grace. There, near the end of their ordeal, they will be allowed to drink from Kawthar, the lake of abundance, which belongs to Muhammad personally and so only his followers and friends may drink from it. Once a soul of a person has drunk a sip, that person will never be thirsty again, and never be ill. The water is sweeter than sugar, whiter than snow and has such a pleasant smell that no one who has ever tasted it will want to go back to earth. The lake Kawthar is so large that it would stretch from Mecca to the Yemen. There is also the *tawba*, that is the tree of remorse, whose fruits are food for every true believer in paradise as often as he wishes. Its branches and rich foliage are so large that they provide pleasant cool shade for all the inhabitants of paradise, sheltering them from the dazzling light that shines down from the Holy Throne above them.

4 RITUAL PRACTICE

See 1.3. The five pillars, outlined in 4.1, are the basic rituals of Islam but are only a part of the over-all structure of the law and of ritual. Prayer, in both its institutionalised (4.2.1) and individual (4.2.2, 4.2.3, 4.2.4) forms, plays a central role here. Acts of devotion such as in Qur'anic recitation (4.3) are highly regarded throughout the Islamic world. See 5.3 for details of giving charity.

Usul al-Din

4.1 AL-BAGHDADI ON THE PILLARS OF ISLAM

Question one of this chapter concerning the five pillars

The prophet said concerning this topic: 'Five things are obligatory upon the children of Islam: witnessing that there is no god but God, rising for the prayer, and giving of charity, fasting in the month of Ramadan, and performing the pilgrimage to the house in Mecca. . . .'

Question two of this chapter concerning the details of the first pillar of Islam

The first pillar of Islam, as is generally reported, is the *shahada*, that is saying: *la-ilaha illa-llah wa inna Muhammad rasul Allah* 'There is no god but God and Muhammad is the messenger of God'. There are a number of aspects to this pillar. First, the person who says the *shahada* will not be heard or rewarded by God for it unless that person knows the truth of the statement and repeats it out of understanding and with heartfelt sincerity. If a hypocrite who firmly believes the contrary of the *shahada* should repeat it, that person will not be considered a believer by God and will have no redemption from the punishment of the hereafter. Anything worse than this, not appearing as a hidden hypocrisy, is a repugnant innovation. When an innovation appears, such as the innovation of the Qarmatians or of the extreme group of the Rafidites,[1] then such persons are to be considered apostates who should be killed, who should not be prayed for, and whose property is considered to belong to the Muslims. However, if the innovation is such as that of the Qadarites, then the severance of inheritance between such innovators and the people of the Sunna is the most the theologians from among our teachers speak of. Therefore al-Harith al-Muhasibi was prevented from obtaining the inheritance of his father because his father was a Mu'tazilite. The jurists among our teachers say that a near relative who is a Sunni would inherit from such a person, just as the protected communities of Jews and Christians inherit from one another, even if they are of different religions. The jurists and the theologians from among our teachers agree that prayer is not permissible standing behind a Mu'tazilite, nor should prayers be said for such a person, nor is it permitted to eat animals which such a person has slaughtered nor to return that person's greeting. Cited in this case is the statement of 'Abd Allah ibn 'Umar which prohibits such things and which disavows the Qadarites. The Karramites claim that hypocrites who conceal their polythesism are truly believers and that their faith is like the faith of Gabriel, Michael, and all of the prophets. The full discussion of this comes in the chapter on faith.

Question three of this chapter concerning the details the second pillar, which is prayer

The number of prescribed prayers is five and the number of *rak'as* for those who do not allow themselves to shorten it is seventeen; whoever shortens the prayer during travel will do eleven. Whoever denies the obligation of some or all of these prayers is an unbeliever. There is disagreement about the obligation of the *witr* prayer; whoever sees it as obligatory is not an unbeliever but neither is whoever denies its obligation. There is also disagreement among the jurists concerning some of the aspects of the prayer. Whoever denies that over which there is disagreement concerning its obligatory character, is not an unbeliever. Whoever denies the obligatory nature of an aspect of it upon which the pious ancestors agree, however, is an unbeliever. We therefore regard the Karramites as unbelievers because they say that the statement of intention to do the prescribed prayers is not obligatory and that the statement of intent made when entering Islam to begin with is sufficient. This is against the policy of the entire community. As for those who refrain from the prayer while firmly believing in its obligatory character, there is disagreement about them. Ahmad ibn Hanbal states that they are therefore unbelievers while al-Shafi'i feels they are apostates and should be killed but that they are not unbelievers. Abu Hanifa too imposes that but not that they should be killed. Anyone who regards refraining from prayer as permitted is an unbeliever; of that there is no doubt. Anyone who does not partake in the Friday prayer and the prayers on the festivals along with the people of the Sunna is also an unbeliever and we shall not pray behind such a person, nor for such a person when dead. Our opinion on this is that the position of such a person is the same as that of the apostates. In our opinion the Friday prayer is obligatory for all those legally capable except women, slaves, the sick, travellers, those tending the sick, and those fleeing oppression if that person is unable. A part of the prescribed part of the prayer is the fixed time; anything before the appropriate time is not permissible. Among the sound requirements of the prayer are the ablutions, entering at the appropriate time, and facing the *qibla*, although this does not apply when riding an animal during the time for the supererogatory prayers. The covering for the genitals is also required. Whoever neglects one of the requirements at its appropriate time will receive the appropriate punishment from God. But as for whoever neglects the supererogatory prayer, there will be no punishment for that person on that account although there will be a reward for those who do perform some of the prayer.

Question four of this chapter concerning the details of the third pillar

The third pillar of Islam is charity (*zakat*). The type of charity about which all agree on its obligatory character is the *'ushr* which consists of the giving of a cow, a sheep, raisins, dates, edible grains which people cultivate, merchandise, and the specific *zakat* at the end of Ramadan. Whoever denies the obligatory character of any one of these is an unbeliever with the exception of the giving of merchandise, in which case personal opinion has free reign. There is disagreement concerning the giving of other kinds of fruit, jewellery, and horses. Once again individual judgement may decide, which is the same in the case of disagreement over giving herbs, saffron, and honey. The decision can rest only on personal opinion. Every kind of charity except the giving at the end of Ramadan is obligatory in two respects: there must be complete payment and the recipient must vary. There is disagreement concerning taking into account the sale when giving a sheep and concerning the obligatory character of the giving of property belonging to children and the mentally deranged. Personal opinion in these matters, and in all matters where the jurists disagree in the giving of charity, is permissible.

Question five in this chapter concerning the details of the fourth pillar of Islam

The fourth pillar of Islam is the fast in the month of Ramadan. There is no excuse for anyone who is knowingly legally capable to omit the obligation of the fast of Ramadan. With the obligation comes the penalty for anyone who breaks the fast whether there is an excuse or not, and there is no escaping the obligation of the fast vowed to God. As for the fast among the unbelievers, the jurists and the élite recognise it as a custom. It is necessary for the fast of Ramadan to begin with the sighting of the new moon or for thirty days to have passed in Sha'ban. Some of the Rafidites say that the fast begins on the given day regardless of doubt about the sighting of the moon but there is really no place for disagreement in this matter. The Jews regard a single fast as obligatory while the Christians fast for 48 days the beginning of which comes between February and March. As for the rules of the fast and its many aspects, that is the matter of which the jurists have specialised knowledge.

Question six in this chapter concerning the details of the fifth pillar of Islam which is the pilgrimage

The obligation of this pillar occurs once in a lifetime for whoever has the ability. The obligatory aspects of the pilgrimage from which there can be no escape are four according to al-Shafi'i: the donning of the *ihram*, the standing at 'Arafa, the circumambulation of the Ka'ba, and the running between al-Safa and al-Marwa. The period for the standing is from the setting of the sun on the day of 'Arafa to the true appearance of daybreak on the day of the sacrifice (10 Dhu'l-Hijja). Whoever stands for an hour of the period has fulfilled the requirement. The minumum which should be performed of the circumambulation according to al-Shafi'i is seven times around and likewise for the run between al-Safa and al-Marwa. There is disagreement concerning the obligatory character of the *'umra* or lesser pilgrimage. Al-Shafi'i makes it obligatory and establishes three parts to it: the donning of the *ihram*, the circumambulation, and the running between al-Safa and al-Marwa. Abu Hanifa eliminates the obligatory character of these three.

Question seven in this chapter concerning the explication of the stipulations of the five pillars

The prayer requires a number of elements including ablution, covering the genitals, arriving at the proper time, and facing the *qibla* when it is determinable or using one's personal judgement when it is not; even this is not necessary when one is struggling with death (as in battle), when it is sufficient to fulfil the requirements in accordance with one's ability. Likewise the supererogatory prayers done while riding may omit the prescription of facing the *qibla*. The various stipulations of the minor ablution according to the traditionists are six: four places to be washed, the statement of intention, and the sequence of actions. For the major ablution there are two obligations, the statement of intention and making sure that water reaches all of the outer skin and the outer hair. The requirements for the Friday prayer are worthiness, being male, being of legal age, being of sound mind, body, and health. The stipulation for charity in giving a sheep is that the recipient vary, that it is from freely grazing livestock under the full ownership of a Muslim, and that it is thereby a complete payment. The main stipulation for the pilgrimage and the *'umra* is the existence of the ability for the person who resides in Mecca or who is

Z ←——|————

Mount of Mercy

Plain of ᶜArafa

Muzdalifa

al-Jamrat al-Ula
al-Jamrat al-Wusta
al-Jamrat al-ʿAqaba

Mina

Marwa   Safa
         Mosque of Mecca
    Kaᶜba

Mecca

2. The pilgrimage road between Mecca and the plain of ʿArafa (distance about 25 km)

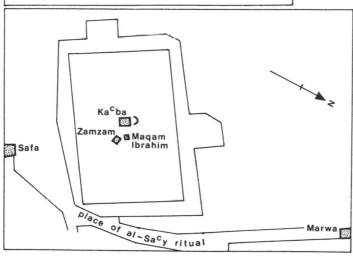

Kaᶜba

Zamzam   Maqam Ibrahim

Safa

place of al-Saᶜy ritual   Marwa

3. The Holy Mosque in Mecca

connected to it bodily and, for those who are far from Mecca, that they also have sufficient supplies and a means of transportation along a secure roadway.

4.2 POPULAR PRAYER

4.2.1 The ritual prayer

The following prayers and statements, repeated in Arabic, make up the prayer ritual of most Muslims. There are minor variations as to what will be said precisely. All are combined with certain physical actions and positions and a number are repeated throughout the ritual.

Glory be to You, O God, and praise be to You. Blessed is Your name and exalted is Your majesty. There is none worthy of worship other than You. I seek the refuge of God from Satan, the accursed.[2]

God is Great. Glory be to God, the Great One.

God listens to whoever praises Him. O our Lord, Praise be to You.

Glory be to my Lord, most High. O God, forgive me and have mercy upon me. All reverence, worship, and sanctity are from God. May peace, mercy, and blessings of God be upon you, O Prophet. Peace be upon us and the righteous servants of God. I bear witness that there is no god but God and I bear witness that Muhammad is His servant and messenger.

O God, pray for our lord Muhammad and the descendants of our lord Muhammad, just as You prayed for our lord Abraham and the descendants of our lord Abraham. Indeed You are the Praiseworthy, the Exalted.

O God, bless our lord Muhammad and the family of our lord Muhammad, just as You blessed our lord Abraham and the descendants of our lord Abraham. Indeed, You are the Praiseworthy, the Exalted.

O my Lord, make me and my offspring keep up the prayer. O our Lord, accept the prayer. O our Lord, forgive me, my parents, and the faithful on the day upon which the final reckoning will take place.

May the peace and mercy of God be upon you.

O God, You are peace and peace comes from You. You are blessed, O our Lord. You are exalted, O Lord of Glory and Honour.

Funeral services include the following prayer:

O God, forgive our living and our dead, those of us who are present and those of us who are absent, our younger members and our older ones, our males and our females. O God, those whom You keep alive among us, keep them alive in Islam; and those whom You cause to die, let them die in Islam. O God, do not deprive us of its reward and do not try us after it. O God, forgive him and have mercy upon him, preserve him and pardon him, ennoble his tomb and widen his place of entering, wash him with water, snow, and hail and cleanse him of faults just as white cloth is cleansed of imperfections.

4.2.2 Swahili prayer-songs

Wedding song

I pray to You, Majesty, Lord, receive my prayer, give me good deeds, may the heavy things become easy. Give me a lawful wife that my destiny may be fulfilled.

Give me a quiet wife, good-natured, diligent, attentive, and modest at the same time. Nor should she be lazy in washing or sweeping.

Furthermore, give me a one-eyed wife who does not see another man, with well-founded legs and well-filled calves, with an elegant gait.

Let those speak who have something to say!

Let her height be just right, let her legs be as fat as elephant's legs. May her colour be that of creamy linen, may her eyes be languid. May her teeth be like diamonds; soft should be her cheeks.

May her voice be silken in conversing; that which is gentle is pleasant, pleasant to hear. And may she have features to be proud of, beauty that pleases.

One who has a good line of ancestors on her mother's side as well as on her father's. Furthermore, put love in her and increase her faith.

When these wishes are fulfilled, let us all be joyful.

Let her shape be natural as I have begged You; let her be humble and gentle, ready to laugh and sing, so that those who may see and know that she is a precious ornament.

When You have given to me, my Lord, this woman of beauty, give us then also mutual understanding and let our lives be long and keep us alive with children who have no problems.

Lord, accept my prayer, O Kind One, and take suffering away from me; let me be well-guided; give me a devoted wife to live lovingly.

Amen, my Lord, Amen. Accept my prayer, Generous Lord.

Wedding song by the contemporary Swahili poet Ahmad Shaykh Nabahani of Malindi.

O Merciful Lord, receive my prayer, by the blessings of the Trustworthy, Your beloved prophet, let it be: 'Exist', and it is.

Give me acceptance.

God, I pray for them, for the bride and the groom; may they live and get accustomed to one another and be completely in love. May their love continue to be fresh so that they can never keep out of each other's eyes.

Give them good children, blessed young ones, and may money come pouring in for them. By night as well as by day may joy increase for them with laughter and chatter.

May they live in peacefulness – You are the All-Powerful, Praised One – like water in a cup. May they increase in mutual understanding. May they see heaven and be there in the garden of paradise.

May they rise in this world, may intrigues avoid them, may they love each other faithfully and show each other kind respect, like Layla and Majnun, always listening to each other.

You who are here present and you ladies who have come, please raise your hands and say: May this prayer be acceptable for us, may our Lord be agreeable.

Prayer for offspring

God will help me and give me a great boon that I may have children, that I may be cheerful and happy. May I give birth to an angel with radiance and grace.

God will help me. Generous Lord, succour! A star will shine on me when my time arrives. May I give birth to an angel with radiance and grace.

Untie my knots

Untie my knots, I pray to You, O Giver. May we be cheerful, may we stretch our necks, may our hearts dwell in joy. Bring us to the gates that are unknown.

Untie my fetters, I pray to You, Lord of the Quintessence. May we be merry and lift up our heads, for love and affection bring us closer to the gates while time is running out.

Open the seals for me, I pray to You, Lord of Power. Poets who hold their heads high may find increasing belief. Bring me closer to the gates which I do not know.

A petition by Mu'allim Saydi ibn Ahmad al-Kumri of Mombasa

We Pray to You, Holy God, who has neither birth nor death, our Lord, known to all, generous God. We raise our hands in supplication, our Lord; You know us, please receive our prayer. Give us whatever has goodness. Lord, our tears are welling, indeed, our tears are bubbling up; we have repented in truth, we, Your slaves, have ceased our sins! Lord, we are Your slaves! We repent, we return to You. We are under Your authority, receive our prayer, generous God! O God, give us knowledge and give us good perception to understand difficult things of Your religion, generous God. Give us Your fruits, let us study untiringly. Lord, preserve our knowledge in our hearts in a good place. My Lord, when judgement comes let it not be hard for us; make us incapable of oppressing our neighbour. May we fear You, generous Lord!

Give us our daily bread quickly, unceasingly; give us also all good things in this world and at the resurrection. Give us our permitted food; may it not be hard to get. Give us good health in this life and at the resurrection. Take irritation away from us and every disaster; give us also patience and Your faith, generous Lord. Allow us to love one another and our children as well, with a love without trickery, in accordance with Your religion, generous God! Give us the gift of speaking properly without flaw; give us much joy in this life and at the resurrection. Let us be at peace in our towns, forgive us our debts before there comes to us, Your deputy – a kindly death. Do not let our efforts break, help us to stand upright; fill us with Your good things in this life and at the resurrection. Bless us, Majesty, lengthen our lives for us and for all just people, for whoever teaches the good word. But whoever brings evil, You know that person's secret; may their intentions be broken so that they cannot stand. My Lord, prayers and blessed greetings may attain the prophet Muhammad and his noble companions and whoever possesses goodness.

Amen, My Lord, Amen. Amen, My Lord, Amen. Lord, receive our prayers.

4.2.3 *Masnun al-du'a'ayn*; the prayers of the prophet *Indian*

Prayers of the people of God of every age

God, there is no god but He, the Living, the Self-Subsisting. *Alif-Lam-Mim.*[3] God, there is no god but He, the Living, the Self-Subsistent.

Downcast will be the faces before the Living, the Self-Subsistent.

There is no god but You. Glory be to You.

Indeed, I am one of the wrong-doers.

O One God, the Absolute who does not beget nor is begotten.

None bears likeness to Him, O Most Merciful of the Merciful. We have wronged ourselves. If You do not forgive us and do not bestow Your mercy upon us, we shall certainly be among the losers. O our Lord, forgive us and turn to us. Indeed You are the Returner, the Merciful.

O my Lord, forgive, be merciful and overlook what You know. Indeed you are the Most Exalted, the Most Generous. O God, You are the Forgiving and the Generous. You love forgiveness. Forgive us, O God. Turner of hearts, turn our hearts to Your obedience. O Director of hearts, keep our hearts steadfast in Your religion.

O God, indeed our hearts, our forelocks, and our limbs are in Your hand. You have not given us control over any of them. Since You have done that with us, be our protector and guide us on the even path.

O God, show us the truth as truth and help us to be able to follow it; show us falsehood as falsehood and help us to be able to avoid it.

O God, give us Your love and the love of Your messenger and the love of those who are beneficent for us according to You.

O the Living One, the Self-Subsistent, by Your Mercy we appeal and ask forgiveness. O our Lord, we ask You for repentance and set our affairs aright and do not entrust us to ourselves even for the blinking of an eye.

If You entrust us to ourselves, You entrust us to weakness, faultiness, sin, and error.

O God, nothing is easy except that which You make so and You are the one who makes the difficult easy when You wish. There is no god but God, the Forbearing, the Generous. Praise be to God, Lord of the highest throne. Praise belongs to God, Lord of all beings. We ask of You that which arouses Your mercy and forgiveness, the opportunity to do every kind of good and protection against every kind of error. Let no sin of ours remain unforgiven, O most merciful. Let no worry be unremoved nor any wish which is in accord with Your pleasure be unsatisfied, O most merciful of the Merciful.

O my Lord, love us and instil in our hearts a yearning for You. And exalt us in the eyes of the people and protect us from adopting incorrect ways. Let us travel firmly in right conduct on the straight path and against our enemies, Your enemies, the enemies of Islam.

Help us O God, help us; do not aid anyone against us.

O God, take care of our affairs but do not control them against us.

O God, make us prosperous and do not make us poor; do not impose upon us a ruler who has no mercy.

O God, open our hearts to Islam.

O God, make us love faith and embellish our hearts with it but make hateful unbelief, immorality, and error.

O God, make us one of those rightly guided.

Prayers for this world and the hereafter

O God, forgive me, take pity on me, preserve me and grant me sustenance.

O God, ennoble all our affairs in their outcome and save us from disgrace in this world and from punishment in the world to come.

God, improve my religion in me, for that is my refuge, and improve my worldly existence which I must live. Prepare me for the afterlife to which I shall return. Make this life a means to achieve every kind of good and turn death into bliss, away from any evil.

O God, I ask of You forgiveness and protection in this world and in the world to come.

O God, forgive me and turn to me; You are the Forgiving, the Merciful.

O God, I have sinned against myself and only You forgive sins. Grant me forgiveness from Yourself and take pity on me. You are the Forgiving, the Merciful.

4.2.4 The *Burda* of al-Busiri   *d.* 1294

Chase the soul's passion away! Beware of it, do not make it a habit. If it rules you along its ways, it will either kill you or be a blemish. Guard your soul wherever you look, with good works, whenever there is one; it has found this place, Earth, pleasant, do not leave it to do as it pleases but seek spiritual peace. How many times has the heart, with its ruses, shown you good things on the outside while there was poison at the inside, it killed the one who followed his lusts.

Do not neglect the hidden pikes and slings, of hunger as well as of satiety, both ways, it happens, my friend, that an empty stomach holds more evil than bliss. Wipe away the tears from your eye; forbidden things will only be remorse, then look for a place to hide, make a resolution not to do it again. Turn away from the passion of the soul and from Satan, do not trust those two rebels, when they give you counsel, O my friend, take good care never to come near them. Do not follow him who is quarrelsome, do not accept him who is clever; you know that their wiles are poison, beware of them from an early age.

My Lord, pardon my words which I have spoken without deeds; it is as if I had attributed posterity to a person who stood at the end of his lineage. I order you always to do good, but in my own heart I break the rules, I am admonishing you to persist, I am teaching you, but I myself did not persist in the good acts. Nor did I do any fortunate deed, preserving its good reward hereafter, nor did I pray more than duty prescribed, I performed no supererogatory duties, not even the fast.

The exemplary custom of the prophet who was always praying, persisting in worship all the nights, until both his footsoles were swollen, I sinned against it, I did not follow it. The dear one closed the belt around his middle to fast, and in addition he put a stone under the leather; to prevent hunger, his breath came with force so that he could persist. Mountains of silver and gold spoke to him, pleading with him: 'Come, use us, beloved!' The prophet refused them and rejected them. His need only strengthened his character, that is what enabled him to reduce his desires.

I will tell you one thing which will suffice you: Lust is not a match for fortitude. How could it be that your prophet could ever yearn for possessions? This cannot be. The very existence of this universe, its cause was our Hashimite.

Muhammad is the lord of the two worlds, the earth and the heavens and the animated beings, spirits and men of every sort, from the Arabs to the foreigners. It is our prophet who rules, ordering good things and denying bad ones, he is the one who defeats people and kills them by saying: 'No' or: 'So be it'. He is the beloved of his Lord, we may hope for his intercession, he is the right guide of his Community, in the midst of terror and turmoil. He has called people towards the true religion, and whoever follows him and believes in him, has an important reason for his trust: God will save him at the resurrection. He surpasses all the other prophets in appearance, character, and nature, they do not even approach him in appearance, nor in his knowledge, nor in his capacity to work miracles. All the other prophets have their rank assigned to them in relation to the prophet; they possess one handful of water from the ocean of his knowledge, or one sip, and that is all, where there is the great and beneficial rainfall. They are all just standing near their lord, each one like a single dot in the great volume of all knowledge, in the celestial tablet. They are just like one vowel mark in the great book of wisdom.

He is the confessor, the form and meaning which have been completed; finally the Omniscient placed him apart to be the beloved of the Generous. In his goodness he has no rival, either among the prophets or the angels, God cleansed him so he became pure, His jewel, His dear beloved. Leave off speaking, I forbid you, the word of praise of the Christians for the prophet Jesus. You may render complete homage to the prophet, praise in any form you like his good qualities. Any form you like for his essence, do not fear, attribute his nobility to his descent, attribute it also to his rank, any form you like for rendering him homage. Because his virtues are very many, their number has no conceivable limit; any form of praise a person can mention, they will never be completed no matter how long that person speaks. If his rank and the miracles he performed would be duly praised, a person, if so able, would have died and even rotted, being called by his name while still persisting.

He did not come to us to bring fear; his whole religion contains God's riches, and we merely have to listen to him and to obey, we do not have to feel doubt nor suspicion. The intelligence of the people is being pressed down, they do not know the reality of the prophet, far away and near by he is the same, the human eye does not accept to look at him. It is like the sun when it appears, your eyesight perceives it as a small object, but when you know its appearance, you do not obtain the reality to pronounce. How could a person who is in human form here in this world, a person whose negligence is like that of one asleep, see the prophet in his true state? A person who knows that the prophet is a son of Adam of exceptional generosity, he surpasses all mortals, he knows with perfect knowledge.

Every miracle that came with every prophet, could only come true because of the light of the prophet, that is why they too received the gift to perform miracles. He is like a sun because of his virtues, and they are like stars, this we know, in order for their light to shine, it is necessary that the sun has not yet come out, that there is darkness. Noble in his mien is the prophet, his character is well disposed. He has gathered goodness, he is exceedingly kind, always appearing cheerful and smiling. His mildness is like a lovely flower, and his nobleness like the full moon, his generosity is like an ocean, his solicitude is like time. The prophet, if you would see him in his full splendour, would be quite unique, like a king, surrounded by many great warriors. Like a pearl in its oyster shell, when he begins to speak it emerges, and its place, my brothers, is when he speaks and smiles. There is no perfume that matches the sand on which he lay down, a tree in Paradise it is, for him who may enjoy the smell, it is his bliss.

4.3 AL-NAWAWI ON THE PROPER ETIQUETTE IN THE RECITATION OF THE QUR'AN

To begin, let us summarise what has come before this chapter. Concerning the etiquette of reciting, we know that this is the most perfect of states and reflects the best of character and that it requires elevating the self above all that the Qur'an forbids as a tribute to that book. One must be protected from base desires, being honourable in the self, rising above the tyrants and the ruffians of the world, behaving humbly towards the pure, the good, and the poor. It also requires that one display humility and devotion as if in the presence of God.

It has been transmitted from 'Umar ibn al-Khattab that he said: 'O group of reciters of the Qur'an! Lift up your heads so that the path may become clear to you. Hold on to the good things; do not be dependent upon the people'. It is also reported of 'Abd Allah ibn Mas'ud that he said: 'It behoves those who wish to transmit the Qur'an that they become acquainted with nighttime when the people sleep and with daytime when the people are awake and with grief when the people rejoice and with tears when the people laugh and with silence when the people discuss matters and with humility when the people are bold'. It is also related of al-Hasan ibn 'Ali that he said: 'If people are before you treating the Qur'an as a message from their Lord, then they have considered it at night and studied it by day'. It is also related from al-Fudayl ibn 'Ayyad that he said: 'It behoves whoever transmits the Qur'an that they have no responsibilities to any leader. Whoever is without such, so much the better!' He has also said: 'The transmitter of the Qur'an is the transmitter of the banner of Islam and it is not fitting that such people occupy their time with worthless people or that they be distracted by such people or that they talk nonsense with such people; this is so that they may be worthy representatives of the truth of the Qur'an.

Chapter 1

The most important thing for a transmitter of the Qur'an to guard against is being occupied with the book as a way of life such that it becomes a means of life. It is reported that 'Abd al-Rahman ibn Shubayl said that the messenger of God said: 'Recite the Qur'an but do not eat by it nor demand riches from it'. From Jabir comes the report that the prophet said: 'Recite the Qur'an before a people arrives who will slander it by demanding a reward for reciting'. A similar report with the same meaning is also transmitted by Sahl ibn Sa'd. Also a report comes from Fudayl ibn 'Amr who said that two of the companions of the messenger of God entered a mosque and greeted the *imam*. A man rose and recited some verses from the Qur'an and then asked them for some money. One of the companions said: 'By the God to whom we shall return, I heard the messenger of God say: "People will come asking for money by means of the Qur'an. Whoever makes a request by means of the Qur'an, do not give them anything" '. The *isnad* for this report is defective because al-Fudayl ibn 'Amr could not have heard reports from the Companions.

As for a reward being taken for knowledge of the Qur'an, there is in fact disagreement among the learned. Imam Abu Sulayman al-Khattabi reports that he prohibited the taking of any reward on the authority of some of the learned class, including al-Zuhri and Abu Hanifa while on the authority of some others it is possible as long as the giving of money is not an obligation of doing the recital. This is the statement of al-Hasan al-Basri, al-Sha'bi, and Ibn Sirin while 'Ata' and Malik and al-Shafi'i and the others tend to allow it even if giving is a condition of the recital. Engaging someone's services brings a sound reward and many sound reports are transmitted which allow reward. The argument against the prohibition of payment is based on the report of 'Ibada ibn al-Samit who said that he knew a righteous man who was given a bow as a reward for recitation. The prophet said to him: 'It would be disbelief that you master a capability from hell. So accept it!' This is a famous report transmitted by Abu Dawud and others on the authority of many of the pious ancestors.

I would respond to those who seek permission to accept rewards on the basis of this report from 'Ibada with two rebuttals. The first of these is that the *isnad* is defective and secondly that the reward was given voluntarily in full knowledge that it was not required and that it was not demanded. So the reward was given to him as a present for the recitation and he was not rewarded because of the demand of anyone with him. God knows best.

Chapter 2

It behoves one to pay attention to the recitation and to increase its portion. The pious ancestors had various habits concerning the amount that they would recite. Ibn Abi Dawud reports that some of the pious ancestors would recite the Qur'an once over a two-month period while others would do the same in one month, or ten nights or eight nights; many of them would recite over the period of seven nights, while some would do it over six, five or four nights. Many others chose to do it over a three-night period while some would do it over two nights. Others would recite the whole book over the period of a day and a night while others would recite it all in a night and then again during the day. Still others would recite it three times while others would recite it eight times, four times at night and four times during the day. 'Uthman ibn 'Affan, Tamim al-Dari, Sa'id ibn Jubayr, Mujahid, al-Shafi'i, and many others used to recite the whole Qur'an over a period of a night and a day. Salim ibn 'Umar, the Qadi of Egypt during the rule of Mu'awiya, used to complete the Qur'an three times in a day and a night. Abu Bakr ibn Abi Dawud reports that each night Salim would recite the Qur'an four times. Abu 'Umar al-Kindi reports in his book about the judges of Egypt that Salim would recite the entire book four times in a night. The pious shaykh Abu 'Abd al-Rahman al-Sulami said that he heard the shaykh Abu 'Uthman al-Maghribi saying that Ibn al-Katib would recite the Qur'an four times at night and four times during the day. This is the greatest amount that we have heard of anyone accomplishing. The honoured Sayyid Ahmad al-Dawraqi reports with an *isnad* traced to Mansur ibn Zadan, one of the generation of successors to Muhammad, that Mansur would recite the entire Qur'an between the midday and the afternoon prayer and also, between the sunset prayer and the evening prayer during Ramadan, he would recite the text twice. The evening prayer during Ramadan used to be delayed for four nights. Abu Dawud reports with a sound *isnad* that Mujahid used to complete the Qur'an between the sunset and the evening prayers. Also on the authority of Mansur it is reported that al-Azdi made a vow to recite the whole Qur'an between the sunset and the evening prayers every night during Ramadan. As for those who recite the whole Qur'an during prayer, their number is countless. Among the previously mentioned people 'Uthman ibn 'Affan, Tamim al-Dari, and Sa'id ibn Jubayr all recited the entire book in each prayer at the Ka'ba.

As for those who recite the Qur'an once a week, they too are many. This act is attributed to 'Uthman ibn 'Affan, 'Abd Allah ibn Mas'ud, Zayd ibn Thabit, Ubayy ibn Ka'b, and many of the successor generation such as 'Abd al-Rahman ibn Yazid, 'Alqama, and Ibrahim. That mode of recitation was the choice of most people but there was disagreement. Most people who manifest little thought about the matter are content with a quantity that can be done comfortably and can be understood as it is recited. As for those who are occupied with serious writing or other important religious matters or affairs connected to the welfare of all Muslims, they should limit themselves to a quantity which does not interfere with what they do. Whoever is not one of those just mentioned should try to increase the amount recited as much as possible without going beyond the limits of tiredness and overly fast speech. Most of the previously mentioned people dislike the recitation of the whole of the Qur'an during a day and a night as is indicated in a sound report on the authority of 'Abd Allah ibn 'Amr ibn al-'As, that the messenger of God said: 'Whoever recites the Qur'an in less than three days does not understand it'. Abu Dawud, Tirmidhi, al-Nasa'i, and others transmit this report. Al-Tirmidhi says this is a very sound report. God knows best.

As for the time of beginning and ending the recitation of the whole of the Qur'an for those who are going to do it in one week, Abu Dawud reports that 'Uthman ibn 'Affan started at the beginning of the Qur'an on Friday night and ended on Thursday night. The *imam* Abu Hamid al-Ghazzali said in his book the *Ihya'* that it is best to recite one complete text by night, another by day. One should begin the daytime recital on Monday during the morning prayer or later and begin the nighttime recital at the nighttime prayer on Friday night at the sunset prayer or later so that the beginning of the night and the end of it may be joined by recitation. Ibn Abi Dawud reports that 'Umar ibn Marrat al-Tabi'i said that they used to like to begin to recite the whole of the Qur'an either at daybreak or at nightfall. Talha ibn Musarrif al-Tabi'i said: 'Whoever finishes reciting the whole of the Qur'an with a verse during any given hour of the day, the angels will pray for them until evening comes. Whoever finishes the recitation of the Qur'an with a verse during an hour of the night, then the angels will pray for them until morning comes'. A similar report comes from Mujahid. Al-Darimi reports in his *Musnad* with a report from Sa'd ibn Abi Waqqas that he said: 'Whenever the completion of the recitation of the Qur'an coincides with nightfall, the angels pray for the reciter until morning; whenever the recitation ends with daybreak, the angels pray for the person until evening'. Al-Darimi says that this is a sound report from Sa'd. Habib ibn Abi Thabit, one of the successors, reported that he used to finish the recitation before prayer times. According to Ibn Abi Dawud, Ahmad ibn Hanbal said the same. Further on this topic will come in a following chapter, if God wills.

Chapter 3, concerning the observance of recitation during the night

It behoves all to pay attention to many things while reciting the Qur'an at night. God has said in Qur'an 3:113–14; *Some of the people of the book are an upstanding nation who recite the verses of God in the hours of the night, prostrating themselves, believing in God and the last day, ordering the good and forbidding the evil, competing with each other in good works. They are the righteous ones*. It is reported in *al-Sahih* that the messenger of God said: 'A man will receive the blessing of God for praying through the night'. In another tradition from *al-Sahih*, Muhammad is reported to have said: 'O servant of God, do not be like So-and-so who arises in the night and then refrains from praying'. Al-Tabarani and others have it on the authority of Sahl ibn Sa'd that the messenger of God said: 'The best of the believers are those who arise at night'. There are many reports similar to these. It comes from Abu al-Ahwas al-Jushami that there was a man who used to go to Fustat at night and he would listen to the sound of its people which was like the sound of bee and he said: 'Why is it that these people who believe are not those who fear?' Yazid al-Raqqashi said: 'I would be asleep, then I would be awakened and then I would sleep but my eyes would not sleep'. I say the following. Prayer at night and recitation during it surpasses all because it is clear to the heart and further from distractions, occupations, and attending to one's needs; it protects one from all types of frustration while bringing all the good things that the revelation comes with at night. For example, the journey of the messenger of God to Jerusalem was at night and there is a report which says: 'Your Lord descends to the worldly heavens every night once half the night has passed. At that time He says: "I must reply to whoever calls" '. Also in the *hadith* it is reported that the messenger of God said that there is an hour every night when God replies to whoever calls upon Him.

Know that the merits of rising at night are as follows. Recitation can occur during the night, either in a small amount or a large amount – the more the better, unless it encompasses the whole night, for God does not like that, and also unless it harms the person. Among the reports which indicate that reciting a little is good is one which comes from Ibn 'Amr ibn al-'As that the messenger of God said: 'Whoever gets up to recite 10 verses will not be recorded among the names of the heedless. Whoever gets up to recite 100 verses will be recorded among the names of the obedient. Whoever gets up to recite 1,000 verses will be recorded among the names of the just'. Abu Dawud and others transmit this report. Al-Tha'labi reports of Ibn 'Abbas that he said: 'Whoever prays two *rak'as* at night, passes the whole night before God prostrated and standing as in prayer'.

Chapter 4, concerning the command to pay attention to the Qur'an and the danger of it falling into oblivion

It is reported on the authority of Abu Musa al-Ash'ari that the prophet said: 'Guard this Qur'an, for, by He who has the soul of Muhammad in His hand, it is easier for it to escape from the mind than it is for a camel to escape'. This is transmitted in the works of al-Bukhari and Muslim. On the authority of Ibn 'Umar it is reported that the messenger of God said: 'The possessor of the Qur'an is like a tied up camel. If one is fastened tight to it, then one can hold it fast but if one loosens it, then it will go'. Muslim and al-Bukhari also transmit this report. Anas ibn Malik reported that the messenger of God said: 'I will reveal the rewards of my community and I will display the sins of my community until the end of time. I do not know a sin greater than a person who forgets a surah or a verse from the Qur'an'. Abu Dawud and al-Tirmidhi relate this report. Sa'd ibn 'Ibada reports that the prophet said: 'Whoever reads the Qur'an and then forgets it, will meet God on the day of resurrection and will be totally cut off from any reward'. Abu Dawud and al-Tirmidhi transmit this report.

Chapter 5, concerning those whose neglect the *wird* prayer
   'Umar ibn al-Khattab reports that the messenger of God said: 'For whoever neglects the portion of the Qur'an or any part thereof to be recited during the night, whatever is recited between the morning and the noon prayer will be counted for that person as if it had been recited during the night'. Muslim transmits this report. Sulayman ibn Yasar reports that Abu Usayd said: 'Last night I slept through my *wird* prayers so when I awoke in the morning I revoked my vow to do it. My *wird* recitation should have been surah 2, the Cow. During a dream I thought I saw a cow pushing me'. Ibn Abi Dawud transmits this report.

5 LAW

See 1.4. 5.1 comes from a text dealing with cases of abrogation of laws in the Qur'an but moves quickly from that to more detailed discussions of the law and various opinions about it. While reading 5.2 compare the modern position on birth control with its Western concerns in 9.3. The alms tax of 5.3 is one of the five pillars; see 4.1. The religious-moral nature of the Islamic law is illustrated in 5.4 where modes of divorce can be morally reprehensible in the eyes of God but legally valid for individuals in this world.

5.1 AL-BAGHDĀDI ON THE LAW IN PRACTICE AND THE VARIATION BETWEEN THE SCHOOLS OF LAW

God has said in Qur'an 6:145: *Say: I do not find in that which has been revealed to me anything forbidden to those who wish to eat thereof except carrion, blood poured out, and pork – for it is an abomination.* This verse was revealed at the beginning of Islam since this surah is Meccan up until God's saying in verse 151: *Say: I will recite what your Lord has forbidden you,* to the end of the verse. The rest of the surah was revealed in Medina. Then God abrogated the delineation of the three items mentioned in this verse by His saying in Qur'an 5:4: *Forbidden to you is carrion, blood, pork, what has been hallowed to other than God, that which has been strangled or killed by a violent blow,* up to His saying: *what has been sacrificed to idols.* Surah 5 is Medinan. Then God revealed in Qur'an 7:157: *He has permitted to them the good things and forbidden them the bad things.* After that the prophet forbade the eating of all wild beasts with eye-teeth, all birds with teeth, the flesh of domestic donkeys and mules, and the flesh of an animal which has been tied up and then dies of strangulation. That is the explanation of the forbidden *bad things* of Qur'an 7:157.

In these verses of the Qur'an and the reports which we shall mention are three topics of concern with regard to their legal implications: one, the explication of what is permitted to be eaten and what is forbidden to be eaten and drunk; two, the description of ritual slaughter by which the eating of meat is then permitted; and three, the explication of the wording of these verses and reports.

Explication of the animals which are permitted or forbidden to be eaten

The followers of al-Shafi'i disagree concerning aquatic animals. One claims that fish are permissible but that frogs are forbidden. Others say that if the animal is in the form of a fish or of an animal ritually slaughtered in good faith, then the eating of it is permitted if it comes from the sea without being ritually slaughtered; however, if it is of a form of something which is not permitted to be eaten in good faith, then one is forbidden to eat it. This is the judgement of Abu Thawr. Others say that everything from the sea is to be judged by the law of fish except the frog which is forbidden because the prophet forbade killing it. This is the judgement of 'Ali ibn Khayran.

Malik and Rabi'a declare all aquatic animals allowable, even the tortoise and the like. This is suggested by a report from Abu Bakr who said: 'There is nothing in the sea besides animals which God would slaughter for you'.

Abu Hanifa forbids everything which does not have the form of a fish among the aquatic animals.

All agree on the allowability of the flesh of the beasts of the flock, including camel, cow, buffalo, sheep, and goats. There is disagreement, however, concerning riding horses and work horses. Al-Shafi'i and al-Awza'i allow them while the Ahl al-Rafd forbids them and Abu Hanifa declares them reprehensible.

There is also disagreement concerning domestic donkeys. Al-Awza'i allows them to be eaten while others forbid them although the jurists concur on the allowability of wild donkeys and wild mares.

There is disagreement as well concerning the fox, hyena, and lizard.

Al-Shafi'i, al-Awza'i, Abu Thawr, and the Medinan jurists allow them to be eaten while Abu Hanifa forbids them. All agree, however, that animals are forbidden if someone kills one of them when that act then requires compensation by that person.

There is disagreement concerning birds also. Malik allows all of them to be eaten while al-Shafi'i and Abu Hanifa forbid those that have claws and also forbid crows and vultures.

The followers of al-Shafi'i disagree concerning killing in those places where one may take refuge. Some declare it allowable and require only that compensation be paid by someone who is in the state of *ihram* or is in the *haram*. Others forbid it and thus do not require compensation for an act of killing. As for vermin, all of them are forbidden except the jerboa which is permitted; whoever kills it while in *ihram* or in the *haram* must pay a compensation.

All animals of which we permit the eating are permitted on the condition of ritual slaughter being done, except in the case of fish and locusts, the eating of which is permitted when they are not ritually slaughtered. All dead fish and locusts are possible to eat; there is no difference between whether it floats or whether it sinks according to al-Shafi'i and Malik although Abu Hanifa forbids that which floats, whether it is in the sea or a river; he does not allow what is floating in a well or a vessel, either.

Discussion of the description of the ritual slaughter of what is permitted to be eaten thereby

Concerning ritual slaughter, there is variation in both the ability to do it and the possibility of doing it.

The ritual slaughter has been decreed for the inner and the outer part of the throat and the upper breast. According to al-Shafi'i, the slaughter is connected to two things: one, the cutting of the windpipe and two, the cutting of the gullet. Likewise, it is recommended that these two be cut along with the two major blood vessels. If the windpipe is cut without the gullet or the gullet is cut without the windpipe or the blood vessels are cut without the other two, that cut will not be considered a proper ritual slaughter. Malik says that the two blood vessels are like the throat and the cutting of the two of them is the only requirement of the ritual slaughter. Abu Hanifa requires the cutting of the windpipe and the gullet and most of the blood vessels; if only one-half or less of the blood vessels are cut, then it is not permitted to eat the animal. Al-Awza'i says that the cutting of the blood vessels is sufficient. The Zahiris require the cutting of the windpipe, the gullet, and both of the blood vessels totally.

It is recommended in the ritual slaughter of the camel that it be done by stabbing in the upper chest but that ritual slaughter for cows and sheep be done as described previously. If the camel is slaughtered rather than stabbed while cows and sheep are standing near-by, eating it is permitted according to al-Shafi'i, but it is considered a reprehensible practice. Malik says that slaughter (rather than stabbing) of the camel is not permitted except out of necessity; he also permits the stabbing of a cow even without dire necessity. Concerning sheep, he says that stabbing them is not permitted without dire necessity and stabbing them without such a condition would mean that they could not be eaten.

There is disagreement concerning slaughter done with teeth or claws. Al-Shafi'i says that what is slaughtered with such implements is carrion unless it is exhausted or injured and thus needs to be slaughtered quickly.

Abu Hanifa and his two followers say that if an animal falls into a pit then eating it is possible although it is reprehensible. If it did not fall in the pit, then it is carrion.

There is agreement that animals slaughtered by Jews, Samaritans, and Christians are allowable but there is disagreement on animals slaughtered by Zoroastrians. Abu Thawr permits such flesh but al-Shafi'i, Malik, Abu Hanifa, and most of the community forbid it. There is agreement that animals slaughtered by idol worshippers, Hindus, Dualists, Atheists, and apostates among the philosophers are forbidden. Al-Shafi'i says concerning the Christian Arabs that their slaughtered animals are not permitted; this is reported on the authority of 'Umar, 'Ali, Ibn 'Abbas, and Ibn Mas'ud.

There is disagreement concerning animals slaughtered by converts. Al-Shafi'i, Abu Hanifa, and most of the community forbid such animals while al-Awza'i says that if the slaughterers have been converted to Judaism or Christianity then their slaughtered animals are permitted but if they have been converted to a religion other than those, then their animals are not permitted.

The followers of al-Shafi'i and most of the theologians agree on forbidding animals slaughtered by various heretical sects including the Mu'tazilites, the Jahmiyya, the Khawarij and the extreme Rafidites. Slaughtered animals are also forbidden from those who forbid for themselves animals slaughtered by the Sunni community. Therefore animals slaughtered by groups such as the Qarmatians and the Batiniyya are not permitted.

Our followers agree upon the allowability of the flesh of an animal which has been slaughtered by all those who master the slaughtering method among those whose slaughtered animals are permitted. This can therefore include a youth, a man, a woman clean or menstruating, a mute person, or a blind person. The flesh of an animal slaughtered by someone who is drunk or crazy is considered reprehensible. The Zahiris, however, say the animal slaughtered by a drunk person or a crazy person is not permissible. Ibn Wahb transmits thusly from Malik.

5.2 AL-GHAZZALI ON BIRTH CONTROL FROM HIS CHAPTER ON THE SECRETS OF MARRIAGE

It is a rule of cohabitation that the emission of semen should not take place outside of the vagina, for what God has decreed must take place. The prophet said likewise. There are differences among the learned class concerning '*azl* or *coitus interruptus*. One group says that '*azl* is lawful in all circumstances while another group says it is unlawful in every circumstance. Another group says it is lawful with the consent of one's wife while another group says it is lawful in the case of female slaves but not in the case of free women. To us, the custom of '*azl* is lawful but it is not commendable for the reason that the merits of ejaculation in the vagina are lost. A similar example is found in the person who sits idly in the mosque without remembering God. The point is that the person is not doing something which is intended to be done in the situation; that is not commendable. There is virtue in producing a child but that is lost in '*azl*. Muhammad said: 'If a man cohabits with his wife, the reward of producing a child is decreed for him – such a child will become a martyr fighting in the way of God'. He said this in consideration of reward, because if a child is born like this, he will get the reward for producing a martyr in the way of God. This is only possible with full intercourse.

That birth control by '*azl* is lawful is supported by legal analogy from the Qur'an. Though there is no clear verse regarding the matter, it can be gathered by analogy such as the following. It is not unlawful to give up marriage or to give up intercourse after marriage or to give up ejaculation of semen after intercourse. It is true that rewards are given up on these actions but absence of actions is not unlawful. There is no difference between these three things. A child is born after ejaculation into the vagina. Before it there are four stages: (1) to marry; (2) to cohabit; (3) to have patience to ejaculate after intercourse; (4) to ejaculate into the vagina and then to stay in that condition until the semen is settled therein. The life of a child coming into existence has a number of stages: (1) semen in the vagina must be mixed with the female egg. If both are mixed, it is a sin to destroy it. There is no sin if they are not allowed to mix; (2) if it is created into a clot of blood and a lump of flesh, it is more hateable to destroy it; (3) if life is infused into that lump of flesh, it is most hateable to destroy it; (4) the last limit of sin is to destroy the child when it is born. If the male semen is mixed with the menstrual blood of a woman, it is condensed, as happens when something is mixed with milk. It is just like proposal and acceptance which constitute an agreement or contract. Both things are necessary for a contract. If there is a proposal but no acceptance, there is no sin in breaking it. The ejaculation of semen is like a proposal and doing that in the vagina is like its acceptance. If it is ejaculated outside the vagina, the proposal is lost. There is no sin in it. Therefore, to ejaculate outside the vagina before the semen is mixed with female egg is not a sin.

Question: if there is no sin in ejaculating outside of the vagina, it must still be considered bad because the object of semen is to produce a child and if that is not done, it is secret polytheism.

Answer: There are four aims of '*azl*. (1) To preserve the beauty and health of one's wife and thus to enjoy her always. If semen is destroyed with this object, then it is not unlawful. (2) To prevent the birth of too many children. It is not unlawful; to maintain too many children is very difficult. The verse in the Qur'an which guarantees maintenance of all creatures means perfection of God-reliance and perfection of merits and rewards but it is no sin to give up the highest stage of merits just as it is no sin to protect one's wealth and properties and to hoard things for a limited period of time. This is the meaning of the verse: *There is no animal in the earth of which the maintenance is not upon God* (Qur'an 11:6). (3) To practise birth control for fear of the birth of daughters. This is unlawful. The Arabs before Islam used to bury their daughters alive and they feared the birth of daughters. This was prohibited in the Qur'an. If with the above object, marriage or intercourse is given up, it will be committing a sin but these actions without that object are not sinful. If semen is ejaculated outside of the vagina with this purpose, then it is unlawful. (4) To protect the honour of a woman, to keep her neat and clean, and to save her from maintaining children. This too is unlawful use of '*azl*.

5.3 ABU BAKR EFFENDI ON THE ALMS TAX

The alms tax consists of the distribution to (certain categories) from amongst the Muslim poor – and from which the descendants and slaves of the Hashimi family are excluded – of part of one's property, which part is specifically laid down by the secred law.

The taxpayer may deduct all the costs he has for maintenance of dependents under whatever heading; the tax is paid for God's purposes only.

Its obligatoriness is subject to the following conditions: sanity, majority, Islam, freedom, ownership of taxable property, i.e. property which has been in his possession (not less than) a year, which is free from debts, in excess of his basic needs (or those of his dependants), capable of increasing, and of which he is in complete possession. The alms tax is not obligatory for (or on) the mentally deficient, unbelievers, slaves, those who have no taxable property, i.e. property which has not been a full year in their possession, those slaves who have made a contract with their masters, debtors of whom repayment is demanded and when the amount of alms tax due would be equal to (or more than) the total of the debt to be repaid, property which is doubtful, i.e. which has gone astray or has fallen in the sea, or which has been misappropriated and possession of which cannot be proven by witness, or which was lost because it was buried somewhere in the country and the exact spot was forgotten; also (it is not due on) property which has been unjustly seized as well as property which was given out in loan which was subsequently disowned by the borrower and for which there are no witnesses.

This is in contrast to a debt which is acknowledged by the borrower, whether he be rich or poor or destitute, or a loan which, though disowned by the borrower, can be proven by witnesses or is known to the magistrate.

(As against all these ways of holding property, and upon which all Canonists agree in declaring them non-taxable), there is some difference of opinion as to property, buried and forgotten, if it had been buried in one's own house, or in one's own plot or vineyard.

Loans are taxable from the moment the borrower receives the money. As to commodities or articles of trade, these are taxable as soon as the minimum of forty *dirhams* is realised on them. As to other articles of property, which are not merchandise, as soon as their value amounts to the taxable minimum (they are taxable). As to property not in the owner's possession, as soon as the taxable minimum returns to his possession, and after it has been for one year in his possession (they are taxable).

The condition *sine qua non* of tax payment is the intention (to pay the alms tax) which must accompany the actual payment or the setting apart of the amount due. If one hands over the amount due *in toto*, and omits the intention, the entire payment counts as not rendered. If one pays only a part (of the amount due), the part as yet unpaid remains payable. It is thus according to Abu Yusuf.

It is reprobated to employ juridical expedients in order to avoid payment.

If one buys a slave as 'merchandise' (i.e. to sell him again at a profit), and subsequently makes the intention to employ him as a servant, then the slave ceases to be considered as a (taxable) article of trade. What was intended for use, does not become 'merchandise' through a (new) intention, but (only) through the actual sale. The same applies to what one inherits. What, however, came in one's possession through a free gift, or a bequest by will, or through marriage, or through divestiture, or through compensatory settlement, becomes 'merchandise' if one makes the intention to use it for trading purposes.

Any specifications of a vow to give on this day, this money to this poor man as a pious gift, are so many idle words.

Chapter on the alms tax on the produce of the fields

On what is watered by rain or river or what grows naturally in the mountains, a tenth is due as alms tax, whether the quantity is small or large, for there is no stipulation as to a taxable minimum nor is it necessary that it has been one year in the taxpayer's possession.

According to the two Canonists, however, the tax constitutes a necessity only on produce which has been growing for one year on the land, provided it amounts to five camel-loads. Produce which cannot be measured by the camel-load, must be assessed as to commercial value, taking as basis five camel-loads of a produce of the lowest possible value. This is a legal decision to be found with Abu Yusuf. But Muhammad has made a decision to the effect that the tax must be paid on the basis of five camel-loads of produce of the highest possible value of its kind. For cotton the taxable minimum is five mule-loads, for saffron five man-loads. No taxes are payable on wood, bamboo, hay, straw, or date-palm branches.

On produce artificially irrigated by bucket, waterwheel, or camel-drawn pump, only one-twentieth is payable as alms tax, to be calculated without deduction of the cultivation costs.

The tax is due on honey, whether the quantity is small or large, when the honey is collected from a mountain or flat land which is under tithe liability. According to Muhammad the tithe must be paid on honey if it amounts to five *farq*. According to Abu Yusuf when it amounts to ten *qarb* (it must be paid).

On land which is liable to the tithe and belongs to a *taghlabi*, one-fifth is payable in alms tax, and this remains so if a non-Muslim under Muslim protection buys it from such a person. Likewise if a Muslim buys that land, or the owner becomes converted to Islam (the tax is still the same).

On women and children rest the same tax obligations as on men.

If a non-Muslim under Muslim protection buys from a Muslim land which is liable to the tithe then he must pay the general tax and if a Muslim takes this land again from him because of the right of pre-emption or the land returns to the seller because of some fault in the transaction, the tithe is again payable on it.

General tax is payable on a house turned into a garden whether the garden belongs to a non-Muslim under Muslim protection or to a Muslim, when it is irrigated by water coming from land on which general tax is payable. But if the garden is irrigated by water coming from land on which the tithe is payable, then the tithe must be paid on the produce of the garden. But no general tax is payable on a house, even though owned by a non-Muslim under Muslim protection.

(Land irrigated by) rain or by a well or dam is liable to the tithe. (Land irrigated by) water from canals dug by foreigners is liable to the general tax, similarly, (land irrigated by) the rivers Oxus and Yaxartes as well as by the Tigris and the Euphrates. Abu Yusuf has given a legal decision to that effect.

No tax of any kind is payable on pitch mines, oil wells, and salt-pans, if these are on tithe land. But if they are on general-tax land, then general tax must be paid on the land surrounding these, if the land would be suitable for wheat or other cultivation, but not on the land occupied by the pitch mines, oil wells, and salt-pans. On no land are tithe and general tax both payable.

Chapter on the distribution of the alms tax

The beneficiaries are the poor, i.e. those who possess something though not enough to become taxable, and the needy, i.e. those who have nothing.

The opposite is also said. (The beneficiaries should be) the collectors, who should be rewarded in proportion to their labour even though they be wealthy, contract-slaves who should be helped to free their neck, the debtors who do not possess a taxable minimum in excess of their debt, those who are unable to go on military expeditions, according to Abu Yusuf, while Muhammad says (those unable) to perform the pilgrimage since they are too poor (to provide themselves with arms and provisions), and (the travellers) who have their property in their country but not with them. It is allowed to pay the alms tax to all of these or to some of these (categories of people).

The alms tax must not be used to build a mosque, or to buy grave linen for a deceased or to pay his debts, nor to free a slave. Nor may it be given to a non-Muslim under Muslim protection. Other (free gifts) may be used for those purposes.

It should not be given to a rich person who possesses the taxable minimum, of whichever kind of property, nor to his slave, nor to his minor children. But it may be given to his major children or to his wife, if these are poor. It must not be distributed to any member of the Hashimite family; (these are the members) of the clan of 'Ali or 'Abbas or Ja'far, Aqil or al-Harith even though they are themselves collectors of taxes, nor to any of their dependants who must be considered as similar to them. A taxpayer should not give taxes to his parents, neither to his grandparents, nor to his children or grandchildren, nor to his wife. Likewise, a woman should not pay her alms tax to her husband, nor to his slave, his contracted slaves or the slave whom he appointed as his executive, nor to the mother of his child, nor to a partly freed slave.

When a taxpayer has given the alms tax to someone whom he thought was a rightful beneficiary and later it appears that he is wealthy or a member of the Hashimite family or an unbeliever or his father or his own son, he is nevertheless deemed to have acquitted himself of his tax obligations. But when it appeared that the recipient was his slave or his contracted slave, then it does not count as correct acquittal of his tax obligations.

When giving the alms tax (to a needy person), it is recommended to give him so much that he need not beg any more for that day. It is reprobated to give the whole amount due or more to one poor person who is not indebted. It is also reprobated to send alms money from one village or province to another unless it is to one's relatives, or to someone who is in greater need than the people of one's own place. He who has sufficient money or food for the day should not ask alms tax for that day.

5.4 AL-MARGHINANI ON DIVORCE

On the three kinds of divorce

The most laudable divorce is where the husband repudiates his wife by a single sentence during the time she is not menstruating; at this time he should not have intercourse with her. He should leave her to pass the waiting period (*'idda*). This is the most laudable means of divorce because the companions of the prophet praised those who only pronounced the divorce once during the waiting period as opposed to giving three divorces by repeating the sentence in successive months. As well, this method is better because the husband still may recover his wife with no shame on him, and there is less harm on the woman since she is still, in fact, lawfully subject to her husband.

The laudable divorce follows the example of the prophet and is where the husband repudiates his wife with three sentences over the period of three months. Malik says that this method is on a level with the third type of divorce, the irregular, because the reason that divorce is even permitted is due to the urgency with which it is felt it must be performed; this urgency is fulfilled by the divorce in a single period. For us, relevant is a saying from the prophet transmitted by Ibn 'Umar: 'The *sunna* requires that you wait for the proper time and pronounce the divorce in each period'. Also since the propriety for divorce is established by the sense of urgency, this urgency is reconfirmed at the beginning of each period when the divorce is to be pronounced because of the desire to have intercourse. Repeating the divorce at the subsequent period is therefore a restatement of the proof of the urgency and is therefore to be allowed. It is also said that the husband should wait until the end of the non-menstruating period of his wife to pronounce the divorce so that the waiting period should not be too long. However, it is better that it be pronounced at the beginning of the period because if he were to delay it, he may be more tempted to have intercourse with her and divorce after that is not permitted.

The irregular divorce is where the husband repudiates his wife by three divorces in a single statement or three times during the non-menstrual period. If this is done, the divorce holds but he has committed an offence.

Al-Shafi'i says that all three of these divorces are permitted because they are codified as a part of the shari'*a* and therefore no danger is to be connected to it. It is even possible, according to al-Shafi'i to divorce a woman during her mestrual period for the prohibition there applies to the extension of the waiting period, not to divorce itself.

For us, however, divorce is to be considered dangerous since it dissolves marriage, an institution which involves within it many religious and worldly circumstances. Only on the grounds of urgency of release is divorce permitted but this does not give the excuse for three divorces at once. Giving three divorces over three months, however, exhibits repeated proof of urgency.

On the execution of divorce

Divorce is of two kinds, by express statement and by implication. The expressed divorce is where a man says: 'I divorce you', or: 'You are divorced'. This results in a reversible divorce, such that the husband may take back his wife before the end of her waiting period. These words are only used in divorce and are never used on any other occasion. . . .

If the husband says: 'You are under the divorce', or: 'You are divorced by divorce', without any particular intention, or intending thereby one divorce or two divorces, only a single reversible divorce is considered to have taken place. If he intended three divorces, then a triple divorce has taken place.

If the husband says: 'You are divorced by the divorce', and says that by that he means a single divorce with the word 'divorced' and a second divorce by the word 'divorce', that is sound because each of these words is valid for effecting divorce. It is as if he had said: 'You are divorced and divorced', such that two reversible divorces have taken place, as long as the marriage has been consummated.

If the husband wishes to divorce his wife and says: 'You are divorced', this is valid since it applies to its proper subject, his wife. The pronoun 'you' implies all of the woman. This is the same where the husband uses words for a part of the body which are understood to apply to the whole: 'Your neck', 'Your body', 'Your head' – 'is divorced', for by such words the whole person is implied in common usage and such words are found used that way in the Qur'an and in *hadith*. According to one tradition, 'blood' may also be used.

6 THEOLOGY

See 1.5. 6.1 is one of the earliest theological tracts from the beginnings of Islam still in existence, arguing the case for free will on the basis of the Qur'an. 6.2 gives a view of what has become orthodoxy; some of the items mentioned will be recognised as having been presented in more elaborate forms in the various legends in chapter 3. The more closely argued stance of 6.3 represents the compromise between the use of reason and the dogmatic assertion of traditionalism which orthodox Islam reached.

6.1 THE LETTER (*RISALA*) OF AL-HASAN AL-BASRI ON FREE WILL AND PREDESTINATION[1]

'Abd al-Malik ibn Marwan wrote to al-Hasan al-Basri:

From 'Abd al-Malik ibn Marwan, Commander of the Faithful, to al-Hasan ibn abi'l-Hasan al-Basri. Greetings to you! May the only God who exists commend you. The Commander of the Faithful has heard about your views on *qadar*, hearing the like of which he has never heard before. Nor has the Commander of the Faithful heard of any of the companions of Muhammad talk about the matter of which he has heard that you are talking. He knows that you are sound in your being, meritorious in your religion and knowledgeable, searching and intent in religious thought. Therefore the Commander of the Faithful does not believe these statements attributed to you. So write to him about your position on this matter and about the affair explaining whether this is on the basis of transmissions from the companions of Muhammad, or according to your own view of things, or on the basis of truth which is known from the Qur'an. We shall listen to no other disputant nor intelligent person on this topic until we hear from you. So let the Commander of the Faithful know your opinion on the matter. Peace be upon you and may God grant you mercy and good blessing.

So al-Hasan al-Basri wrote to him:

From al-Hasan al-Basri to 'Abd Allah 'Abd al-Malik:

Greetings to you, O Commander of the Faithful. May God grant you mercy. May the only God who exists commend you. May God cause the Commander of the Faithful to prosper and to make him one of His followers who are obedient, attain His pleasure, and hasten the following of His command. May God make the Commander of the Faithful prosper, making him progress from small things to ever larger ones and let those small things be visible to the good people (of the community) such that they will rely on them and copy them in their deeds. We know, O Commander of the Faithful, that the pious ancestors followed the command of God and considered His wisdom and followed the *sunna* of the messenger of God. They did not reject the truth nor did they accept the false as truth and they did not ascribe to the Lord more than that which He allowed Himself and would not use any arguments other than those used by God in addressing His creation in scripture. God said in Qur'an 51:56–7: *I have created jinn and men only so that they will worship me. I do not require nourishment from them nor do I need them to feed (me).* So He ordered them to worship Him which is why He created them. God would not have created them for a purpose and then come between them and (the purpose) because He does not do harm to His servants. None of the pious ancestors denied this statement or quarrelled about it because they were all of one accord on the matter. We have started to discuss the matter only because some people have started to deny it. They have adopted misleading positions and committed grave sins while distorting the book of God. God's religion is not according to man's desires as God has said in Qur'an 4:123: *It is not according to your desires nor the desires of the people of the book. He who does evil will gain his reward for it.* Any statement for which there is no proof in the book of God is erroneous as God has said in Qur'an 2:111: *Bring your proofs if you are truthful,* that is (proofs) concerning that which you create lies about Me and invent opinions. *They will know that the truth is with God and that which they were forging will go astray from them* (Qur'an 28:75).

Therefore, O Commander of the Faithful, know what is incumbent upon you in the book and leave aside the opinions of those who do not know about God's decree (*qada'*) and His judgement. Indeed God says this, that He will not alter a favour which He has bestowed upon a people until they change what is in their souls. The beginning of the blessing came from God but the change came from the servants (of God) because of their being contrary to what He commanded for them. This is just as God has said in Qur'an 14:28–9: *Have you not considered those who traded God's favour for disbelief and caused their people to descend into the house of the fires, Hell.* Thus favour was from God and the trading was done by man because they omitted what He commanded them to do and did what they were forbidden to do. God has said in Qur'an 6:151: *Do not approach the abominations, outward or inward*. What God has forbidden is not from Him because He does not approve of what He is displeased with nor is He displeased with what He approves because He has said in Qur'an 39:7: *If you disbelieve God has no need of you but He does not approve of disbelief in his servants; if you are grateful, He does approve of it in you*. If disbelief was from God's decree and determination (*qadar*), He would approve of one who did it. God would not decree something and then disapprove of His own decree. Oppression and wrong are not from the decrees of God; rather, His decree is His command to do good, justice, and kindness, and to give to relatives. He forbade abomination, evil, and injustice. He said in Qur'an 17:23: *Your Lord has decreed that you serve only Him and that you are kind to your parents*. O Commander of the Faithful, it is the book of God which speaks – and who is better than God, *He who determines and guides* (Qur'an 87:3)? He did not say: 'He commands and leads astray'. God has made this clear to His servants and has not left them in confusion concerning their religion nor left them with any doubt about their command such that He has ascribed guidance to Himself and error to His prophet as He has said Qur'an 34:50: *Say: If I err, I err against myself while if I am guided it is by that which my Lord reveals to me*. Do you approve of (the idea) that error is from Muhammad when he errs and disapprove of that from ourselves? God has said in Qur'an 92:12: *Indeed it is for Us to guide* and He did not say that 'It is for Us to lead astray'. The book of God has been revealed in its place, O Commander of the Faithful; do not alter it or interpret it falsely. God would not openly prohibit people from something and then destine them to do it secretly as the ignorant and the heedless say. If that were so He would not have said in Qur'an 41:40: *Do what you wish* but would have said: 'Do what I have destined you to do'. Nor would He have said in Qur'an 18:29: *Whoever wills shall believe and whoever wills shall disbelieve* but would have said: 'Whoever I will shall believe and whoever I will shall disbelieve'. He also said in Qur'an 33:38: *The command of God is a determined decree* so the command of God is His decree and His decree is His command because He does not command abomination or evil. Some people said that, however, and God denounced them saying in Qur'an 7:28: *When they commit abomination they say 'We found our fathers practising it and God has commanded us to do it'. Say 'God does not command abomination; do you say things about God that you do not know?'* The book of God is a light in the darkness and life at the time of death. God has not left another proof after His book and prophets for His servants: *Whoever is destroyed is destroyed by a clear sign and whoever lives lives by a clear sign* (Qur'an 8:42).

Consider, O Commander of the Faithful, the words of God in Qur'an 74:37: *Whoever among you wishes to go forth or go back*, because God has given them the power by which they go forth or go back, so that whoever does good should deserve paradise and whoever does evil should deserve hell. If the matter was in accord with those who hold false opinions, then they would not have been able to go forth or go back. Whoever goes forth would not be praised nor would whoever goes back be blamed for what they had done, because, according to their assertion, this is not from them and not in their hands but is something done with them. God would have said concerning their reward: 'A reward for that which has been done with them' and: 'A reward for what I have recorded for them' and would not have said in Qur'an 32:17: *A reward for what they have done*. The people opposed the book of God, O Commander of the Faithful, and they altered it and distorted some of it into what it was not. Rather it was just as the best of narratives describes a book, some of which resembles other parts of it and there is no disagreement between the parts of it, because it is *a revelation from the all-Wise, the all-Laudable* (Qur'an 41:42). Notice, O Commander of the Faithful, the statement of God in Qur'an 91:7–8: *By the soul, and that which shaped it and revealed to it lewdness and godfearing*, and then He said in Qur'an 91:9–10: *Whoever purifies it will prosper while whoever corrupts it has failed*. If it was Him who corrupts it, His self would not fail. Then, O Commander of the Faithful, consider the words of God in Qur'an 38:61: *They say 'Our Lord, whoever presents this for us, give him a double punishment in the fire'*. Now if it were God who presented this to them . . . [omission in text]. But God has made it clear to us who it is that presents that to them and who it is that leads them astray saying in Qur'an 33:67: *And they say 'O Lord, we obeyed our chiefs and elders and they led us astray from the path'*. So it was the chiefs and the elders who presented them with disbelief and led them astray from the path after they had been on it. Also consider, O Commander of the Faithful, Qur'an 41:29: *O Lord, show us those who led us astray of jinn and people so that we may put them under our feet that they may be of the lower ones*. And He said in Qur'an 76:3: *We have guided him on the path whether he is grateful or disbelieving* meaning that We have made the way known to him, he being grateful so that We reward him or disbelieving and ungrateful so that We punish him for his disbelief. *Whoever is grateful is grateful for his own soul's sake and whoever disbelieves, God is all-Sufficient, all-Praiseworthy* (Qur'an 31:12). Likewise God has said in Qur'an 20:79: *Pharoah led his people astray; he did not guide them*. So say, O Commander of the Faithful, just as God has said that it was Pharaoh who led his people astray. Do not be contrary to what God has said and attribute to God only that which is pleasing to Him. He has said in Qur'an 92:12–13: *Incumbent upon Us is guidance and to Us belongs both the hereafter and this world*. Guidance is from God and error is from His servants.

Consider also, O Commander of the Faithful, the statements of God in Qur'an 26:99: *Only the evil-doers led us astray*, and 20:85: *The Samaritan led them astray*, and 17:53: *Satan is an obvious enemy for people*, and 41:17: *As for Thamud, We guided them but they preferred blindness over guidance because of what they had earned*. So, the beginning of guidance was from God but the beginning of their deserving blindness was in their erroneous opinions. My statements and my letter do not demand a lot from you, O Commander of the Faithful, for the proofs are quite clear in them for whoever's soul is free of guilt. Consider our father, Adam, who was the most truthful of those who set an example, who said, when defying his Lord: *We have wronged ourselves and if You do not forgive us and have mercy upon us we shall be among those lost* (Qur'an 7:23). He did not say: 'Your determination and your power'. Likewise Moses said when he killed someone: *This is of Satan's work; he is a misleading manifest enemy. He said: 'My Lord I have wronged myself. Forgive me!' So God forgave him* (Qur'an 28:15–16). Moses said: 'This is the responsibility of Satan and the ignorant while this is from the actions of the Merciful'. None of those whose stories are recounted by God to us in His book acknowledge that. God also said in Qur'an 5:30: *Then his soul prompted him to kill his brother and he slew him and thus became one of the inhabitants of Hell.* To no one would it be said: 'You are evil and from you is its beginning' without him detesting that (ascription). They ascribe to God that which does not please Him and they ascribe to themselves what they covet. A community will not be destroyed for that unless there is a deviation in their hearts. They follow what the desire of temptation resembles. They quarrel and say that God has said in Qur'an 13:27: *He leads astray whoever He wishes and He guides,* but they do not look at what precedes those words and what follows them. They would not have erred if they had observed the verses which come before and after it. God said in Qur'an 14:27: *God strengthens those who believe in His lasting word both in this life and the hereafter. He will lead the wrong-doers astray. God does as He pleases.* Therefore among those things He wishes to do is to strengthen those who believe in their belief and their righteousness and to lead astray the wrong-doers in their denial and their enmity. He has also said in Qur'an 61:5: *When they went astray, God led their hearts astray,* so it is because they have gone astray that God led their hearts astray. He also said in Qur'an 2:26–7: *He misleads many thereby and guides many by it but He only misleads those who are evil-doers, those who break the covenant of God after they join in alliance (with it) and they sever what God has commanded should be joined and they do evil in the world. They will be the dwellers of Hell.* Among those things about which they dispute is the statement of God in Qur'an 39:19: *Shall he who has the word of punishment invoked against him have you deliver him out of the fire?* God explained to His creation about he who has the word of punishment invoked against him with His statement in Qur'an 40:6: *Thus the word of your Lord is invoked against those who are corrupt; they will be the inhabitants of the fire.* So the word of punishment is invoked against them after they have done acts of corruption.

Another verse about which they dispute is Qur'an 10:100: *It is not for any soul to believe except by the permission of God.* Permission here means that it is allowed. God has already allowed this and faith as well and has given it power to do it and has said in Qur'an 4:63: *We have sent Our messengers so that they will be obeyed by the permission of God.* God is not one to send a messenger to be obeyed and then prevent His creation from obeying him. How far this would be from the description of God and His justice and wisdom!

Another verse about which they dispute is Qur'an 74:37: *To whoever of you wishes to go forward or follow behind,* and Qur'an 81:28–9: *To whoever of you wishes to go straight but you will not unless God wills, Lord of all beings.* The truth of God is that we cannot will good without God willing it for us, but rather (it will only come) from Him willing us good before we will it ourselves. He has explained that to us. God has said in Qur'an 2:185: *God desires ease for you and does not desire hardship for you,* and in 4:26–7: *God desires to make clear to you and to guide you in the ways of those before you and to turn towards you. God is all-Knowing, all-Wise and He desires to turn towards you.* God does not wish to turn towards us and (at the same time) prevent us from turning nor have we ever been prevented.

They also dispute about the creation of children born of fornicators and similar people. God does not punish the fornicators for their children. Rather He punishes them for contradicting His command: it is their fornication, not their children (where the blame lies). Similar to this is someone who impregnates a woman unlawfully like the farmer who sows his seed in land which is not his and then cultivates what he wishes of it and leaves the rest, which he does not want, uncultivated.

They also dispute concerning Qur'an 57:22: *No affliction falls on the earth or on yourselves unless it is in a book before We created it.* They interpret this by their opinion as concerning unbelief and faith, and obedience and disobedience. That is not so. Rather, this 'falling' concerns possessions, souls, and fruits. We are informed of that. It is our temptation in this world with deviation and comfort, poverty and riches, but we are not grieved for what escapes us and we do not rejoice at its enjoyment; whoever observes it, rejoices. Then He has made it clear to those who are patient by saying in Qur'an 2:156–7: *Give good tidings to the patient who, when they are visited by an affliction say 'Surely we belong to God and to Him we shall return'; upon them are the prayers and mercy of their Lord. They are the truly guided.* If that had to do with faith and disbelief, He would not have said in Qur'an 57:23: *So that you are not grieved for what escapes you nor rejoice for what comes to you,* but would have said 'So that you do not grieve at what escapes you of faith nor rejoice for what comes to you of it'. So why are the people saddened when they are not saddened at what escapes them of His religion? God has said in Qur'an 10:58: *Say: In the bounty of God and His mercy – in that let them rejoice. It is better than what they gather together.* The truth is plain for those who understand but most of them are ignorant. Know, O Commander of the Faithful, that God is more just than to blindfold His servant and then say to him: 'Look! I will not punish you!' or to make him deaf and then say to him 'Listen! I will not punish you!' or to make him mute and then say to him 'Speak! I will not punish you!' This, O Commander of the Faithful, is plainer than that which is hidden from an intelligent person.

They also dispute about Qur'an 11:105: *Some of them will be unfortunate, others fortunate.* They interpret this such that God created people in their mothers' wombs either fortunate or unfortunate so there is no way for whoever is fortunate to become unfortunate nor is there a way for the unfortunate to become fortunate. If the matter was as they interpret it, God and His messengers would not have decreed something and then issued the call of the messengers to them to fear God and provoke them to righteousness. He did not mean something without there being some profit in it. But the interpretation is other than that which they take from it. God has said in Qur'an 11:102: *That this is a day upon which the people are to be gathered, a day of witnessing,* that is the day of resurrection. Then He said in Qur'an 11:105: *A day comes; no soul shall speak except with His permission. Some of them will be unfortunate, others fortunate.* The fortunate ones on that day will be those who hold fast to the command of God while the unfortunate will be those who scornfully neglect the command of God about His religion. Know, O Commander of the Faithful that those who disagree with the command of God, His book and His justice are a people who are lax in the affairs of their religion and who reveal their ignorance in a like manner.

6.2 THE CREED OF IBN QUDAMA

This is the creed of the most learned Hanbali Imam Muwaffaq al-Din ibn Qudama.

In the name of God, the Merciful, the Compassionate, and may the prayers and peace of God be upon our lord Muhammad, and his family and companions.

So says the Shaykh of Islam Muwaffaq al-Din Abu Muhammad 'Abd Allah ibn Ahmad ibn Muhammad ibn Qudama al-Maqdisi, may God sanctify his soul, Amen.

Introduction

My brothers! May God give you success and defend you from heresy and bestow upon you firmness in Islam and the *sunna* and make you cling to the *sunna*. Preservation of it brings salvation. Persist in following the book of God, the most praised and glorified, and the *sunna* of his prophet, may the prayers and peace of God be upon him, and know that the roots of Islam are to be found in God's decree and man's submission to the command of God and being firm in following the laws of God and following what God orders and staying away from what God has forbidden.

Faith

Iman (faith) is verbal confession, action, and intention and is increased by obedience and decreased by disobedience.

Predestination

The decree, of both good and evil, sweet and bitter, little and big, loved and detested, is from God. What comes to you of the decree could not have come by mistake, nor could what has missed you have been intended for you. The pen (writing down the deeds of people) will become dry with all that occurs by the day of resurrection.

The Qur'an
The Qur'an is the speech of God, the revelation of what He spoke. It is uncreated. The Qur'an originated with God and to Him it will return. Whatever is recited of it, or chanted or heard or written, in whatever form, is the uncreated speech of God. This includes the surahs and the verses, the words and the letters, although God spoke without letters or voice.

Moses heard God speak
As for Moses, God entrusted him with His address and Moses heard the speech of God in reality.

The Vision of God
Believers will see God on the day of resurrection with their eyes and will hear His speech. The reports from Muhammad agree with this and on this topic our predecessors also agree.

The Qur'an [ii]
Imam al-Hafiz Abu Fadl ibn Nasir said: You have asked me about the statement: 'The Qur'an originated with God and to Him it will return'. Know that many sound *hadith* reports have been transmitted about that and they have been accepted by the leaders of the community in their books. You may accept them on the authority of the prophet of God, his companions and their successors, may God be pleased with all of them. Among these reports is the one transmitted by 'Uthman who reported that the messenger of God said that the merit of the Qur'an over all other types of speech is like the merit of God over His creation and that means that the Qur'an came from Him and will return to Him. Abu al-Qasim al-Lalaka'i has transmitted this report in his *Kitab al-sunna*. 'Abd Allah ibn 'Amr ibn al-'As reported that the messenger of God said that all of the revealed Qur'an will most certainly return to God and will echo around His throne just like the buzzing of the bees. God, who knows best about these things, will say: 'What are you?' to which it will reply thrice: 'I am your revelation; I came from You and to You I am returning. I do not return to be recited nor to have anything done with me'. 'Ali ibn Abi Talib said: 'The Qur'an was neither creator nor created but is the speech of God, may He be exalted and praised; it originated with Him and to Him it will return'. A similar report is also transmitted from Ibn 'Abbas. 'Amr ibn Dinar said that for seventy years prior to the generation of his teachers, people had been saying that the Qur'an was the speech of God and that it originated with God and to Him it will return. The prophet said that whoever recites the Qur'an with the correct inflection will receive fifty rewards for each letter. He who recites it but

fails to inflect it properly will receive ten rewards for each letter. The prophet also said that when God speaks via revelation the inhabitants of the heavens hear His voice. The pious ancestors agree on the number of surahs, verses, words, and letters in the Qur'an. Hisham ibn 'Ammar said that the number of surahs in the Medinan, Syrian, and Kufan traditions is 114 while the number of verses in the Medinan tradition is 6119[2] and the number of letters is 321,250.

Attributes of God

According to the *sunna* accepted by Muslims concerning the attributes by which God described His Self or by which the messenger of God described Him, it is required that one have faith in these attributes such that they are unrejectable, uninterruptable, not subject to doubt nor allegorical interpretation nor anthropomorphisation nor comparison. Rather we acknowledge them just as they come and we believe in them and do not ascribe to them attributes of created things. We know that: *There is nothing like unto Him. He is the Hearing, the Seeing* (Qur'an 42:11), which is similar to God's saying in Qur'an 5:67: *Rather, His hands are outstretched*, and in 55:27: *The face of your Lord remains*, and in 54:14: *[The Ark of Noah] floats under Our eyes*, and in 5:119: *God will be pleased with them*, and in 48:6: *God has cursed them*. The prophet said: 'God descends each night to the heavens of the world'. This report is transmitted by twenty-three of the Companions, seventeen men and six women, as well as all the religious leaders. The prophet also said: 'Nothing comes from the heart unless it is between the fingers of the all-Merciful'. This report and other sound reports like it are transmitted on the authority of the messenger of God. Our religious school, being the school of the pious ancestors, holds to the affirmation of this idea and has faith in it and acknowledges it in a statement of faith in its plain sense. Both modality and anthropomorphisation are rejected and allegorical interpretation is disdained. The learned ones of the pious ancestors say in the reports about the attributes of God that they acknowledge the attributes in a plain sense, for speaking of attributes surpasses speaking of essences. The affirmation of God is in fact the affirmation of His existence and not of His modality. Therefore, the affirmation of the attributes is the affirmation of their existence and not their modality. Therefore God has said in Qur'an 7:54: *Then He was firmly established on the throne*, and in 67:16: *Are you secure about He who is in heaven?*[3]

Punishment in the tomb

Faith also requires belief in the reality of punishment in the tomb and the squeezing which will really take place and that Munkar and Nakir, the two angels, will come to the people in the grave asking about their Lord and their helper and their prophet. *God will strengthen those who believe with the everlasting word in this world and in the hereafter; but God will lead astray the wrong-doers for God does as He wills* (Qur'an 14:27).

Pool of Muhammad

The pool of the prophet stretches between the two extremities of paradise, as if it were between Aden and Oman. The number of cups (available for people to drink from) will be as many as the stars in the heavens.

Intercession

Intercession by the messenger of God is such that people will be brought out of the fire after having resided therein and become a group and arrive at the door of paradise at the river of life. They will flourish there just as grain flourishes in the garden. Then God will bring them into paradise. This will continue until there does not remain a single person in hell with any measurable amount of faith in his heart.

The balance

The balance exists in reality. It has a tongue and two scales to weigh the deeds of the believers. *As for those whose deeds weigh heavy, they will attain salvation but those whose deeds weigh light they will lose their souls in Hell where they shall live forever* (Qur'an 23:102–3).

The bridge

The bridge exists in reality. The pious will cross it while the unbelievers will slip off it. It is an arched bridge across hell. Hooks, spikes, and thorns will pull the unbelievers down.

The trumpet

The trumpet is a horn in which Israfil will blow twice, once to stun and once to raise the dead as God has said in Qur'an 39:68: *The trumpet will be blown and whoever is in heaven or earth will be stunned except those whom God wills. Then it will be blown again and behold, they will be standing, watching.*

The resurrection

Resurrection after death is a reality, both for the body and the spirit.

Heaven and hell

Heaven and hell have both been created for the purpose of reward and punishment. They will not cease to exist. Heaven is the home of the saints and hell is the prison of the enemies. Indeed, God seizes each one by his right hand and says: 'These are destined to heaven by My mercy as I wish!' and He seizes the others and says: 'These are for hell, as I wish!'

The prophets

God created Adam by His own hand and breathed in him with His spirit. *And he took Abraham as a friend* (Qur'an 4:125), and *He spoke to Moses* (Qur'an 4:164), and He revealed Himself on the mountain and devastated it. And our prophet travelled by night from the Mosque in Mecca to al-Aqsa Mosque then ascended to the heavens. *He saw the greatest of the signs of his Lord* (Qur'an 53:18). *And he was at a distance of two bows-length or nearer* (Qur'an 53:9).

Submission to authority

We hear and obey whomever God delegates our leadership to, even if that person be a mutilated Ethiopian slave. We will not have armed battles against the leader even if that person has deviated from Islam. We pray for our leader at the Friday prayer and on festival days.

Holy war

Jihad or holy war will be practised by every pious as well as immoral person such that they will all fight Dajjal[4] when the end time of this community is reached.

Previous generations

It is an obligation to beg for mercy for the past generations of the pious, may God have mercy on all of them! The best of all centuries was that of our prophet and those who followed after that century. The best of all people after the messenger of God was Abu Bakr, then 'Umar, then 'Uthman, and then 'Ali. They were the rightly guided Caliphs to whom homage must be paid. No one was more entitled to the Caliphate than them. The messenger of God saw ten people in paradise: Abu Bakr, 'Umar, 'Uthman, 'Ali, Talha, al-Zubayr, 'Abd al-Rahman ibn 'Awf, Sa'd, Sa'id, and Abu 'Ubayda ibn al-Jarrah. 'A'isha, the truthful one, daughter of Abu Bakr, the truthful one, mother of the believers, was free of every impurity, free from every suspicion, and most beloved of God. Likewise, all the wives of the messenger of God were pure and mothers of the Believers. We pray that God will be pleased with all of the companions of the messenger of God and we seek God's forgiveness for them just as God commands us. We refrain from speaking of the quarrels between them and we know that God will forgive them just as He has informed our prophet and just as He has said in Qur'an 48:18: *God was pleased with the believers when they pledged allegiance to you under the tree; He knows what was in their hearts.* No Muslim will go to heaven or hell without the messenger of God testifying on his behalf. We wish success to the good but are fearful for the evil-doers.

Heresy

The *sunna* or right practice requires the avoidance of the people of innovation, the study of their books, and listening to their talk.

Epilogue

These statements comprise the *sunna* upon which all the religious leaders are agreed; they come from the messenger of God and all the religious leaders of the Sunni community are agreed upon them and transmit them. Anyone who disagrees with any portion of them is a misguided heretic and should not be spoken to, greeted as a Muslim, prayed behind, helped when he is sick, honoured at his funeral, or listened to. It has been transmitted in a *hadith* from the prophet, among that which Abu al-Qasim Yahya ibn Thabit ibn Bundar told us that he was informed by Muhammad ibn 'Umar ibn Bukayr al-Bazzaz al-Muqri', that he was told by Abu Bakr Ahmad ibn Ja'far ibn Salim that he was told by Ahmad ibn 'Ali that he was told by 'Abd al-Rahman ibn Nafi' that he was told by al-Husayn ibn Khalid on the authority of 'Abd al-'Aziz ibn Abi Dawud from Nafi' from 'Abd Allah ibn 'Umar ibn al-Khattab who said that the messenger of God said that whoever turns away from an innovator will have his heart filled with riches and faith by God and whoever rejects an innovator will be safeguarded by God on the final judgement day; but whoever greets an innovator as a Muslim, and wishes him well and greets him in a way that is pleasing, has scorned that which has been revealed to Muhammad. It is also transmitted from the prophet that he said that a repulsive affair, an overburdening load, and evil which does not cease are all manifestations of innovation.

May God guard you against the approach of heretics and listening to their talk and help you in their removal and elimination. Indeed, their presence is a disease which naturally is alienated from faith and hopes for no reward. Perhaps he will alter the faith of those who live close to him or cause them to doubt their religion. Perhaps they will sow the seeds of discord among the people and perhaps they will teach the youth of innovation while they are young so they will grow up in it and the *sunna* will become hateful to them and they will be beckoned to error after having received guidance and the *sunna* of God and His prophet which has existed since the time of the pious ancestors who came before us will become altered. It is incumbent upon you to practise that which you know and to reject that which you detest and not to be changed by the powers of falsehood with their great number of supporters as compared to the paucity and weakness of the people of truth. This is the age which the prophet mentioned that true religion would become more rare but it is also transmitted that people will hold on to the religion in this age waiting for the final reward.

May God grant us fair reckoning and may His representative be blessed and may the prayers of God be upon our lord, Muhammad, our lofty prophet, foretold in the Torah and the Gospels, and on his family and his faithful companions who are free from falsehoods and may the peace of God be upon them. Glory be to God, Lord of the Worlds.

6.3 A POPULAR THEOLOGICAL STATEMENT

God possesses twenty-nine qualities of which fourteen are necessary, fourteen are impossible and one is possible.

1. God's first necessary quality is being or existence

All created beings possess this quality only from the moment they are created until the moment they cease to exist. Since God is not created nor caused by any other being His existence does not have a beginning. Since nothing caused His beginning, nothing can end His existence, which is therefore necessary. For example, a weaver may destroy the cloth that he has woven. God created Adam and later caused him to die. God himself, however, cannot be destroyed by anything. For example, a man may die of hunger or of an arrow piercing his heart. God, however, needs no food nor could any weapon ever hit Him. It follows that His existence does not end. It is, therefore, necessary to assume it.

It is impossible to assume the opposite, namely, that God would not exist. It would then be necessary to assume the existence of another God who had created the creation.

2. God's second necessary quality is His eternity which means that there is no time at which God did not exist. Every creature has its first moment. In the case of a man that is the moment when God creates the drop out of which he will grow. There is no such first moment in the existence of God, because it would follow that God had been created, in which case the created one would not be God but his creator would be God. It is impossible to suppose that there would be an unending chain of causes or creators. It is therefore impossible to suppose that God had a cause other than Himself, so that it follows He has always been there. His beginning did not take place in time at any moment.

3. God's third necessary quality is His unendingness, or his immortality, which means that His last moment will never come. Proof for this dogma is that if God's existence could at any time be followed by His non-existence, then His non-existence must also have preceded Him in which case the objections of the second dogma would apply: if God had at any time not been there, He would have been caused or created, etc.

If a thing ceases to exist, it is not eternal. If there are things which can cause its end, there must have been things which once caused its beginning. If a thing ends its existence, it follows that it is only possible; its existence is not necessary. We have seen, however, that God's existence is necessary since it is impossible to assume His non-existence.

A thing which exists is 'possible' when it could also not exist. Since God is eternal His non-existence is impossible. All 'possible' things will perish. God alone will persist since His existence is unconditional: whatever is eternal cannot not be there.

Conclusion: if God did not possess the necessary quality of endlessness then He would also have a beginning. This, however, is impossible since we have seen that there is nothing that can have caused His beginning.

4. The fourth quality which God possesses by necessity is His difference, God is unlike any temporary thing. He resembles nothing in any of His aspects. God is remote from comparison with any of His creatures.

The proof for this dogma is as follows: suppose a thing which was in any way comparable to God if only with one of its qualities. It would follow that God had one quality in common with one of His creatures. It would follow that God Himself had originated in time, so that He would have been in need of a creator.

If God had only one quality in common with the temporary things, then He would Himself be temporary. When we deny that God is temporary, we also deny that He is comparable to anything, since all things are temporary and God is the only eternal one. Since neither His beginning nor His end has been, or can be, caused, He is essentially different from all other existing things.

5. God's fifth necessary quality is His substantiality. God stands on His own without any support. He is independent. He does not fall. He needs no floor to stand on. He needs nothing to give Him existence or to keep Him alive. Human beings need breath, water and food, and firm land to stand on but God needs none of those.

It is for this reason that God is called *al-Ghani*, i.e. independent or rich, for He needs nothing and no one. It follows that His existence is not relative but absolute.

6. God's sixth necessary quality is His unity or uniqueness in essence, in substance, and in activities, i.e. the absence of plurality.

God is unique in the sense that there is nothing else of the same substance and He is one in the sense that there is no one else like Him, and that He is not divided nor divisible. This means that He is not composed of parts like a ship nor can part of Him be taken away like a hand or foot. God has no plural, He cannot be counted like people. The plural 'gods' does not refer to God but to false gods invented by liars who make idols to mislead the people.

God's necessary qualities are also unique, like eternity, omnipotence, omniscience, etc., which are shared with no one else. This follows also from God's difference. Even in His actions, God is quite unique since He creates the actions of all His creatures. None of His creatures creates his own actions. God is the doer of all deeds, the maker of all things. Even when you raise your hand to hit a man, it is God who creates the action. *He created you and what you do* (Qur'an 37:94).

Thus God possesses oneness in five respects: (1) He is not composed of parts; (2) there is no other god; (3) His qualities are unique, i.e. He has only one of each: one eternity, one omnipotence, etc.; (4) He alone has those qualities, no one else shares any with Him; (5) He alone creates activities. No creature can act on his own, not even free human beings.

The proof for God's uniqueness is that the world cannot have been created by two creators, since each thing has only one cause. More likely would be that two gods would wish to create different worlds, so that one would destroy the creation of his rival. This does not happen so that there is only one god. The same applies if only one God succeeds in creating, for then He is the true God.

It follows that no one except God succeeds in creating anything at all.

Nothing can have effect without God. The fire cannot burn, the knife cannot cut, the food cannot satisfy the hunger except that God makes them do so.

It is an error to believe that the fire owes its heat to its own nature. On the contrary, God makes the fire hot and He makes it turn wood into ashes. Likewise it is an error to believe that the water slakes the thirst without God willing it to do so.

7. God's seventh necessary quality in His omnipotence. It is the power which has the effect to make the possible real. It brings the non-being into existence. This effect is contingent, i.e. God will act from time to time, when He wishes, but His power to do anything is always there. God creates anything at any time and then having created it, He makes His creature act according to His wish, at any time, according to, or in spite of, that creature's character.

God's omnipotence has seven relations to its objects, viz.: (1) A potential one which is eternal. (2) A relation of extent: God's power extends to that which He has not yet brought into existence. (3) An actual relation, when God actually creates a thing. (4) A relation of negative extent: God's power extends to that which exists and which He can destroy at any time. (5) An actual relation of destruction when a thing ceases to exist. (6) A potential relation of reviving a thing after its destruction. (7) An actual relation of reviving which God will use for us on the day of resurrection.

The faithful must remember that God has at any time the power to create what He wishes, e.g. a new child, to terminate its existence at any time, e.g. when a person dies, and to call resurrection at any time.

8. The eighth necessary quality of God is His will. Out of the endless mass of possible things God selects at any time what He wishes to create and gives it qualities to His taste, then He gives them reality, i.e. existence. It is by His will that He creates, destroys, changes anything at any time. He has completely free choice. God may will the following things: (1) being (i.e. creation); (2) non-being (i.e. destruction); (3) qualities (e.g. shape, colour, etc.); (4) time; (5) place; (6) direction.

God's will is potential before His action has begun and actual when He is busy carrying out His decision. God's will relates to every event in the universe: nothing happens that He does not will. If anything happened against His will, it would have been willed by another God, which is unacceptable. God's will is always related to an object which may be anything since nothing is impossible for God.

If you are healthy it is that God wishes you to be so, therefore be grateful. If you suffer, God wishes to test you. If you think, your thoughts have been willed by God. If you decide something, it is God's decision, so do not be proud of your virtues or achievements.

9. God's ninth necessary quality is His omniscience. It is an eternal, real quality. God's knowledge is complete, i.e. there is no ignorance in God. There is nothing that He does not know completely. Everything is knowable for God,

even the things that do not exist, and He knows everything completely. He knows all real and unreal things, all possible and impossible things. He knows our beginning and our end, our thoughts and our deeds, our past and our future.

Knowing refers to an object which includes the knowing subject. Thus God knows Himself better than we know ourselves.

If God knew only real things and not potential things it would mean that He was ignorant of things that could happen but had not yet happened. It follows that God knows the future completely. Thus God can never learn anything that He does not know already.

10. The tenth necessary quality of God is His life. It is unacceptable to assume that God is dead. How could He will, speak, hear, see, know without life? A creature may live and be blind but a seeing creature lives. A stone is not alive, therefore it cannot act, nor see nor hear, nor think, nor speak. The quality of living is not related to an object.

11. God's eleventh quality is hearing. It is always related to an object and to that extent it is contingent unlike God's life which is there all the time. It is conceivable that at certain times there reigns complete silence in the universe, but in practice it is probable that there is always something to be heard so that God will always be hearing something. Since God never sleeps He is never unreceptive to sound.

God can hear many things which we cannot hear, because they are either too far away or hidden. For God, distance does not matter so He will hear even the most distant bodies moving. He can even hear the creatures hidden in the earth or in the depth of the ocean. God does not hear by means of ears; God can hear without them.

It is unacceptable to suppose that God could be deaf. In some cases we do not know whether God receives knowledge from hearing or from seeing. For instance, God can perceive our thoughts but we do not know whether He hears them or sees them, or both.

12. God's twelfth necessary quality is seeing. God sees all things which happen, will happen, and have happened. Seeing is always related to an object. God is never not seeing since He never sleeps. God can see even objects that are too far away or too small for human beings to see, or hidden from view such as the worms in the earth or the crabs on the sea bottom. He can also see our souls, the spirits and jinns, the angels and the devils without difficulty. God's seeing is not limited to what human eyes can see.

13. God's thirteenth necessary quality is the faculty of speech which He must possess since it is unacceptable to suppose that God could be dumb. The faculty of speech is always there and is related to an object only when He actually speaks. The object is what He says. Speaking itself is a sequence of words such as was revealed to the prophet, but the immutable word of God is different. The words are temporary, they come and go, but the Qur'an is eternal, non-sequential, free of consonants and vowels. If, however, the veil of

ignorance could be lifted from our spiritual eye, then we would perceive that the meaning of the two books, the eternal one and the one in word sequences, is identical. But we cannot now understand this meaning. The material words of the Qur'an have been created and written on the well-preserved tablet in heaven. The angel Gabriel descended with these words from the lowest heaven to where they had been lowered in the night of power, and gave them to the prophet. Other scholars have a different opinion but only God knows. We believe that the Qur'an was taught to Muhammad with all the words and all the meanings as we know them today. He did not add a word to what he was told to recite, nor did he omit one.

The proof that God possesses the faculty of speech is in the Qur'anic verse where God spoke to Moses in the valley of Tuwa (Qur'an 19:52; 20:12; 27:9; 28:30). It follows that God Himself says that He has spoken. The word has the same objects as the knowledge: the necessary, the possible, and the impossible. In addition the word expresses these matters and communicates them. If only the veil were lifted off our minds we could understand all this.

When the soul speaks to itself, that too, is the word, is language, but it is not comparable to the word of God because that is eternal while the language of people is temporary.

14. The fourteenth necessary quality of God is, according to al-Maturidi, the power to give existence to things, to give them shape and reality, in brief His creativity. Seven times the Qur'an states that if God wishes a thing, He only says it to *kun* ('Be!'), and it becomes. From this *kun* comes the word *takwin* 'giving existence'. The word *kun* is often cited by writers to denote God's creative activity. The effect of His pronounciation of this syllable is immediate. No sooner has the *n* joined the *k*, then whatever it is that God wishes is there, already created, with every quality and feature in place. This is how He created the prophet Jesus in the womb of the Virgin Mary, without a man. For God, anything is easy.

These positive qualities are paralleled by a series of negative qualities which cannot be applied to God. They are the following. 1. Non-existence or absence. 2. Beginning in time, e.g. birth or genesis. 3. Mortality or perishability. 4. Homogeneity with created things as opposed to diversity or difference. For example, God is not limited in space like all things and creatures. One can therefore not say: 'I am beneath God'. Popular expressions like: 'I am under God' or: 'The Lord is above me', are to be rejected because they entail the risk of unbelief. 5. Denial of substantiality or causelessness. God needs no substratum; He is no *accidens* to anything nor is He caused by an *agens*. He exists by Himself. 6. Complexity (as opposed to simplicity) or multiplicity, or multitude (as opposed to singularity or uniqueness); or duality (as opposed to unity). 7. Impotence as opposed to power. 8. Constraint as opposed to freedom to act, or aversion as opposed to wish. It is inconceivable that God would not be free to do whatever He wishes. Nor is it conceivable that God could do anything against His will, e.g. that He could be forced by anyone or by circumstances to do something He does not wish to do or even something He dislikes. Thus it is unthinkable that God has created anything He does not want. He makes everything out of His own free will.

It follows that the scientists are wrong if they believe that the things that exist are caused by blind causality and that God is forced to accept their existence as a result of the laws of nature. God can never be forced and He does not have to accept anything He does not wish.

It cannot be that the philosophers who pretend that God Himself has only acted as blind causality by generating things mechanically could be right. Even less acceptable is the hypothesis that God has generated things in conjunction with other causes such as the heavenly spheres or the stars, as if God himself were only a force of nature, like the *Physis*, an invention of infidel philosophers.

The distinction between the true and the false notion is as follows. An effect may be caused automatically by a cause. For example, when a man moves his finger, his ring will also be moved, without any other condition that has to be fulfilled, e.g. an impediment. For instance, fire can burn trees on condition that it touches them, and that the trees are dry. If a log is far away from the fire, or is soaked, it will not be burned by it. Those are the impediments in the chain of cause and effect. Should both conditions be fulfilled however, i.e. should both impediments be absent, then the fire will burn the log, according to this theory, whose defenders may be cursed by God.

The true doctrine is as follows. When we see that the fire is beginning to burn the log, what happens is that God creates the burning at that moment in the log, at the occasion of the fire touching it. Similarly, God creates the movement of the ring when the finger moves. It follows that no thing has its existence as a result of natural causality or force or nature.

God is unique in His work. That is why it is impossible that there could be a cause present in the universe which has caused the world without God's will, or a force of nature which has effected the world. God's power is far too great for that.

9. Ignorance. It is impossible to attribute this to God. It is inconceivable that God would be even partially ignorant. For example, that He would ever create something without knowing what it would look like is not possible. He knows the future actions of every man and woman He creates. He knows what goes on in every corner of His creation; He cannot be ignorant of anything any of His creatures is doing. Even more unacceptable is the idea that God could make a mistake because His knowledge of a thing or an event is incomplete. Nor could God ever forget anything that He had known previously. Nor could God's attention ever flag so that He was not fully aware of every occurrence in His universe at every moment.

10–13. As we have already seen it is unacceptable to suppose that God might be lifeless like a stone, or deaf, or blind, or mute.

14. Finally it is impossible to suppose that God could not create things.

Indeed God's creativity is one of His most essential qualities. If God did not have it, then some other god would be the creator, and we would have to worship Him who created us all, and has therefore the power to stop our existence at any time, for He is all-Powerful, Omniscient, and One.

God's one possible quality is His power to create good or evil at any time He wishes, i.e. His decree. God creates faith in one man, infidelity in another, knowledge in one, ignorance in another. Both good things and evil things are the result of God's decree. It is the duty of every Muslim to believe this. God's decree was previously resolved upon by Him. God's will may intend to make you a scholar or a king, but God's predestination, i.e. God's fixing of your destiny is the creation in you of knowledge or of royal dignity after you have been given existence in accordance with that will of His.

Modern theologians sometimes teach that God has the duty to be good, to do good for people, to will the good, but that is naïve optimism. God, they say, must give people good things. That is a proud sort of faith. It is wrong and mendacious. God has no such duty. If He had, it would follow that it would be impossible for God to do the opposite of His duty, in other words, His free will and power would be limited which is clearly contrary to the dogma of omnipotence and the divine will.

Thus, if God creates faith in a man and gives him knowledge, then this is God's voluntary kindness, without any obligation on His part. Evidence for this is that babies suffer pain and illness which is not 'good' for them. If it were God's duty to perform only the good things, then babies would never come to any harm. The 'liberal' theologians maintain that God will not fail to fulfil his obligation for that would be a shortcoming. However, according to the consensus of the community of Islam, God is free of shortcomings.

When God rewards the pious, that is pure kindness and when He punishes the sinners, that is pure justice, since the piety of humans is not useful for God, nor does the sinner do Him any harm. It is He who causes harm and good. Rather the good works of some and the evil of others are signs that God wishes to punish some and to reward others. So, if God wishes to draw someone close to Himself, then He will give him the grace which will make that person do good works. If He wishes to reject someone and put that person to shame, then He will create sin in him. God creates all things, good and evil. God creates people as well as their actions: *He created you as well as what you do* (Qur'an 37:94).

Muslims further have the duty to believe that God can be seen by the faithful in the hereafter (Qur'an 7:139). However, we shall not see Him in the way that we see each other, in a given quantity, shape, and colour, since God has no body, so that He is not in one place only. One can see Him in more than one direction.

The liberal theologians (may God shame them) teach (incorrectly) that humans create their own actions, even though they are slaves of God. This is their love of freedom. Hence they are called the Qadariyya, because they teach that all human actions are based on this *Qudra*, the power to act freely, or *Qadar*, free disposition.

Similarly, the representatives of extreme predestination are called Jabariyya, for they teach that people are forced, *majbur*, to act as they do, by God's *jabar*, compelling power. This doctrine is also incorrect.

The truth is the golden road between two extremes: people are not compelled nor do they create their own actions. God creates the actions which people perform, but at the same time people have a free choice to act.

It is, however, impossible to explain this free choice. Any person discovers a difference in moving a hand or when the air moves it. The human freedom can therefore only be established in hindsight, as a fact, whether the hand moved out of free will or not.

God has sent His messengers to humanity out of His own free will, without any obligation to us, for God has no duties.

The prophet Muhammad is the best of men. The other four possessors of God's highest mission were Abraham, Moses, Jesus, and Noah. They all taught Islam.

It is our duty to believe that God supported these five prophets with miracles. He made Muhammad excel by his special favour in that He made him the seal of the prophets so that Muhammad's words would not be contradicted by any other prophet. When Jesus comes back before the resurrection, he will teach Islam and apply its law. The prophets always speak the truth. They cannot lie, nor hide the truth, nor speak foolishly. Proof: if the prophets were liars, then God's message would be deceptive, but God has proved their truthfulness by means of miracles. Therefore, if the prophets had been liars, then God would have been one too.

7 SECTARIAN MOVEMENTS

See 1.6. 'Ali and his family figure prominently in Shi'ism as a whole; these themes are shown in the popular liturgical material 7.1.2 and 7.1.3 as well as in 7.1.1 which is taken from a prose work considered to be of the highest eloquence and whose contents are ascribed to 'Ali. For modern Iranian Shi'ism, see 9.4. The Isma'ilis (7.2.1, 7.2.2) would accept the status of 'Ali and his family as it is set out in 7.1. The Baha'is (7.3) and the Ahmadis (7.4) are both more recent offshoots, the former emerging from a Shi'i background, the latter from a Sunni.

7.1 SHI'ISM

7.1.1 The speeches and letters of 'Ali ibn Abi Talib

(NB)

1. God has placed His trust in the family of Muhammad. They are the strongholds where His commandments receive protection and are those who explain and interpret the law. They are the fountain-heads of knowledge created by Him, shelters for His teachings, refuges for divine books and mountain-like citadels in the defence of His religion. Islam in its beginnings was weak and helpless but they came to its defence and help; Islam was nervous of the unbelievers around it but they made it strong and powerful.

2. I stood up alone among my contemporaries to welcome the order of God while they were timidly holding back. I boldly came forward to defend the faith while they were nervously hiding their heads in the sand. Without hesitation I testified to the message of God while they were tongue-tied out of fear of the unbelievers. I walked in the path of truth under the divine light while they stood under clouds of uncertainty and doubt about religion and God. I never spoke aloud of my virtues and was never concerned about my reward even though I surpassed everyone in attaining divine favours.

Possessing these attributes and distinctions, I rose higher than any of them and stood alone in eminence. My stand was firm like that of a mountain which cyclones cannot shake nor tornados break. No person has any justifiable cause to blame me or to find fault with me.

All those whom society has wronged or who have been unjustly humiliated are respectable before me and dear to me and I shall secure for them their just claims and rights. I hold in contempt those who take away the rights of others and I shall make them give back the rights and privileges wrongly usurped.

I have happily resigned myself to the will of God and have willingly bowed my head at His commands. Can you believe that I would lie about our prophet? I was the first person to witness that he was the prophet of God; how could I be the first to lie about him? Therefore, when I deliberated upon my state of affairs, I came to the conclusion that I must give priority to the fulfilment of promises made to the prophet concerning the problem of asking people to take the oath of allegiance to me.

3. For those who wish to approach the realm of God through good deeds, the following are the best ways to achieve success.

The first and foremost is to have complete faith in God and His holy prophet. The second is to exert oneself in the service of God to the best of one's capability because such endeavours are sublime heights of the glory of Islam. The third is the repetition and belief in the statement of faith because it is the basic concept of the religion of Islam. The fourth is continuing to offer daily prayers because these services are the soul of religion. The fifth is continuing to offer the alms tax because it is a compulsory obligation. The sixth is fasting during the month of Ramadan because it saves one from the wrath of God. The seventh is going on the pilgrimage to the house of God during the days of the *hajj* and at other times because journies on these occasions reduce poverty and cleanse the soul of sin. The eighth is pitying one's poor relations and helping them when they are in financial distress because this charity causes an increase in the wealth of people. The ninth is giving charity and help to every needy or crippled person because this charity, when given secretly, washes away one's sins and, when given openly, prevents accidental death. The tenth is being kind, sympathetic, and solicitious to the creatures of God because this habit prevents one from falling into calamities, degradation, and disgraces.

4. These are the people who having given up the straight path of religion are wandering in the wilderness of error and delusion. Do not make haste in inviting the future nor try to put it off; wait for it, for it is inevitable. There are many people who often eagerly desire something and when it reaches them, they wish that it had not come at all. Today is so near to tomorrow. The future is the inevitable result of the present and is inseperable from it.

O people! Remember that the present time is the time when something which has been promised will happen and events which you do not know or cannot foresee or forecast will take place. During the trials and temptations those who recognise the significance and worth of the family of the prophet will, like people walking in the dark with lamps in their hand, not only go safely through the times but will be of help to others and will act like pious people. This will continue until the true *imam* of the time will clear the doubts created by heresy and schism, will free the people from oppression and tyranny, will educate the ill-informed and the ignorant, will introduce reforms in the society, and will cement the gaps which wickedness and impiety may have created in the true teaching of Islam. For some time he will be hidden from the eyes of people in such a way that the greatest searcher of the day will not be able to find a trace of him, however exhaustive the search. But when he appears, he will educate people in such a way that human vision will expand through the teachings of the Qur'an, people will be able to acquire true wisdom, and their minds will be able to rise to higher planes of science and philosophy.

5. Prayers to God and praise of Muhammad! Let it be known to you that I am in receipt of your letter wherein you write to me that the Lord selected Muhammad as the messenger of His revelations and He helped those companions of the prophet who sincerely exerted themselves to assist him.[1] Is it not an irony that circumstances have favoured you to such a position that you dare remind us of the favours which God bestowed upon us and the blessings conferred by Him upon His chosen apostle who was one of us. You have nothing to do with them and you have no share in these blessings and favours. Your condition is like that of a person who carries dates to the date-growing districts or that of a person who tries to teach archery to the master from whom that person has learned the art. You believe that the best of the people among the Muslims are such-and-such a group and you have started discussing a subject which if it is proven correct will not be of any use to you – it will not

enhance your status – and if it is repudiated, will not harm you, because you are neither a descendant of the emigrants nor of the helpers of Muhammad. What have you to do with their status and prestige? What is it to you if one is considered superior to the other? How are you concerned in their affairs? You are a freed and liberated slave and even freed slaves and their offspring cannot aspire to the exalted status of these two groups and they have no right to introduce an unholy classification among those groups. Do you realise your limitations? You do not belong to either group; you are a liberated slave and the son of liberated parents and you want to introduce an unhealthy division between these two groups. The false status which you have tried to grasp is not going to enhance your prestige. Can you not think of remaining at the place where your age-long enmity of Islam and Muhammad has kept you? How is the lower status or defeat of one class or of a person of that class – to whom you do not belong – going to harm you and how is the success or higher status of the other going to do you good? You have gone astray from the straight path and are lost in the depths of ignorance.

Listen! I want to give you a short description of the blessing of God upon us. A party of the emigrants received martyrdom by being killed in the cause of Islam and God. Every one of the them was favoured by God with a status and rank and those of them who belonged to my family and tribe, the Banu Hashim, were granted excellent ranks by God. My uncle Hamza received the title of Chief of the Martyrs; Muhammad himself called him by this name after his death and at his funeral service Muhammad praised God seventy times as a mark of distinction for him alone, something which is not for any other Muslim. Some emigrants lost their hands in the battlefield but when one of us, namely Ja'far my brother, lost both his hands and died on the battlefield, God favoured him with angel's wings and Muhammad informed us that this martyr had received the title of One who flies through heaven. If God had not disapproved of people eulogising and praising themselves then I would have given several instances which speak of the enhancement of my prestige and rank before God, instances which are accepted and can be testified to by faithful Muslims and which hearers will have no reason to doubt. Do not be like a man whom the devil has led astray. Accept the obvious truth when it faces you.

Listen, O Mu'awiya! We are supreme examples of the creation of God. For such a status we are not under an obligation to anyone but the Almighty Lord who granted us these favours. Humans have received and will receive perfection through us. This perpetual supremacy and natural superiority does not prevent us from forming family connections with your clan even though you are not of our status. How can you be our equal when Muhammad comes out of us and Abu Jahl, the worst enemy of Islam, was from you.

We were faithful followers of the orders of God and you and your clan always opposed Islam and accepted it simply to save yourselves from humiliation and disgrace. Our sincerity in Islam and our services to its cause are known events of history, at the same time history cannot deny your enmity of Islam and Muhammad. The credit which you want to take away from us and the honour of which you want to deprive us is the one which the Qur'an is carefully guarding for us. It says: *Some relatives are superior and have excellence over others according to this book*[2] (Qur'an 8:75) and God has also informed humanity that: *The people most liked by Abraham are those who follow him and those who follow the prophet and God is a friend of the faithful Muslim* (Qur'an 3:68). Therefore, we hold two excellences: that of near relationship to the prophet and that of faithfully accepting his doctrines.

You also want to taunt me by saying that when I refused to accept the caliphate of the first Caliph I was dragged like a camel with a rope around my neck and every kind of cruelty and humiliation was brought upon me. I swear by my life that by talking like that you want to bring disgrace upon me but you are actually doing the greatest service to me and are disgracing yourself as well as the cause that you wish to support. There is no disgrace for a Muslim if subjected to tyranny and suppression so long as that person is firm in faith and believes in God and religion. And this is exactly what I say that every cruelty and tyranny was levelled against me to deprive me of the right which God and Muhammad had given me and this is exactly what you do not want to acknowledge and accept. Your taunts against me suggest that in reality there was no election, that the position was simply taken and that was followed by brute force; that decided the fate of the caliphate, making it neither hereditary nor elective but rather occupative. I had no desire to go into these matters but you brought up the subject and I have been forced to explain a few points about it.

You have referred to the murder of 'Uthman and declared yourself to be his relative; you claim vengeance and blood. I must say something about this insinuation and propaganda carried on by you in this respect. My reply to you is that, first of all, you should try to find out who was the worst enemy of 'Uthman. Can he be the worst enemy who offered his help and services but who 'Uthman refused to have anything to do with and told him plainly to go and sit at home as his help was not required and his services not needed? Or was the worst enemy of 'Uthman the one whom 'Uthman asked to come to his aid but who purposely and intentionally delayed the help and allowed the events to take their course until what was fated to happen, happened? No! These two people cannot be considered in the same category. I swear by the all-Knowing God that He knows about this very well and as He has said in his book: *He knows the people who put obstacles in the ways of those who wanted to go to war and also to those who did not stay to face a battle* (Qur'an 33:18).

Just wait a little; then you will have to face the attack of a brave fighter. He will shortly invite you for the encounter you are waiting for. The event which you wish for is not as far away as you imagine it to be. I am coming towards you with an army of emigrants, helpers, and those companions who have sincere faith in me. Theirs is a powerful congregation. Their movements will raise huge clouds of dust. They are prepared to die or to kill. They believe that the best which could happen to them is to receive the favours and blessings of the Lord by their good deeds. Sons of those warriors who routed your clan in the battle of Badr are with them. The swords of the Banu Hashim are with them. And you have already realised the sharpness of these swords when some of your relatives were killed at Badr and Uhud. These swords are now nearing the tyrants who have tyrannised the Muslim world!

7.1.2 The death of Husayn

The family of the prophet lived happily in Medina until his death. Then Abu Bakr took power and was succeeded by 'Umar who appointed Mu'awiya as governor of Damascus. This was the beginning of the Umayyad dynasty which caused so much suffering to the people of the House. Mu'awiya made Marwan ibn Hakam governor in Medina as soon as he had taken power after the assassination of 'Ali. Marwan attempted to confiscate some lands that belonged to Husayn but the latter successfully resisted this illegal appropriation.

Before his death, Mu'awiya insisted that all the notables in his empire recognise his son Yazid as the successor to his throne, but Husayn refused to accept as a ruler a man whom he knew as a corrupt and sinful character. Yazid never forgot this affront. When Mu'awiya had died, Yazid demanded Husayn's submission to himself as the new Caliph, but again Husayn refused, stating that a man who drank wine and consorted with male friends was unfit to rule the community of the faithful lawfully and honestly. Husayn had to leave Medina secretly together with his kinsman 'Abd Allah ibn Zubayr, to seek refuge in the sanctuary at Mecca where they were safe for the time being. Mecca remained in the hands of Ibn Zubayr until his capture under 'Abd al-Malik.

The Caliph Yazid used to organise banquets for his friends, at which pork was consumed. He would take other men's wives to his bedroom and he once coveted Ibn Zubayr's wife. He tricked 'Abd Allah into divorcing her, but when his envoy Ash'ari came to bring Yazid's proposal, she said she preferred Hasan. This enraged Yazid so much that he had Hasan poisoned. Hasan died but his great-grandson Idris ibn 'Abd Allah ibn Hasan escaped to become king of the West where he founded Fez.

In order to pay for his extravagance, Yazid extracted taxes from the people, especially from the citizens of Iraq which was rich at that time, and the leaders of its capital Kufa complained by letter to Husayn in Mecca that he must come and take command. The letter stated that no ruler should be a burden 'bending the heads' of the people, but that every healthy man ought to work for his bread. The tradition narrates that one day Fatima was crying. When her father Muhammad asked her why she was crying, she complained of being hungry because she had not eaten in three days. 'Neither have I', answered her father, 'but it would be a sin to use the money of the treasury to buy food for ourselves. The faithful have entrusted that money to me for the orphans and widows.'

The Caliph 'Umar likewise took no money from the people but provided for his livelihood by making bricks which he sold.

Husayn wept when he received this letter from the citizens of Kufa, and he prayed that God would soon end this tyranny. Then he received a second letter from the citizens of Kufa, urging him to come and take command of their city, 'where an oppressor now rules, who takes wedded wives and virgin daughters for his own pleasure, and extracts money with threats and violence. It is better to execute a tyrant than to allow the government of sinners. If you, Prince Husayn, do not come to rescue us from corruption and injustice, we shall accuse you on the Day of Judgement of neglecting your duty, we swear this by the Almighty'.

When he read this, Husayn wept again, but there was no more doubt in his heart; he could now go and take power from the tyrant without fear of accusations that he acted for his own glory. He set out from Mecca with only seventy-seven followers, across the desert in the direction of Kufa. On the way they were suddenly confronted by a large army of animals of prey, with sharp claws and mighty jaws, under the command of a huge lion, king of the beasts. The lion bowed his big head down to the ground before the feet of Daldal, Husayn's horse, begging to be allowed to help him in his battle against the oppressor of the faithful, and to restore the rule of God's laws among the sons of Adam. Husayn thanked him, but sent him away, saying: 'Nothing happens on earth that He does not will. If it is His will that I shall win, God will strike down His enemies before my face'. They rode on, until suddenly the sky became dark. Many hundreds of birds of prey hovered over the modest army, headed by a large eagle who likewise offered to tear Husayn's enemies to shreds for him, but again Husayn, knowing that God was only testing him, declined, saying: 'Thank you, my winged friends, go back to your mountains, God has already decided who will live and who will die, nor can we alter His decision'. The final vision of temptation in the desert was an army of *jinn*, whose king, a monstrously big ogre with long teeth like sabres, threw himself at Husayn's feet, saying: 'Not since king Solomon has any man subdued us, but you Prince Husayn, may command, and we will obey. Please order us to destroy your enemies and none will survive'. Even though Husayn knew that he might not live to see the day after the battle, he sent the *jinn* away, thanking them courteously for their offer to help him. They disappeared at once.

Just when all their waterskins were empty, they arrived within sight of the Euphrates river where an army of Syrians was waiting for them, preventing them from reaching the riverbank and hoping that their enemies would die of thirst. The Syrians avoided a man-to-man battle because Husayn and his men had a great reputation as warriors and the Syrians were cowards who limited themselves to shooting arrows at the 'Alids from behind safe positions. For the sake of the women and children who were with them, Husayn's men tried to fight their way through to the river in the hope of fetching water for those parched creatures, but each of them was killed after many hours of heroic battles against vast armies shooting thousands of arrows. 'Ali Akbar, Husayn's eldest son, rode into battle, calling to his father: I am tired of waiting. / Our death is in God's writing. / We all die by His decision. / I will fight. Give me permission.

'Ali rode into battle and was soon killed. Husayn fought his way through the ranks of the enemies and picked up his son's body which was so full of arrows sticking out on all sides that it could not be laid on the ground. It received a proper burial.

Then Husayn saw how his youngest son, 'Ali Asghar, suffered from thirst, because his mother's milk had dried up in her bosom. The women sat there in their hastily erected tent, praying and praising God.

When Husayn saw the patience of the women, / He took the child which had not yet been weaned, / And carried it to where the river flowed, / Calling the enemies who lay in ambush / 'Do not shoot now! This child is sick with thirst! / Have pity on this babe who cannot speak / And soon will be an orphan, when I die . . .' / Before he finished speaking, all the Arabs / Had shot their arrows at the little child. / One arrow pierced his ear. He screamed with pain / Until the shadows sank over his eyes. / The women wept and all the men wept with them. / Husayn interred the little child near-by, / Praying the prayers that suit a proper service.

Then 'Abd Allah ibn Hasan asked permission to ride into battle. After killing 3,000 enemies, he too, was slain by arrows. When Husayn had retrieved his body, the dying young prince exclaimed: 'Look, uncle, do you see, they are all there, they can see us from above, they call me, do you hear? There is my father Hasan and my grandfather 'Ali and grandmother Fatima, all inviting me to join them!' At that moment the young hero died, leaving his uncle Husayn alone to defend the women against the enemies who were now closing in. Husayn prepared for the unavoidable battle and mounted his Daldal.

He sat upon his faithful charger Maymun / like a raincloud hanging above a mountain, / he took his spear with points like monsters' teeth, / he took his sword, Swift Lightning was its name. / It flashed sharp warnings to the evil-doers. / He took his shield of steel, his heavy helmet, / black was the colour of his iron armour. / Husayn turned in the saddle and pronounced / a prayer to God and to His holy prophet, / then to the women of his household he declared: / 'Farewell, beloved ladies of my house! / I have to go, such is my destiny; / God has ordained that I shall not return. / His will be done, His name be always praised, / what He decrees is inescapable. / Pray do not weep too much for no one dies / a moment earlier than He decides. / Be quiet, bear your lot with fortitude, / My task ends here but for you life goes on. / Goodbye Shaharbanu, daughter of kings, / Goodbye Sukina, daughter of my heart, / Goodbye my son, jewel of faithful men, / Goodbye Zaynabu, daughter of my mother!' / Thus Husayn took his leave of those who were / left in his care and now alone, without / a leader or protector to depend on.

In spite of his admonition, all the women wept bitter tears, and so did the children. Even the angels in heaven cried sadly, and the animals in the wilderness and the birds in the sky lamented in mournful songs; even the fish in the ocean wept.

When Husayn rode out, the army of the Syrians ran away, but he pursued them, for he knew this was his last day. He mowed down his enemies like a fire raging through the tall grass of the savannah. The earth grew bloodied and the sky grew dark as if the Day of Judgement had begun. Dark clouds veiled the sun even in Mecca so that its people wondered what caused this gloom which covered Arabia, Syria, and Egypt, reaching as far as Iran and Khurasan.

The angels prayed to God with the women that He might rescue Husayn. But God's intentions are unknown to man / Not even angels understand His plan. / Husayn called loudly to the Syrians: / Here is the water's edge. Have you all fled? / Prevent my horse from drinking if you can! / The faithful horse bent down its neck to drink / But Husayn scolded it: My dear Maymun, / How can you drink before the women have / Relieved their thirst and let the children drink? / The loyal horse obeyed and raised its head. / That was the moment when a voice was heard: / Husayn! The enemy has overrun your tent! / The women have been taken and the children killed! / It was a trick, an evil strategem. No one would dare, / while Husayn was alive, to touch his wife, / his sister or his daughters, nor his son. / He turned his horse and hurried back to camp. / There in the shrubs the enemy were waiting. / They shot at him without their faces showing / Hundreds of arrows flew into his face / Seventy arrows hit his tender body / and pierced his skin and spilled his precious blood. / He knew that he did not have long to live, / Just enough time to say: There is no god / but God and Muhammad is His prophet. / His soul flew up into the cloudless sky / Where it was met by those who loved him most: / His parents and his brother and his sons. / His body meanwhile fell from the strong horse. / Maymun escaped, it would obey no man / No enemy could lay his hands on it. / Alone it carried sweet Shaharbanu / Princess of Persia, home to fair Iran. / Here ends the sad account of Prince Husayn / Who lived and died a witness for the faith / A ransom for his people, for Mankind.

7.1.3 The death camp

There was Husayn lying in the sand, felled by an arrow shot from afar, the last arrow as we now know, the one that would cause his death. Husayn had fought most valiantly with his few surviving faithful men against a numerous army of heavily armed professional soldiers who had completely surrounded him, his men, their wives, and the children who were sitting huddled together in temporary makeshift shelters while the fighting raged.

The army from Damascus had occupied both banks of the Euphrates river, so that the people of the prophet's family were shut off from all sources of water. Shimar, the enemy commander, had decided on a siege, expecting that Husayn would soon surrender, overcome with thirst. In battle, Husayn could not be conquered by force of arms, for he was too strong and brave, even for a whole army. So the soldiers contented themselves with raining arrows on the camp and waiting. In his efforts to fetch water for the thirsty children, Husayn had had to expose himself and was hit by several arrows. One finally struck him fatally so he had to lie down, exhausted, waiting to die soon. Meanwhile he prayed his last prayer: 'O God, Thou always full of mercy and compassion! / My wounds hurt me like fire. I will soon die. / I did my best to fight Your cruel enemies / but now my time has come, I feel death is approaching. / O God have mercy on my faithful people! / Their lot is hard, their enemies are many / It pleases You to let me die alone / without my eldest son Akbar. Alas! / If only I could see grandfather here!

At that moment his grandfather the holy prophet Muhammad appeared to him in visible form by the grace of God, speaking: 'My dear Husayn, here I am, your grandfather Muhammad, to give you consolation in your last hour. Your wounds are many. I am proud of you, my grandson, how you suffered for Islam! You are a great martyr for the true faith. If you have a last wish, behold, here I am, speak and I will pray God on your behalf'.

The dying Husayn pleaded for his followers: 'Dear grandfather! I am not attached to my life! May it soon be over, may I come with you and see my mother and my sons in Heaven, especially Akbar'. 'Grieve not for him, my child, he is with me in a happier world. He died for the good of our sinful people, to lighten their burden on the Last Day'. 'Grandfather! My last wish is to offer my soul a thousand times for the salvation of my people, of those who believe in you as God's prophet!'

The latter answered: 'My dear grandson, your wish is granted. You will be a mediator on behalf of your people. Tomorrow you will help me distribute life's water from Kawthar, my holy well, on the frontier of paradise, for all our faithful Muslims who are dying for the sake of Islam. Come to Heaven!'

Feeling death approaching his heart, Husayn cried out: 'Oh Mother! Your son is dying, a soldier in a foreign land. I am still young but have no mother to attend my deathbed. . . .' At once, it pleased God to send Husayn's mother, Fatima, down from Heaven to console her dying son: 'O my child! So many wounds in your beloved body which I have so often washed and caressed, fed and protected. Look, your blood is flowing, there is a pool of blood, you are lying in it!' 'O mother! Come and let me see you! You are late in coming, I am almost dead!' 'O my son! May my soul be offered for your defaced and wounded body! I am only a mother, O God, give my son a gentle death, let me carry him to Heaven!' After more prayers, Husayn finally died, while on his lips were words of his repeated request to God that He might grant him the right to intercede for his people. Fatima and Muhammad flew back to Paradise accompanying Husayn's soul.

Without a leader to guide them out of their death-camp, the women and children could do no more than lament their fate. To add to their distress, it appeared that Rukayya, Husayn's daughter, was missing. Zaynab, Husayn's sister, prayed to God by the soul of her father 'Ali, that he might help them at least to find Rukayya. It pleased God to send 'Ali's soul down to earth where it appeared in visible form to his descendants in the camp. To Zaynab, he spoke, pointing out that Rukayya had fainted of thirst in the desert while she was trying to find some water in a pool which, however, had dried up. Rukayya was found and the family was reunited.

That night Rukayya, though tired and thirsty, could not sleep; she got up and walked around the camp, lamenting in her heart her father's death. Suddenly she heard soft words spoken to her by her father's voice. It had pleased God to give Husayn's body the power of speech so that the fatherly voice could console the poor orphan girl. For a long time the daughter conversed with her father's dead body, then she lay down next to it, saying: 'There is no place more suitable to me than by the side of my beloved father'.

In the camp, meanwhile, Zaynab her aunt, and Kulsum her sister, were discussing their sad condition when suddenly they saw a black apparition in the moonlight. It was the spirit of 'Ali, their father, who was watching over his daughters. Frightened, Zaynab asked the ghost for his name, saying firmly: 'Unless you tell me what your name is, stay where you are, come not near to us, the daughters of 'Ali, the hero of Islam. Have respect for us who are bereaved of our brother'. 'Ali's ghost then revealed himself and spoke consoling words to the poor weeping women of his household, admonishing them to have patience, and to pray during the night, 'that all those who belong to my *shi'a* may drink the sweet waters of paradise on the Day of Judgement. More trials are awaiting you'.

Zaynab replied firmly: 'If it is for the salvation of your followers, father, for God's chosen people, I will endure suffering like a bird being burned by the fire, even if they make me ride a camel without a litter!' Little did she know the disgrace that was awaiting her.

During the same moonlit night the spirit of Hasan, 'Ali's eldest son, appeared to his wife, and together they lamented the death of Qasim whose throat was cut by the soldiers of Yazid, the tyrant, earlier in the battle, on what was intended to be his wedding night. Husayn's spirit, already separated from his body by death, was raised by the grace of God, and permitted to appear in visible form to his daughter Sukayna who was sitting in her tent and sobbing in deep despair. Thus did the spirits of 'Ali and his two sons comfort their wives and daughters who were left bereft and surrounded by enemies in the camp at Karbala.

7.2 THE ISMA'ILIS

GINAN

7.2.1 Prayers and hymns

The following is a prayer taught in Isma'ili schools.

Our Lord Nur Mawlana Shah, Karim al-Husayni Hazar Imam! We humble students humbly pray to thee: Give us your divine guidance to discharge our duties! Give us the courage and strength to obey the holy *firmans*! Our saviour, have mercy upon us and bless us with the holy *Nurani Didar* in this world and the next.

There is no salvation without our *imam*. O 'Ali! O 'Ali! Better than written guidance, we have the living *imam*. O 'Ali! O 'Ali! All-wise, omniscient, sinless.

Ginan (hymn)

The *imam* will give the kingdom to his followers and they will rule until eternity. — *12% of income*

Pay *dashond* and obey his incarnation. After these good deeds the soul attains salvation.

Pay your tithes to our teacher, the *imam*; it will help you to secure salvation, bliss, and happiness. Without it you may be reborn 10,000 times. O believers! Pay your dues to our Lord accurately. You will be doubly rewarded for all the things you offer. O believers! Come to the prayer-house and partake of the water of purity.

While serving him devoutly we recognise him as *imam*. Only those who give all the *dashond* which they owe, only those who sacrifice all they possess with love, only they are the true believers.

He is true and just. He is pure and sinless. He is our gracious Lord, sustainer of creation. He is the judge of judgement, the maker of us all. Serve the *imam*, we are his slaves. There is no salvation without the *imam*. He is all in all. O 'Ali!

Du'a (prayer)

O Karim al-Husayni! Forgive our sins. Amen.

O Karim al-Husayni! Fulfil our wishes. Amen.

O Karim al-Husayni! Remove our troubles. Amen.

O Karim al-Husayni! Destroy the enemies of our faith. Amen

O Karim al-Husayni! Grant us a temporal and spiritual glimpse. Amen

O Karim al-Husayni! Grant us health for our sick. Amen.

O Karim al-Husayni! Grant us goodness to know you and believe in you. Amen.

O Karim al-Husayni! Keep us perfect in partaking in *sukrit* and in paying *dashond*. Amen.

O Karim al-Husayni! Make the community prosperous by giving them long life, wealth, and children. Amen.

O Karim al-Husayni! Please bless those that give money generously. Amen.

7.2.2 The Aga Khan Karim 'Ali on the Qur'anic 'light'

Before we endeavour to interpret the Qur'anic symbols [in Qur'an 24:35 *God is the light of the heavens and the earth. The likeness of this light is a niche in which there is a lamp, the lamp in a glass, the glass like a glittering star, kindled from a blessed olive tree, an olive that is neither of the east nor the west, the oil of which could shine without being touched by fire. Light upon light; God guides whom He pleases*], it is better to make it plain as to what we mean by the four garments,

From "Unpublished" sources (!)

which our traveller has acquired from the 'Strangers at the Gates'. The first was his spiritual body, the function of which is knowing. The second was his mental body, the function of which is thinking. The third was his emotional body, the function of which is feeling. The fourth was his physical body, the function of which is doing. He is endowed with certain faculties: Fire, Air, Water, and Earth – the four basic elements, which compose the human body. The Qur'anic verse, with its own fundamental symbols is a manifestation of this truth. The mystery surrounding the whole of the verse must be appreciated at the very outset. God's divine light cannot be revealed directly to man. Why there has never been a direct divine revelation is a definite mystery, but this begins to be unfolded if a human soul by intense meditation reaches its ultimate reality. But as far as we are imprisoned within these physical shells, God shall always speak to humanity in parables.

Now we come ultimately to the mystic path to unfold this verse. To all those who wish to tread this path, I beseech: let us walk together in love and prayers and tolerance, so that we may fathom the deepest mysteries of God.

The hint given earlier by me can now be revealed more fully and clearly, that this verse and its five symbols stand for man's reincarnation upon this earth – and that within his body, mind, heart, spirit, and what we call 'Life' is hidden his Soul, the Light of God – and it is through his 'Life' upon the earth that he must search the inner reality and find himself and God.

Thus the *Niche* in the verse symbolises his physical incarnation, his body or the temporal vehicle. But it is not an ordinary vessel. The Creator has blessed it by enshrining within it a lamp, within which shines eternally His Light. It is the presence of this *Lamp* in man and only those who are aware of its Divine Presence, or have had its glimpse, can be said to have lived their lives truly.

The next symbol is the *Lamp*. The *Lamp* is the core of the spiritual truth, and which is the true source of illumination. Let us try to study this 'Lantern' which we all carry within ourselves. The Qur'anic symbols, which follow after the *Lamp* clearly show its structure, – the *Glass*, the *Olive Tree*, and the Olive *Oil*, the last being the real source of divine illumination. Thus the *Lamp* although far higher than the *Niche* is still at a lower level than the pure light itself. Thus with these five symbols, the life-energy as manifested within the human body becomes finer and subtler, that is, *Niche* is the body, the *Lamp* is the entire, whole, indivisible, indwelling spirit, sustaining, nourishing man, yet encased within the *Glass* with three significant meanings: (i) a transparent medium through which the light passes to illuminate the humanity and if it is in true harmony with the indwelling spirit can become the brilliant rising star of the human destiny; (ii) it is a protective shield against the lower and baser motives in man, and (iii) by failing to harmonise with the spirit, it may transmit a false image of the external world to the inner being. In a larger sense the glass truly and logically stands for the mind. Between the external world of the senses and the inner realm of reality, stands the mind. The *Olive Tree* is the source of oil. I must admit that I found this symbol difficult to understand, and before we attempt its interpretation, we have to retrace our footsteps and attempt a brief recapitulation.

According to our logical thinking, we represented the human body as the *Niche*, whose function is to transmit to the human mind through its five sensory mediums, the external world. The *Lamp* is the entire life-force or the living spirit, whose first layer is the *Glass* or the mind, which is subtler and finer than the body. Its function is to record the data conveyed to it by the senses and to create out of its power of imagination a realm of knowledge. This line of thought I believe should lead us to the 'tree' as the heart, which 'manufactures' the oil, the essential fuel. In the physiological sense the heart is very much like the tree. From the psychological point of view, it is the discursive spirit, which on receiving the data of reasoning from the mind, combines them and creates pure reason. It is also a seat of human emotions and feelings. The heart like the tree is a creation of two worlds. The tree has its roots deep down into the dark earth, and its crown uplifted to meet the finer elements from the above. So also the heart has lower animal instincts and yet it inspires man to strive for the supreme pinnacles of life. How does it do this? By producing and generating the essential fuel to ignite and enkindle the light of divine illumination, the Olive *Oil*. The oil produces the most radiant illumination in man. This is of course in the symbolic sense of man being the lantern. This fuel represents a spirit higher than the mind and the heart, for in its composition there is no base element. It is so luminous, that it seems to be as if self-igniting, and bestows the transcendental prophetic spirit to man. I believe it to be immortal and continuous in its memory, . . . knowledge and wisdom.

But it awaits the ultimate spark from the Divinity, and until that spark ignites it, it remains dormant. At this stage our spiritual quest into the mysteries of this verse reaches its climax. This indwelling lantern, having the fuel and the glass and placed in a niche, shall only be ignited by the grace of God – this is clearly manifested in the words: *Light upon Light; God guides to His Light whom He pleases*. And when God's infinite love descends upon his spirit, he is awakened and enlightened from the deep slumbers of all births and deaths. That moment is a moment of reawakening, when man sees himself as Himself. That moment is a moment of rebirths, for man is reborn a superman, a prophet. That is his true birth, the birth of an ever living spirit, the dawn of Cosmic Consciousness, in which his past, present, and future all become one. In that supreme moment man achieves his ultimate Destiny – the Spiritual Union with God.

Amen.

7.3 THE BAHA'IS

7.3.1 The writings of the Bab: from the Persian *Bayan*

Worship thou God in such wise that if thy worship lead thee to the fire, no alteration in thine adoration would be produced, and so likewise if thy recompense should be paradise. Thus and thus alone should be the worship which befitteth the one True God. Shouldst thou worship Him because of fear, this would be unseemly in the sanctified Court of His presence, and could not be regarded as an act by thee dedicated to the Oneness of His Being. Or if thy gaze should be on paradise, and thou shouldst worship Him while cherishing such a hope, thou wouldst make God's creation a partner with Him, notwithstanding the fact that paradise is desired by men.

Fire and paradise both bow down and prostrate themselves before God. That which is worthy of His Essence is to worship Him for His sake, without fear of fire, or hope of paradise.

Although when true worship is offered, the worshipper is delivered from the fire, and entereth the paradise of God's good pleasure, yet such should not be the motive of his act. However, God's favour and grace ever flow in accordance with the exigencies of His inscrutable wisdom.

The most acceptable prayer is the one offered with the utmost spirituality and radiance; its prolongation hath not been and is not beloved by God. The more detached and the purer the prayer, the more acceptable is it in the presence of God.

7.3.2 The Glad-Tidings of Baha'u'llah

O people of the earth!

The first Glad-Tidings

which the Mother Book hath, in this Most Great Revelation, imparted unto all the peoples of the world is that the Law of holy war hath been blotted out from the Book. Glorified be the All-Merciful, the Lord of grace abounding, through Whom the door of heavenly bounty hath been flung open in the face of all that are in heaven and on earth.

The second Glad-Tidings

It is permitted that the peoples and kindreds of the world associate with one another with joy and radiance. O people! Consort with the followers of all religions in a spirit of friendliness and fellowship. Thus hath the day-star of His sanction and authority shone forth above the horizon of the decree of God, the Lord of the worlds.

The third Glad-Tidings

concerneth the study of divers languages. This decree hath formerly streamed forth from the Pen of the Most High: It behoveth the sovereigns of the world – may God assist them – or the ministers of the earth to take counsel together and to adopt one of the existing languages or a new one to be taught to children in schools throughout the world, and likewise one script. Thus the whole earth will come to be regarded as one country. Well is it with him who hearkeneth unto His Call and observeth that whereunto he is bidden by God, the Lord of the Mighty Throne.

The fourth Glad-Tidings

Should any of the kings – may God aid them – arise to protect and help this oppressed people, all must vie with one another in loving and in serving Him. This matter is incumbent upon everyone. Well is it with them that act accordingly.

The fifth Glad-Tidings

In every country where any of this people reside, they must behave towards the government of that country with loyalty, honesty, and truthfulness. This is that which hath been revealed at the behest of Him Who is the Ordainer, the Ancient of Days.

It is binding and incumbent upon the peoples of the world, one and all, to extend aid unto this momentous Cause which is come from the heaven of the Will of the ever-abiding God, that perchance the fire of animosity which blazeth in the hearts of some of the peoples of the earth may, through the living waters of divine wisdom and by virtue of heavenly counsels and exhortations, be quenched, and the light of unity and concord may shine forth and shed its radiance upon the world.

We cherish the hope that through the earnest endeavours of such as are the exponents of the power of God – exalted be His glory – the weapons of war throughout the world may be converted into instruments of reconstruction and that strife and conflict may be removed from the midst of men.

The sixth Glad-Tidings

is the establishment of the Lesser Peace,[3] details of which have formerly been revealed from Our Most Exalted Pen. Great is the blessedness of him who upholdeth it and observeth whatsoever hath been ordained by God, the All-Knowing, the All-Wise.

The seventh Glad-Tidings

The choice of clothing and cut of the beard and its dressing are left to the discretion of men. But beware, O people, lest ye make yourselves the play-things of the ignorant.

The eighth Glad-Tidings

The pious deeds of the monks and priests among the followers of the Spirit [i.e. Jesus] – upon Him be the peace of God – are remembered in His presence. In this Day, however, let them give up the life of seclusion and direct their steps towards the open world and busy themselves with that which will profit themselves and others. We have granted them leave to enter into wedlock that they may bring forth one who will make mention of God, the Lord of the seen and the unseen, the Lord of the Exalted Throne.

The ninth Glad-Tidings

When the sinner findeth himself wholly detached and freed from all save God, he should beg forgiveness and pardon from Him. Confession of sins and transgressions before human beings is not permissible, as it hath never been nor will ever be conducive to divine forgiveness. Moreover such confession before people results in one's humiliation and abasement, and God – exalted be His glory – wisheth not the humiliation of His servants. Verily He is the Compassionate, the Merciful.

The tenth Glad-Tidings

As a token of grace from God, the Revealer of this Most Great Announcement, We have removed from the Holy Scriptures and Tablets the law prescribing the destruction of books.

The eleventh Glad-Tidings

It is permissible to study sciences and arts, but such sciences as are useful and would redound to the progress and advancement of the people. Thus hath it been decreed by Him Who is the Ordainer, the All-Wise.

The twelfth Glad-Tidings

It is enjoined upon every one of you to engage in some form of occupation, such as crafts, trades, and the like. We have graciously exalted your engagement in such work to the rank of worship unto God, the True One. Ponder ye in your hearts the grace and the blessings of God and render thanks unto Him at eventide and at dawn. Waste not your time in idleness and sloth. Occupy yourselves with that which profiteth yourselves and others. Thus hath it been decreed in this Tablet from whose horizon the day-star of wisdom and utterance shineth resplendent.

The most despised of men in the sight of God are those who sit idly and beg. Hold ye fast unto the core of material means, placing your whole trust in God, the Provider of all means. When anyone occupieth himself in a craft or trade, such occupation itself is regarded in the estimation of God as an act of worship; and this is naught but a token of His infinite and all-pervasive bounty.

The thirteenth Glad-Tidings

The men of God's House of Justice have been charged with the affairs of the people. They, in truth, are the Trustees of God among his servants and the daysprings of authority in His countries.

O people of God! That which traineth the world is justice, for it is upheld by two pillars, reward and punishment. These two pillars are the sources of life to the world. Inasmuch as for each day there is a new problem and for every problem an expedient solution, such affairs should be referred to the Ministers of the House of Justice that they may act according to the needs and requirements of the time. They that, for the sake of God, arise to serve His Cause, are the recipients of divine inspiration from the unseen Kingdom. It is incumbent upon all to be obedient unto them. All matters of State should be referred to the House of Justice, but acts of worship must be observed according to that which God hath revealed in His Book.

O people of Baha! Ye are the dawning-places of the love of God and the daysprings of His loving-kindness. Defile not your tongues with the cursing and reviling of any soul, and guard your eyes against that which is not seemly.

Set forth that which ye possess.[4] If it be favourably received, your end is attained; if not, to protest is vain. Leave that soul to himself and turn unto the Lord, the Protector, the Self-Subsisting. Be not the cause of grief, much less of discord and strife. The hope is cherished that ye may obtain true education in the shelter of the tree of His tender mercies and act in accordance with that which God desireth. Ye are all the leaves of one tree and the drops of one ocean.

The fourteenth Glad-Tidings

It is not necessary to undertake special journeys to visit the resting-places of the dead. If people of substance and affluence offer the cost of such journeys to the House of Justice, it will be pleasing and acceptable in the presence of God. Happy are they that observe His precepts.

The fifteenth Glad-Tidings

Although a republican form of government profiteth all the peoples of the world, yet the majesty of kingship is one of the signs of God. We do not wish that the countries of the world should remain deprived thereof. If the sagacious combine the two forms into one, great will be their reward in the presence of God.

In former religions such ordinances as holy war, destruction of books, the ban on association and companionship with other peoples or on reading certain books had been laid down and affirmed according to the exigencies of the time; however, in this mighty revelation, in this momentous Announcement, the manifold bestowals and favours of God have overshadowed all men, and from the horizon of the Will of the Ever-Abiding Lord, His infallible decree hath prescribed that which We have set forth above.

We yield praise unto God – hallowed and glorified be He – for whatsoever He hath graciously revealed in this blessed, this glorious and incomparable Day. Indeed if everyone on earth were endowed with a myriad tongues and were to continually praise God and magnify His Name to the end that knoweth no end, their thanksgiving would not prove adequate for even one of the gracious favours We have mentioned in this Tablet. Unto this beareth witness every man of wisdom and discernment, of understanding and knowledge.

We earnestly beseech God – exalted be His glory – to aid the rulers and sovereigns, who are the exponents of power and the daysprings of glory, to enforce His laws and ordinances. He is in truth the Omnipotent, the All-Powerful, He Who is wont to answer the call of men.

7.3.3 The writings of 'Abdu'l-Baha('Abbas Effendi): predestination

Question: If God has knowledge of an action which will be performed by someone, and it has been written on the Tablet of Fate, is it possible to resist it?

Answer: The foreknowledge of a thing is not the cause of its realisation; for the essential knowledge of God surrounds, in the same way, the realities of things, before as well as after their existence. It is a perfection of God. But that which was prophesied by the inspiration of God through the tongues of the Prophets, concerning the appearance of the Promised one of the Bible, was not the cause of the manifestation of Christ.

The hidden secrets of the future were revealed to the Prophets, and They thus became acquainted with the future events which they announce. This knowledge and these prophecies were not the cause of the occurrences. For example, tonight everyone knows that after seven hours the sun will rise, but this general foreknowledge does not cause the rising and appearance of the sun.

Therefore, the knowledge of God in the realm of contingency does not produce the forms of things. On the contrary, it is purified from the past, present, and future. It is identical with the reality of the things; it is not the cause of their occurrence.

In the same way, the record and the mention of a thing in the Book does not become the cause of its existence. The Prophets, through the divine inspiration, knew what would come to pass. For instance, through the divine inspiration They knew that Christ would be martyred, and They announced it. Now, was Their knowledge and information the cause of the martyrdom of Christ? No; this knowledge is a perfection of the Prophets and did not cause the martyrdom.

The mathematicians by astronomical calculations know that at a certain time an eclipse of the moon or the sun will occur. Surely this discovery does not cause the eclipse to take place. This is, of course, only an analogy and not an exact image.

7.3.4 Shoghi Effendi on the goal of modern society

Politically a similar decline, a no less noticeable evidence of disintegration and confusion, can be discovered in the age we live in – the age which a future historian might well recognise to have been the preamble to the Great Age, whose golden days we can as yet but dimly visualise.

The passionate and violent happenings that have, in recent years, strained to almost the point of complete breakdown the political and economic structure of society are too numerous and complex to attempt, within the limitations of this general survey, to arrive at an adequate estimate of their character. Nor have these tribulations, grievous as they have been, seemed to have reached their climax, and exerted the full force of their destructive power. The whole world, wherever and however we survey it, offers us the sad and pitiful spectacle of a vast, an enfeebled, and moribund organism, which is being torn politically and strangulated economically by forces it has ceased either to control or comprehend. The Great Depression, the aftermath of the severest ordeals humanity had ever experienced, the disintegration of the Versailles system, the recrudescence of militarism in its most menacing aspects, the failure of vast experiments and new-born institutions to safeguard the peace and tranquillity of peoples, classes and nations, have bitterly disillusioned humanity and prostrated its spirits. Its hopes are, for the most part, shattered, its vitality is ebbing, its life strangely disordered, its unity severly compromised. . . .

With no less than ten million people under arms, drilled and instructed in the use of the most abominable engines of destruction that science has devised; with thrice that number chafing and fretting at the rule of alien races and governments; with an equally vast army of embittered citizens impotent to procure for themselves the material goods and necessities which others are deliberately destroying; with a still greater mass of human beings groaning under the burden of ever-mounting armaments, and impoverished by the virtual collapse of international trade – with evils such as these, humanity would seem to be definitely entering the outer fringes of the most agonising phase of its existence. . . .

Humanity is now experiencing the commotions invariably associated with the most turbulent stage of its evolution, the state of adolescence, when the impetuosity of youth and its vehemence reach their climax, and must gradually be superseded by the calmness, the wisdom, the maturity that characterise the stage of manhood. Then will the human race reach that stature of ripeness which will enable it to acquire all the powers and capacities upon which its ultimate development must depend.

Unification of the whole of mankind is the hall-mark of the stage which human society is now approaching. Unity of family, or tribe, of city-state, and nation have been successively attempted and fully established. World unity is the goal towards which a harassed humanity is striving. Nation-building has come to an end. The anarchy inherent in state sovereignty is moving towards a climax. A world, growing to maturity, must abandon this fetish, recognise the oneness and wholeness of human relationships, and establish once for all the machinery that can best incarnate this fundamental principle of its life. . . .

The unity of the human race, as envisaged by Baha'u'llah, implies the establishment of a world commonwealth in which all nations, races, creeds, and classes are closely and permanently united, and in which the autonomy of its state members and the personal freedom and initiative of the individuals that compose them are definitely and completely safeguarded. The commonwealth must, as far as we can visualise it, consist of a world legislature, whose members will, as the trustees of the whole of mankind, ultimately control the entire resources of all the component nations, and will enact such laws as shall be required to regulate the life, satisfy the needs, and adjust the relationships of all races and peoples. A world executive, backed by an international Force, will carry out the decisions arrived at, and apply the laws enacted by, this world legislature, and will safeguard the organic unity of the whole commonwealth. A world tribunal will adjudicate and deliver its compulsory and final verdict in all and any disputes that may arise between the various elements constituting this universal system. A mechanism of world intercommunication will be devised, embracing the whole planet, freed from national hindrances and restrictions, and functioning with marvellous swiftness and perfect regularity.

A world metropolis will act as the nerve centre of a world civilisation, the focus towards which the unifying forces of life will converge and from which its energising influences will radiate. A world language will either be invented or chosen from among the existing languages and will be taught in the schools of all the federated nations as an auxiliary to their mother tongue. A world script, a world literature, a uniform and universal system of currency, of weights and measures, will simplify and facilitate intercourse and understanding among the nations and races of mankind. In such a world society, science and religion, the two most potent forces in human life, will be reconciled, will co-operate, and will harmoniously develop. The press will, under such a system, while giving full scope to the expression of diversified views and convictions of mankind, cease to be mischievously manipulated by vested interests, whether private or public, and will be liberated from the influence of contending governments and peoples. The economic resources of the world will be organised – its sources of raw material will be tapped and fully utilised, its markets will be co-ordinated and developed, and the distribution of its products will be equitably regulated.

National rivalries, hatred, and intrigues will cease, and racial animosity and prejudice will be replaced by racial amity, understanding and co-operation. The causes of religious strife will be permanently removed, economic barriers and restrictions will be completely abolished, and the inordinate distinction between classes will be obliterated. Destitution on the one hand, and gross accumulation of ownership on the other, will disappear. The enormous energy dissipated and wasted on war, whether economic or political, will be consecrated to such ends as will extend the range of human inventions and technical development, to the increase of the productivity of mankind, to the extermination of disease, to the extension of scientific research, to the raising of the standard of physical health, to the sharpening and refinement of the human brain, to the exploitation of the unused and unsuspected resources of the planet, to the prolongation of human life, and to the furtherance of any other agency that can stimulate the intellectual, the moral and spiritual life of the entire human race.

7.4 AHMADIYYA: MIRZA GHULAM AHMAD ON THE SOURCES OF KNOWLEDGE AND REVELATION

The comprehensiveness with which the holy Qur'an has dealt with this subject cannot be set forth at this stage for want of time. We shall, therefore, confine ourselves to a concise statement by way of illustration.

The holy Qur'an has drawn attention to three types of knowledge, knowledge by way of certainty of inference, knowledge by way of certainty of sight, and knowledge by way of certainty of experience. . . .

The meaning of revelation

It should be kept well in mind that revelation does not mean that an idea should arise in the mind of a person who sets himself to ponder over a thing as, for instance, a poet having thought out half a verse seeks the other half in his mind and his mind suggests the other half. This is not revelation but is the result of reflection, in accordance with the law of nature. When a person reflects upon something good or bad, a corresponding idea arises in his mind. For instance, one person who is pious and truthful composes verses in support of truth, and another one, who is wicked and vicious, supports falsehood in his verses and abuses the righteous. Both these would, no doubt, write a certain number of verses, and it is quite possible that the verses of the one who is the enemy of the righteous and supports falsehood might be better than the verses of the other one, on account of his greater practice in writing poetry. So, if the arising of an idea in the mind should be accounted as revelation, a vile poet who is the enemy of truth and of the righteous and writes in opposition to the truth and has recourse to imposture, would be called a recipient of divine revelation. Many novels are written in excellent style and set forth altogether false but continuous well arranged tales. Then would these stories be designated as revelation? If revelation were to mean merely an idea arising in one's mind, a thief would also be called a recipient of revelation, for an expert thief often thinks out surprising ways of theft and robbery, and many clever plans of robbery and murder pass through his mind. Would all these unclean projects be called revelation? Indeed not. Such is the thinking only of those who are not aware of the true God Who comforts the hearts of His servants with His converse and bestows the understanding of spiritual knowledge upon those who are not familiar with it.

What then is revelation? It is the living and powerful converse of the Holy and Mighty God with a chosen servant of His, or with one whom He deigns to make His elect. When this converse starts in an adequate and satisfactory manner, being altogether free from the darkness of false concepts, and is not composed merely of a few inadequate and meaningless words, and is full of delight and wisdom and grandeur, then it surely is the word of God with which He designs to comfort His servant and to manifest Himself to him. Sometimes revelation is vouchsafed to a person by way of trial and is not equipped with full blessings. In such a case the recipient is put on his trial at this elementary stage so that having tasted somewhat of revelation he should order his life along the lines of those who are true recipients of revelation, in default of which he would encounter frustration. If he does not adopt the ways of the truly righteous he is deprived of the fullness of this bounty and is left only with vain boasting.

Millions of the virtuous have been recipients of revelation, but they were not of equal standing in the estimation of God. Indeed, even the holy Prophets of God, who are recipients of divine revelation at the highest level, are not equal in rank, as God Almighty has said: *Of these Messengers some have We exalted above others* (Qur'an 2:254). This shows that revelation is pure divine grace and is not evidence of exaltation. Exaltation is according to the degree of truth, sincerity, and faithfulness of the recipient, which is known only to God. If revelation possesses all its blessed conditions it is also one of the fruits of such qualities. There is no doubt that if revelation takes the form that the recipient submits a question and God responds to it, and there is a sequence between question and answer, and the revelation is characterised by divine majesty and light, and comprehends knowledge of the unseen and true understanding, it is truly the word of God. It is necessary that divine revelation should be like a dialogue between two friends. When the servant submits a question he should receive a delicious and eloquent response from God Almighty in which his own self and thinking and reflection should have no part. If such a dialogue is bestowed as a bounty upon a person, it is the word of God and its recipient is held dear by God. That revelation should be bestowed as a bounty, and a living and holy series of revelations should be bestowed upon a servant by God clearly and in a pure form, is not the portion of anyone except of those who attain a high level of faith and sincerity and righteous action, and of that which we cannot here disclose. True and holy revelation displays many wonders of the Godhead. Very often a brilliant light is generated and along with it a majestic and shining revelation is vouchsafed. What could be a greater bounty than this that a recipient of revelation should hold converse with the Being Who is the Creator of the heavens and the earth. God can be seen in this world only through converse with Him.

This does not include the condition of a person from whose tongue an idle word, or sentence or verse proceeds unaccompanied by any dialogue. Such a person is under trial by God, for God sometimes tries a slothful and neglectful servant of His in this manner that a sentence or a statement issues from his heart or tongue and he becomes a blind person not knowing whence the statement has proceeded, whether from God or from Satan. Such a one should implore for pardon in respect of such an experience. But if a righteous and virtuous servant of God should experience unobstructed dialogue with the Divine and should hear bright, and delicious, and meaningful, and wise, and majestic divine utterances in a state of complete wakefulness in the shape of question and answer at least ten times, that is to say he put a question and God replied to it and then in complete wakefulness he made another submission and God made answer to it, and he made another humble supplication and God replied to that. This should have happened ten times. If in the course of such dialogue God should accept his prayers and should instruct him in excellent insights and should inform him of coming events and should honour him repeatedly with His clear dialogue, such a one should be deeply grateful to God Almighty and should be more devoted to Him than anyone else, because God, His pure grace, has chosen him from among His servants and has made him the heir of those faithful ones who have passed on before him. This bounty is most rare and is the highest good luck. For him on whom it is bestowed everything else is utterly without value.

A characteristic of Islam

Islam has always produced persons of this rank. It is Islam alone in which God approaches a servant and holds converse with him and speaks inside him. He builds His throne in the heart of such a one and pulls him from inside towards heaven. He bestows upon him all the bounties that were bestowed on those before him. It is a pity that the blind world does not realise how far a person can reach in nearness to God. They do not step forward themselves, and if another one does so, he is either declared a disbeliever or he is deified and is put in the place of God. Both these are great wrongs which proceed from one extreme or the other. A wise one should not lack high resolve and should not persist in the denial of such an exalted rank being conferred on anyone, and should neither denigrate such a one nor deify him. When a person attains such high rank God Almighty manifests such relationship with him as if He covers him up with the mantle of His Godhead and such a one becomes a mirror for beholding God. That is why the holy prophet, peace and blessings of Allah be upon him, said: 'He who has seen me has seen God'. This is the last stage in the spiritual progress of man in which he is bestowed full satisfaction.

The speaker is honoured with divine converse

I would be guilty of doing great wrong to my fellow beings if I were not to declare at this stage that divine bounty has bestowed upon me the status which I have just defined and has honoured me with the kind of converse the features of which I have just set out in detail, so that I should bestow sight upon the blind and should guide the seekers of the One Who has been so far lost, and should give to those who accept the truth the good news of that holy fountain of which many speak but which few find. I wish to assure the listeners that the God, meeting with Whom is the salvation and eternal welfare of man, cannot be found without following the holy Qur'an. Would that the people were to see that which I have seen, and were to hear that which I have heard, and should lay aside mere tales and should run to the truth. The cleansing water which removes all doubt, that mirror through which that Supreme Being can be seen, is converse with the Divine that I have just mentioned. Let him whose soul seeks the truth arise and search. I tell you truly that if souls are charged with true seeking and hearts develop true thirst, people would search for that way and would seek that path. How can that way be discovered, and how can the intervening veil be removed? I assure all seekers that it is Islam alone which conveys the good news of that path. All other people have long since sealed up divine revelation. Be sure however, that this seal is not imposed by God, but is an excuse that is put forward by man on account of his privation. Be sure that as it is not possible that we should be able to see without eyes, or should be able to hear without ears, or should be able to speak without a tongue, in the same way it is not possible that without the help of the Qur'an we should be able to behold the countenance of the True Beloved. I was young and am now old but I have not encountered anyone who has the cup of this visible understanding except out of this holy fountain.

8 MYSTICISM

See 1.7. The Qur'an (8.2) and Muhammad (8.1) both play central roles in Sufism. Popular saint worship accounts for much of the growth of mysticism in Islam, however, as revealed in 8.3 as well as in 8.4 which consists of texts chanted in order to induce mystical experience. Sufism has been responsible for much of the spread of Islam as revealed in the text from Java, 8.5. 8.6 presents one view of the nature of the mystical quest and its stages.

8.1 IBN HANBAL'S TRADITIONS ON MUHAMMAD'S ASCETICISM

Abu Hurayra said that the prophet said: 'For whoever goes to the mosque in the morning or in the evening, God prepares a place in paradise whenever that person goes in the morning or in the evening'.

'Abd Allah said that a man mentioned to the messenger of God that he slept all through the night and only got up in the morning. The messenger of God said: 'That man has the attention of Satan in one or both of his ears!'

'Alqama said that he asked 'A'isha about the prayers of the messenger of God. She said: 'Whoever of you is able to do what the messenger of God was able to do, your actions will be ever-lasting'.

'A'isha said that the messenger of God frequently said during his prayers and prostrations: 'Glory be to You, O God, our Lord, and praise be to You, O God; forgive us for interpreting the Qur'an'.

'A'isha said: 'The messenger of God bought some food from a Jewish merchant on credit and gave him armour as security'.

Abu 'Abd al-Jadali said that he asked 'A'isha: 'How was the messenger of God born into his people?' She said: 'He was the best of all people created; there was nothing repugnant about it, no noise in the market places, evil not repaying evil. Rather, he was pardoned and forgiven'.

A certain man said that 'A'isha was asked what the messenger of God did in his house. She replied: 'He patched clothes, fixed sandals, and did similar things'.

Al-Aswad said that he asked 'A'isha what the messenger of God did when he came home. She said: 'He used to occupy himself with the work of his family and when it was prayer time, he would go out and pray'.

'A'isha said that when the messenger of God died, he did not leave a dinar nor dirham nor any sheep nor cattle and did not bequeath anything.

Ibn 'Abbas said that when the messenger of God died, leaving neither a dinar, dirham, slave, or offspring, he left his armour as security for thirty measures of food with a Jewish merchant.

Abu Hurayra said that the messenger of God never found fault in food; when he craved it, he would eat it, and when he did not crave it, he would leave it.

Jabir ibn 'Abd Allah said that when the messenger of God was not asked about anything he would not say anything. He would not say no to any question he was asked.

Anas said that the messenger of God said one day, by He who has the soul of Muhammad in His hand: 'At one time, the family of Muhammad did not have any grain or any dates; there were nine children in the family and Muhammad had nine wives'.

Abu Hurayra said that he never saw the messenger of God find fault in food; when he craved it, he would eat it, and when he did not crave it, he would be silent.

Anas said that a Jew offered the messenger of God some barley bread and some rancid melted fat and he accepted it from him.

Mu'awiya ibn Qurra said that his father said to him: 'We lived this way with our prophet and we had no food other than the two "black things"'. So he said: 'Do you know what the two "black things" are?' Mu'awiya said: 'No'. His father replied: 'They are dates and water'.

'A'isha said: 'My dear father – she means the Prophet – went out of the world without becoming fed up with wheat bread'.

'A'isha said: 'By God, a month would pass in the family of Muhammad without any bread being available'. He said that he asked her: 'O mother of the believers, what did the messenger of God eat?' She replied: 'Some of the Ansar, may God reward them well, were our neighbours. They had some milk which they would give to the messenger of God'.

'Ata' ibn Abi Rabbah said that a man came to the prophet while he was reclining on a cushion and in front of him was a plate of bread. He put the bread on the ground and pushed aside the pillow, saying: 'I am a slave. Therefore I will eat like a slave and sit like a slave'.

Abu Salih said that the prophet called for some food and when he was finished, he praised God and said: 'I have not filled up my belly with hot food for such and such time'.

Al-Hasan said that when some food came which the messenger of God had ordered, he would put it on the ground and say: 'I am a slave. Therefore I will eat like a slave and sit like a slave'.

Yazid ibn 'Abd Allah ibn Qasit said that the messenger of God was brought some almond paste. When he was given it, he said: 'What is this?' to which they replied that it was an almond paste. The messenger of God said: 'Take this drink of the rich from me'.

8.2 SUFI QUR'AN INTERPRETATION: IBN 'ATA' ON SURAH 1

bismi ('In the name of'). It is related on the authority of Abu al-'Abbas ibn

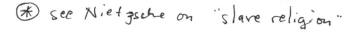
(*) see Nietzsche on "slave religion"

'Ata' that he said: 'The "b" (of *bismi*) stands for the piety (*birr*) belonging to the spirits of the prophets with the inspiration of messengerhood and prophethood. The "s" (of *bismi*) stands for the secret (*sirr*) which the people of knowledge have by the inspiration of divine proximity and intimacy. The "m" (of *bismi*) stands for the granting (*minna*) to the disciples of the continuance of His gazing at them with the eyes of compassion and mercy'.

Allah ('God'). Abu al-'Abbas ibn 'Ata' said that *Allah* (the word) is the manifestation of His awe and greatness.

The Merciful. Ibn 'Ata' said concerning the name *the Merciful*: 'That is His help and His assistance while *the Compassionate* is His friendship and His love'.

Praise belongs to God, Lord of all beings. Ibn 'Ata' said: 'The meaning of this is thanks to God for bestowing the blessing of our knowledge of Him, such that we may praise Him'.

It is reported on the authority of Ibn 'Ata' or somebody else that he said that: *Praise belongs to God* is the affirmation by the believers of His unicity. The first is the affirmation of His Divineness, the second of his Lordship, and the third of His all-Powerfulness.

It is mentioned on the authority of Ibn 'Ata' concerning the statement: *Lord of all beings*, that it means gracing the souls of those who know with the light of surety and fortune; it is also gracing the hearts of the believers with patience and devotion, the hearts of the disciples with righteousness and faithfulness, and the hearts of those who know with thoughts and warnings.

Ruler of the judgement day. Ibn 'Ata' said: 'This is a metaphor for the day of judgement on which everything will be judged by its intention and its importance; those who know will be rewarded for their nearness to Him and will gaze upon the face of God, and the masters of deeds will be rewarded with the gardens'.

The path of those whom You have blessed. That is, the station of those whom You have blessed with faith and knowledge; they are the ones who know. He blesses the saints with righteousness, approval, and certainty, blesses the pious with insight and mercy, blesses the disciples with the pleasure of obedience, and blesses the believers with sincerity. This is the statement of Ibn 'Ata'.

Not of those against whom You have sent Your wrath nor those who are astray. Ibn 'Ata' said: 'Not those whom You have abandoned, driven away, or humbled. *Nor those who are astray*: those who have strayed from the path of Your guidance and knowledge and the path of Your saint'.

Amen. Ibn 'Ata' said: 'That is: So, do it! Do not entrust me with my soul for one moment!'

8.3 LEGENDS OF 'ABD AL-QADIR AL-JILANI *1077-1166*

The beginning
Before he was born, 'Abd al-Qadir already received a hundred visions from

(above?)
p. 2? "the most universal of all the Isl. saints"

God. As a baby, 'Abd al-Qadir refused his mother's breast during the days of Ramadan, so his mother had to feed him at night.

One day 'Abd al-Qadir was playing with other boys in the fields when an ox passed, pulling a heavy plough. The ox turned to 'Abd al-Qadir and said in good Arabic: 'You boy, have you nothing better to do than play? Why don't you go and study the Qur'an?' Deeply impressed, young 'Abd al-Qadir went to his mother and said: 'I want to go to Baghdad to study the Qur'an!' His mother gave him eighty golden dinars' 'Abd al-Qadir gave his brother forty dinars, half his stipend, and departed, joining a caravan of pilgrims. In the hills, the travellers were attacked and captured by robbers. One robber asked 'Abd al-Qadir if he had any money on him. 'Yes,' said the latter, 'forty dinars.' The robber would not believe him and took him to the chief, to whom 'Abd al-Qadir gave the same reply. The robber chief was so impressed when he discovered that the boy had spoken the truth that he let him go along with all his companions. At the end of his life, a student asked 'Abd al-Qadir what had made him a saint. He said: 'I never lied in my life'.

The snake
One day, as 'Abd al-Qadir was explaining the Qur'an in the mosque, a huge snake fell from the ceiling and crept up the saint's legs, inside his robe, coming out at the neck. 'Abd al-Qadir quietly finished the verse he was reciting, though all the men had fled from the mosque. 'Abd al-Qadir conversed with the snake in the snake's language for a long time. Then it vanished. When the people came back they asked 'Abd al-Qadir what the snake had said. It had said: 'I tried all the saints, but you are the only intrepid one!'

The lunatic woman
In Baghdad a man once came to 'Abd al-Qadir and asked him to cure his wife's madness. 'Abd al-Qadir told him: 'Your wife is possessed by a *jinn* called Hanis. Go home and stand in front of her, then address the demon thus: "Go away and never come back. If you ever come near my wife again, 'Abd al-Qadir will destroy you!" ' The man did exactly what the saint had told him and, not only was his wife healthy and happy, but in forty years there was no more madness in the city of Baghdad.

The chicken bones
One day, 'Abd al-Qadir was eating a chicken when the mother of one of his pupils came to see him. She complained that her son had only dry bread to eat. 'Abd al-Qadir covered the chicken bones on the plate with his hand and recited Qur'an 36:78: *He will return dry bones to life*, and at once the chicken jumped up alive from under his hand. 'When your son can do this, he too may eat chicken', concluded 'Abd al-Qadir.

The harrier

One day, as 'Abd al-Qadir was teaching in the open air, a harrier flew over the students' heads, shrieking loudly. When it did not fly away but wheeled round, it completely disrupted the lecture since the superstitious students believed that a harrier's cry spelt misfortune. 'Abd al-Qadir, realising that the students were being prevented from acquiring knowledge by a bird of prey, suddenly called to an invisible person in the air: 'You, go and cut his head off'. At once, the bird's head was severed from its body by the invisible hand; head and trunk fell separately to earth. 'Abd al-Qadir rose, walked over to where the head and body had fallen, picked them up, put them together and spoke: 'In the name of God, the Merciful, the Compassionate'. At once head and body grew together again and the bird straightened itself, perching on the saint's hand. The latter addressed it with admonishing words, as one would address a naughty child: 'Now go, fly away, and leave us in peace. We are studying the Book of God'. The bird bowed its head humbly, then flew away.

The naughty birds

One day, as 'Abd al-Qadir was performing the ablution, a bird came flying over and dropped its dirt on the saint's robe. The latter looked at the bird and it fell down. As 'Abd al-Qadir was cleaning his robe, another bird let fall its droppings on the saint's hand. A look from the old teacher brought it down too. 'Abd al-Qadir called one of his students and told him to pick up the two birds which were alive but unable to fly, and to use the revenues for alms.

The stolen girl

One day, a man came to 'Abd al-Qadir in a state of agitation and despair: 'O friend of God!' he cried, 'my only daughter disappeared in the middle of the night; what can I do to get her back? Where is she? God forbid that she has eloped!' 'Abd al-Qadir reassured the poor father that he could help him find the apple of his eye and recover her. He spoke thus: 'Your daughter has been imprudent enough to go up to the flat roof of your house in the night for a breath of fresh air. No mortal man could see her, but a *jinn* saw her as he was flying over the city of Baghdad. He fell in love with her, lifted her off the roof and flew away with her. Now, in order to get her back you will have to go and see the king of the *jinn*. He will be holding an audience tonight, but of course mortals cannot normally see the *jinn*. Therefore listen carefully: here is what you must do'. 'Abd al-Qadir instructed the bereaved father regarding the details of the place where the king of the *jinn* would hold court that night, and taught him the prayers he had to recite in order to see the *jinn*. The man thanked 'Abd al-Qadir and wended his way out of the city and into the wilderness. After nightfall he reached the magic valley and recited the pre-scribed prayers. Suddenly he saw strange beings in all shapes and sizes: humans, animals, and hideous monsters; these were the *jinn*. In their midst he saw a huge figure in resplendent garments with a shining crown on his head and surrounded by *jinn*-servants. That was obviously the king of the *jinn*, so the man stepped forward into the circle of servants and addressed the king as he had been instructed: 'Sir, Shaykh 'Abd al-Qadir sends me to ask that you do justice. One of your subjects has stolen my daughter, and I do not know where she is or what he has done to her. Can you find her for me?' On hearing the name of 'Abd al-Qadir, the king immediately summoned his captains to go and find out which of the *jinn* had captured a human girl. After some time they came back with a big male *jinn* and the man's daughter. The king spoke to the man: 'Here is your daughter back. We do not want to harm any of 'Abd al-Qadir's friends, for he could bring down the wrath of the Almighty upon our heads!'

How 'Abd al-Qadir killed two robbers
The holy man was teaching in his classroom one day when two men arrived in a state of great agitation. 'O learned Shaykh!' they cried, 'we have been robbed of all our possessions! We were travelling in a caravan along the narrow path that leads through the forest of Nisabur when we were set upon by robbers. They were led by two gang-leaders who took our pack animals and also the animals that carried our wives. We two escaped. What can we do? We will give you all our goods if we can at least be reunited with our wives!' 'Abd al-Qadir rose without speaking, picked up his wooden slippers, stepped outside the school building and flung his slippers into the air, one after the other. His footwear disappeared without being seen to fall down anywhere. Thereupon 'Abd al-Qadir spoke: 'You can now go back safely to the forest and recover your possessions and your wives'. Deeply puzzled, the two men set off and rode as fast as they could to the forest whence they came. After some searching they found the robbers' camp. Their wives were there unhurt, and all their goods and money were there, and more: all the robbers' loot from years of plundering caravans. The wives told the men: 'Suddenly a wooden object came whistling through the air and hit one of the gang-leaders, then another thing came down and crushed the other one's head. Upon seeing their leaders dead, the other robbers fled in panic'. The dead bodies of the two gang-leaders were still there, and the two merchants recovered the two wooden slippers belonging to 'abd al-Qadir which were lying beside the men's broken heads.

In high spirits the caravan drivers packed the animals and resumed their journey to Baghdad. The two merchants kept their word and offered all their wares as well as the robbers' plunder to 'Abd al-Qadir, but the latter wanted only his slippers back. He asked the merchants to spend the money as charity, which they did. They built a mosque and a religious school out of the proceeds; the Qur'an was taught there for many years.

'Abd al-Qadir's generosity
Once when 'Abd al-Qadir was living in Baghdad there was a famine in the city. Many people went to see relatives in the country and 'Abd al-Qadir went

to his native village where his kinsmen gave him a loaf of bread. He did not eat it, but took it back to the city where he broke off pieces and gave them to the hungry citizens. When all the people had eaten enough there was nothing left and the next day 'Abd al-Qadir had nothing to eat. He never took money from anyone and if, as often happened, a pious admirer arrived to offer money, 'Abd al-Qadir would ask one of his followers in attendance to accept it on his behalf and then hand out coins to passing beggars.

The small religious community that had sprung up around 'Abd al-Qadir provided its livelihood by growing fruit and vegetables on the land surrounding their dwellings near the river. One day a poor student arrived complaining about the ferryman who had refused to take him across the river for free. Just at that moment a rich man arrived with a bag full of silver which he offered to 'Abd al-Qadir, so that the latter might pray to God on his behalf for a safe journey. 'Abd al-Qadir asked the student and the merchant to follow him to the riverside where the ferryman was waiting for paying passengers. 'Abd al-Qadir lectured the ferryman about his miserly conduct. 'Students are travellers on the path of God. We must all help them to arrive at their destination so that they may gather knowledge and become teachers of the Holy Law. Here is a bag of money which will pay you for all the poor students who will want to cross this river in the future as sons of the road.' To the rich man he said: 'God may convert your silver into a white horse which will carry you across the *sirat*, the great bridge over the fire of hell on the Day of Judgement'.

8.4 SUFI PRAYERS

Dhikr ceremonies
Allahu O Merciful, O Giver of Grace, O Giver of Sustenance. *Allahu* O Merciful, O giver of Grace, O Giver of Sustenance. *Allahu* O Worshipped One, Make us achieve our intentions. Forgive us with Your generosity. O Giver of favours and kindness, O Lord, O Creator, O Giver of our Daily Bread, Give us the brilliance of Your Light at all times. O Lord, O Forgiver, preserve us from troubles, Multiply the Light and purify all our uncleannesses. O Lord, O Giver, Holy One, Accepter of repentance, Open for us the gates (of paradise), With kindness and Your pleasure.

O Lord, O Merciful One, O God of Great Wonders, We ask of You forgiveness. O You exalted in kindness, O Forgiving Lord, shower Your light upon us, Widen our breasts. May all beings be filled with Your light. Forgive us again, O Forgiver, And change all troubles into Light. Forgive our mistakes for our good intentions, O Great One in evidence.

The following prayer for 'Abd al-Qadir al-Jilani is chanted after the prayers to God.
Peace, peace be upon the Shaykh, the Teacher and their good hearts. O You,

refuge hidden in space, help us from Your abundance, and quench us from Your cup of Salvation. O lineage of Jilani, help us with our vows, Your nobility is like that of the prophet's family. The Lord has illuminated the earth with you, It was made bright because of you, our Jilanis. Praise and gratitude to our Creator. Yes, the Qadiriyya is our path. It excels above all other fraternities, like the new crescent our fraternity is a guiding light. There is nowhere where God's praises are performed better. Nor is there glory that outshines our recital, like water in the desert. I am satisfied with it, and cured by it, it relieves our worries and our sadness. The sweetest pleasure is to be near your *dhikr*, when our brethren are reciting. With passionate love, with grace and devotion, Your *dhikr* has become the highest summit of our delight. Prayers and peace-wishes for Mustafa, the holy prophet, his family, his companions, and for our Jilani.

The following are the praises sung for the prophet Muhammad during the Mawlid *celebration*

Peace be upon you, ornament of the prophets. Peace be upon you, most God-fearing of all men. Peace be upon you, purest of all men. Peace be upon you, chosen of all men. Peace be upon you, by the Lord of Heaven. Peace be upon you, forever without end. Peace be upon you, O beloved prophet. Peace be upon you, O curer of ills. Peace be upon you, O fragrant medicine. Peace be upon you, O obliterator of sins. Peace be upon you, O helper of the stranger. Peace be upon you, O you who follow the sunset. Peace be upon you, O you informed of heavenly secrets. Peace be upon you, O you, our guide, save us and help us fulfil our purposes. Peace be upon you, O you of unique beauty. Peace be upon you, greatest of all the angels.

The following is a ceremonial prayer used in the Qadiriyya order

In the name of God, the Merciful, the Compassionate. He is God other than who there is no god, the Glorious, the Merciful, the Compassionate, the Kind, the Clement, the Mild, the Forgiving, the Believer, the Helper, the Answerer, the Near One, the Noble One, the Patient One. Lord dress me in the fresh beauty of Your light rays which overwhelm the innermost hearts of Your beings and may we turn towards the reality of existence which no ugliness can replace nor suffering can cut off.

Make me beatified with the judgement of the inclination of my love unsullied by vengeance, undiminished by anger, unabridged by any cause. Turn towards me with thy eternal judgement, Inheritor. O Merciful One, He is indeed Merciful Lord, all Succour is His. O Hidden One who is not manifest. O Manifest One who is not hidden. Delicate are the secrets of His exalted existence. You are visible in all existence. Exalted are the lightrays of Your Manifestation, most sacred, and they are evident in all that is witnessed. You are the Lenient One, the Generous Giver, the Forgiver quick with forgiveness, a place of surety for the hidden ones, a Helper for those who beg for succour.

You are near-by in the obliteration of dimensions of proximity and remoteness from the eyes of those who know. O Generous One, Glorious One, Noble One. Peace is the word from the Merciful Lord. Praise be to God, the Lord of all the beings.

8.5 JAVANESE MYSTICISM

The signs of Islam in a person are the following: (1) love for the Lord; (2) love for the prophets; (3) love for the saints; (4) resistance against the enemies of the Lord; (5) fear of the Lord's punishment; (6) faith in the Lord's mercy; (7) praising the Lord's commandments and rejecting what He has forbidden. Hazrat 'Ali has said: 'To suspect a good person of evil is the heaviest sin'.

The honest person is softer than earth. The heart of a hypocrite is harder than stone. A content heart has the abundance of the ocean. An unjust ruler is hotter than fire. Offending the hearts of people is colder than Zamharir (Qur'an 76:13).

A believer has three enemies: the world, Satan, and his own weakness. A believer also has three strengths: ritual prayer, reciting the Qur'an, and staying in the mosque.

Asceticism is ritual prayer and reciting the Qur'an, staying in the mosque and finally selecting a companion to live far away from the crowds.

The prophet said: 'The true faith is: (1) confession with the tongue; (2) confirmation by the heart; (3) resolution with the statement of intention; (4) knowledge of the *sunna*; (5) practice with effort'. Furthermore he said: 'A rich man who is dissatisfied is like a poor man. He who has knowledge without good words is like the ignorant. A *faqir* who wants to be rich is like a dog. A free woman who wants to go outdoors is like a slave girl. If you want this world, go into business. If you want the next, become an ascetic. If you want both, study first to get complete knowledge. Whoever feeds the poor, the Lord will keep that person from hell'.

He said: 'I have been sent to all people. Follow the path of truth. Try to get three things: (1) the poor and needy to give away your possessions to; (2) judgement, to get rid of your pride; (3) the vision of God to get rid of yourself'.

The dead of heart are those who say they love God but never remember His word, those who say they love Muhammad the prophet but do not follow him, and those who say they love paradise but make no effort to arrive there.

If there were no honest merchants the poor would be starving. If there were no honest princes, criminals would be ruling. If there were no honest fighters, Islam would be decaying.

A person can have three types of purposes. The lowest purpose is to obtain enjoyment from other people. This is cursed by God. The middle purpose is to receive enjoyment from God. The highest purpose is to love God and to serve Him even in suffering. God said: 'I love my servants who love Me and long to meet Me. I made My paradise for them and will keep them close to Me'.

When you are united in prayer with the Lord, there is no more distinction between you and He. When you know His being and qualities, you will mention God in the deepest sense of the word. You will see the Lord with your interior eye, your heart will be before Him, and all your parts will be in His presence. Never will you deviate from His will. This state will lead you to utter astonishment.

The highest stage on the upward path is the *haqiqa*. In this stage you will have no more thoughts except for God. Liberated from the world you will remember only God, burning with desire to meet Him soon, having already seen His light. Having once seen that great vision and having come back, you will be like a walking corpse on earth. You will travel at any speed you wish. You will see all things, even those behind walls, and you will travel like lightning. All this because such people have achieved complete unity of thought. The first meeting with Him will cause confusion, giddiness, and trembling. The actual meeting is hidden, mysterious, and indescribable. *Haqiqa* is seeing the Secret close by. It is interior knowledge. The love of God will cause poverty, hunger, isolation, shame, and contempt from others. These are the signs of the ultimate happiness of those whom God loves.

Husayn ibn 'Umar has said that God the Highest loves those persons who open the door of remembering Him so that they know Him intimately and will find themselves in the exalted state of unity. As soon as they settle in it, the veil is lifted for them and they are within sight of the Lord. Such persons are ruled by God's love. God's glory and beauty are revealed to them and they cease to be as individuals in the vision of God, as they go up in unity. Only God the eternal One, is. After this experience, God makes those persons return to their previous state, but from now on they possess knowledge. From then on, and for that reason, those persons will long to come back to God, who said: *To us they will return* (Qur'an 2:28 and *passim*). They need Him and are completely dependent on Him, Who alone is Independent.

This yearning to return to Him makes those persons uninterested in the world so that they have no desires and no wish to sin. They can never be godless, nor wicked. They have peace, they wish nothing in this world, they are truly free. Such a man is perfect; he will want solitude, vigilance, fasting, and absence of distraction. First and foremost he wants to meditate on His word: *We have made the night into a garment and the day into food* (Qur'an 78:10–11). This means that we must praise God from the evening prayers to the morning prayers. This is the true *garment*. *Food* means that we must be patient and forgiving.

There are six degrees of *dhikr*. The *dhikr* of the mouth is merely mentioning. The *dhikr* of the soul is expressed by the voice, when the heart reflects. The *dhikr* of the heart is unforgettable remembering. The *dhikr* of the interior is the complete concentration on God. The *dhikr* of the spirit is seeing the Lord's face and knowing that He sees us and pours over us the light of His manifestation.

The *dhikr* of the subtle being is the final revelation of God without a vestige of doubt that He is the Lord in glory and beauty. One should strive to extinguish the self, through the stage of seeing His face.

No one may speak of the power over his actions, neither before nor after they are accomplished. It is God who has created the power in us to achieve actions. The best treasure is someone with great knowledge. The best possession is resignation. There is no greater joy than a good deed. There is no better deed than to forsake's one's desires. No worship is better than the fear of God. There is no better medicine than sleep. The truth is always the best message. The best asceticism is contentment. Solitude is the best protection. The best proof is the face. Pride is the greatest evil and the most terrible pain is hell-fire. Ignorance is your worst friend and a multitude of desires is the worst wealth. The most contemptible person is a greedy *faqir*.

Admonitions of Shaykh Muslim

My children, follow the prophet in all he did. Do not befriend women. Obey your parents so that God may bless you. Do not listen to the modernists, for they bring evil. Never make friends with the propagandists of new ideas. Be satisfied with what you have and eat only permitted food. Pray often at night and live in harmony with your congregation. Do not covet the position of head for among the leaders of men there is little good and many evils. Be pure in all your intentions.

Be gentle in your dealings with others and humble yourself. Whoever humbles himself will be raised up by God, thus spoke the prophet; and whoever raises himself up will be humbled by God. Have pity on your neighbours and do not mock them for the innermost self of the mocker is killed thereby. Speak little, for the more you talk, the more mistakes you will make. Never let God's charity cease. Believe in Him and fear Him. Do not rejoice when you are praised and do not be angry when you are criticised, for the true believer loves the truth. My children, always be conscientious, meek, and wise. Do not perform asceticism without knowledge. Serve only those religious leaders who covet no earthly goods and are not full of their own greatness. Do not be pleased when people ask you questions; do not argue, joke, or contradict others. Be kind, never envy others. Let your heart be good. Never be a liar or a miser. Do not think yourself better than your neighbours. Do not spend much time on your appearance, for you would neglect your soul. Watch the signs of God's intentions. He has meted out everyone's destiny. Do not fear to speak the truth, always for God's sake. Never eat without hunger, nor sleep without fatigue. Speak no words that may not be used. Love God's creatures only for His sake. Do not try to appear great in people's eyes. Remember, one day you will die. Remember to live on earth as a temporary resident. Remember, you must leave this world the way you arrived: without possessions.

Shaykh al-Hasan al-Basri was once in the market place where he saw a doctor whose assistant claimed that his master knew a medicine for every illness.

Shaykh Hasan asked the doctor: 'Master of Medicines, do you have a remedy against sin and heart-burning?' 'I do Sir', spoke that doctor, 'You will need ten ingredients for that. Firstly, the roots of the trees called the Fear of God and Humility, to be fumigated with burning confession; then add Joy in the Lord's Commandments. Rub these together with the rubbing-stone of contentment, then boil it in the kettle Devotion, having added the water of Piety. Heat it well over the first Love of God. Pour it into the vessel Acceptance, eat it with the spoon Effort, then clean your hands with the cloth Gratitude. You will assuredly be healthy in this world and purified for the next.'

One day the prophet spoke to Hazrat 'Ali saying that the *bismillah* can work wonders. If you pronounce it regularly your sins will be forgiven; you will not fall into error or heresy. You will loosen your ties with this world and will no longer be chained to evil. Your wrongs will be covered, your ailments cured, and on Judgement Day even sinners will be absolved if they have often repeated: In the name of God, the Merciful, the Compassionate.

The meaning of God's *rahma* (Grace) is as follows. He cares for all created beings, for the unbelievers, the ignorant, and even for the idol worshippers, for all that lives and grows, for Muslims and non-Muslims. He will forgive the Muslims on the Day of Judgment with His *rahma*, for the meaning of *rahma* is that God covers sins and wrongs.

Those who pray to God out of pure longing for Him, all their prayers will be heard and answered. Those who do not pray to God will be struck by His wrath. It is with His *rahma* that God has given paradise to His servants as a favour, that He has saved the believers from hell, and has caused light to shine in their minds.

God causes all evil in the world as well as all the good. The prophet said: 'It is God's will to love all things He has created. Those who love His creatures are loved by Him. Those who do not love His creatures are not loved by Him either. Those who show mercy towards all creatures, to him will God show mercy. We must love all created things, in the whole world'.

It is incomprehensible for people that God is constantly active without ever resting, yet He never goes in any direction since there is no place where He is not already. It follows that He is alive and never dies for how could He create the heavens and the earth and keep everything in them going, growing, and flowing, such as the stars, the plants, and the rivers, without being alive and alert all the time, seeing and hearing everything, making new things by His will, His word, and His power. Yet He has no sex, no children, and He will never grow old. He knows all our actions, even those we keep secret and He will remember them.

Sayyid 'Umar said the following. He who speaks less will receive more knowledge. He who looks less at others will receive more insight. He who does not interfere in other peoples' lives will be more pious. He who stops laughing will receive more memory. He who keeps secrets will become virtuous. He who does not love this world will receive paradise. He who is not worried is also free of hypocrisy. He who desires paradise will talk rarely. The highest knowledge is knowing God. The rarest gift for the law scholar is honesty.

Whoever enjoys serving the Lord will receive knowledge, saintliness, devotion, and righteousness.

Before a Muslim dies, that person has to make sure that the following presents are taken:

1. For Gabriel, four: conversion, gratefulness for suffering, regular prayer, and the love of God.
2. For the grave, also four: unwillingness to slander, disinclination to sow discord, keep the heart free of sin, pray all night long.
3. For the Place of Judgement, four: inclination to study the Qur'an, to do good, to be kind to God's creatures, to thank the Lord.
4. For Munkar and Nakir, four: repeating the *shahada*, obeying the prophet, speaking the truth, loving fellow Muslims.
5. For the Angel of the Record, four: never use bad language, never be jealous, never be satisfied with yourself, be generous in charity.
6. For the Narrow Bridge, four: love the Lord, honour your parents, keep what is entrusted to you, love children and kinsmen.
7. For the guardian of hell, four: never stop reciting the Qur'an, weep with the fear of God, be totally devoted to the Lord, stay far away from all forbidden things.

- a Kubraw.
- ca. 1280

8.6 AL-NASAFI ON THE MYSTIC QUEST

Of the traveller, the goal, the stages, and the road

The traveller in the path of mystic philosophy is the perceptive sense, which as it becomes further developed results in intelligence, not however the intelligence of life, but such as is described in the words of Muhammad: 'Intelligence is light in the heart, distinguishing between truth and vanity, not the intelligence of life'. After a time our traveller merges into Divine Light, but of the thousands who start upon the road scarcely one attains thereunto. The goal is the knowledge of God, and the acquisition of this knowledge is the work of Divine Light alone, perception or worldly intelligence having no lot or portion therein. The latter is represented as the sovereign of this world, and the perceptive faculties are the executive officers of his rule, to whom both the cultivation and devastation of the face of the earth is due. The idea is suggested by the following passage of the Qur'an: *When God said to the angels: 'I am about to place a vicegerent in the earth',* they said: *'Will you place therein one who shall commit abomination and shed blood? Nay; we celebrate Your praise and holiness'.* God answered them: *'Verily I know what you know not'* (2:28). This answer implies that God knew that although such might even be the conduct of the bulk of mankind, there would still be some who should receive the Divine Light and attain to a knowledge of Him; so that it is clear that the object of the creation of existent beings was that God should be known. Existence was made for man, and man for the knowledge of God. To the same purport is the answer given to David, 'David inquired and said, Oh Lord! why hast thou created mankind? God said, I am a hidden treasure, and I would fain become known'. The business of the traveller then is to exert himself and strive to attain to the Divine Light, and so to the knowledge of God; and this is to be achieved by associating with the wise. The received notion of the 'stages' in the 'road', involves a paradox, the disciple who asks concerning them being told that there is not even a single stage, nay more, not even a road at all. This statement is differently explained by two sects, the Sufis and the *Ahl-i Wahdat*, whom I shall call the Unitarians. The Sufis say that there is no road from man to God, because the nature of God is illimitable and infinite, without beginning or end or even direction. There is not a single atom of existent things with which God is not and which God does not comprise: *Are they not in doubt concerning the union with their Lord? doth he not comprise everything?* (Qur'an 42:54). Nor is there aught that he does not comprehend with his knowledge: *Verily God comprehends all things with his knowledge* (Qur'an 42:54). The traveller who has not attained to this Divine Light can have no lot or portion with God, but those who have reached it gaze always upon His face; they go not forth by day and retire not to rest at night without an abashed consciousness that God is present everywhere; for with Him they live, and in Him they act.

The whole universe compared with the majesty of God is as a drop in the ocean, nay infinitely less than this. But perception or intelligence can never lead to this conviction, or reveal this glorious mystery; that is the province of the Divine Light alone. Such is the Sufi explanation of the proposition, 'There is no road from man to God'.

The Unitarians interpret it as follows. They hold that existence is not independent, but is of God; that besides the existence of God there is no real existence, nor can there possibly be: for that which exists not, cannot exist of itself, but that which does not exist, exists of itself, and that which is self-existent is God.

When man imagines that he has an existence other than the existence of God he falls into a grievous error and sin; yet this error and sin is the only road from man to God; for until the traveller has passed over this he cannot reach God. A certain Sufi poet has said: Plant one foot on the neck of self, / The other in thy Friend's domain; / In everything His presence see, / For other vision is in vain. That is, while you are looking up to the self, you cannot see God, but when you are not looking up to the self, all that you see is God. Such is the Unitarian solution of the proposition that 'there is no road from man to God', namely that the error or imagining an existence separate from God is the only road to Him; the stages on this road are innumerable, and some philosophers even assert that it has no end.

Illumination = Sufis
Doubt = Unitarians } ?

Concerning the nature of God

The Sufis consider it an axiom that the world must have had a Creator. They affirm that He is One, Ancient, First and Last, the End and Limit of all things, Incomparable, Unchangeable, Indivisible, and Immaterial, not subject to the laws of time, place, or direction; He also possesses the attributes of holiness, and is exempt from all opposite qualities. In this their account agrees with the opinion of the Oriental thinking world in general; but they further assert that He is Infinite and Illimitable, by which they mean not only without beginning or end, but also without determinate position of time, place, or direction. The nature of God, according to them, is an infinite and illimitable light, a boundless and fathomless ocean, compared with which the entire universe is more insignificant than a drop of water in the sea. There is no single atom of existent beings which God does not pervade, comprise, and comprehend. God is always near to man, but man is always far from God, because he is not aware of His proximity. The proximity of God to all created beings is the same, for the highest and lowest are alike in His sight. The light of God is the only thing that can reveal this proximity to the traveller.

There are three grades of proximity to God which are out of the reach of human intelligence: the proximity of time, place, and attributes. We can say, for instance, that Muhammad was nearer our own time than Christ; that the moon is nearer to the earth than the planet Jupiter; that Bayazid Bistami more closely resembled Muhammad in qualities than did any even of the prophet's contemporaries; but we cannot predicate this proximity of God. The verse of the Qur'an: *He is with you wherever you are* (57:4), alludes to this mysterious proximity. Intelligence has no road to the discovery of it, but when its majesty has overshadowed the Illuminati, they perceive that in the sight of God saints and prophets, unbelievers and heretics, the loftiest of mankind and the meanest of brutes, are alike compared with Him. This is their explanation of the passage: *You will see no distinction in the Creation of the Merciful One* (Qur'an 67:3), and: *God's is the East and the West, and wherever you turn your faces God is there* (Qur'an 2:109).

The traveller who has discovered this proximity possesses the one thing needful, and has completed the journey to God, but until he shall have overcome the restraints of time and place his steps can never border on the threshold of eternity. Eternity, in the Sufi sense, is the primal element of cosmos, and takes in at one glance both past and future time. This idea is contained in the words of the *hadith*: 'There is no morning or evening with the Lord'. The passage in the Qur'an: *O assembly of jinn and men! if you are able to pass out of the confines of Heaven, then pass out of them; but you will do so only by the authority which God gives you* (Qur'an 55:33), points to the majesty of Him of whose proximity we are speaking.

This Sufi account of the nature and proximity of God gives rise to many questions among their disciples. For instance: 'In what way is the nature of God infinite and illimitable, in reference to the sensible and invisible world separately considered?' The answer, however, follows plainly from the previous statements. For, since the nature of God is infinite and illimitable, and no notion of time, place, or direction attaches to it, it is equally above the highest conception of the invisible world, and below the lowest material object of the sensible world. Again, their statement concerning the proximity of God to all things alike, and His comprising and comprehending all things, seems irreconcilable with any conception that human intelligence can form of His nature. This objection they meet by the following illustration.

Earth is dense, water compared with earth is subtle, air is more subtle than water, fire is more subtle than air; and the subtle occupies a higher position in the scale of creation than the dense. Now, although each of these four elements occupies a distinct position in nature, they are susceptible of commixture, and are determined the one by the other. If, for instance, a vessel be completely filled with earth there will still be space for water, and when it will contain no more water it will still admit of the introduction of air, and when it will contain no more air it will still admit of the introduction of fire; the comprehensive and penetrating capacities of each is in proportion to their relative densities. It will now be observed that there is no particle of the earth in the vessel but is commingled with the water, and so on of the other three elements, each occupying its distinct and proper position according to its density. It is from the proper gradation and arrangement of these four elements in the world that the phenomena of nature arise; but they are nevertheless susceptible of commixture and conjunction. This again may be proved by experiment. If one thrust his hand into water it is moistened and not burnt, if into fire it is burnt and not moistened, but if he thrust it into boiling water it is both moistened and burnt, thereby proving that these two elements are susceptible of commixture and conjunction. That the four elements do occupy their distinct and proper positions in nature, is evident from the premises concerning their relative densities, for the denser cannot disturb or confine the more subtle. If all this be possible then in the case of material elements, how much more possible is it in the case of the nature of God, which is immaterial and indivisible!

Another and closer illustration is that taken from the connection of the human soul with the body. The soul is conjoined with the body, and does not merely reside in it; so that there is no atom of the corporal frame distinct from or not pervaded, comprised, and comprehended by it. The limbs may be separated one by one, and the body itself even cut into pieces without any wound or hurt accruing to the soul; for the body, which is the denser of the two, cannot disturb or confine the soul, which is the more subtle. In like manner the nature of God pervades, comprises, and comprehends everything, and is incapable of being disturbed or confined by anything.

Again, since the nature of God is infinitely subtle, nothing can ever veil or conceal it, for the more subtle a thing is the greater is its capacity for penetration. Thus the Sufis explain the expression of the Qur'an: *He is the Subtle, the Wise*, with reference to the nature of God, as the only truly subtle nature. They

say that this sentence would convince everyone of the truth of the Muslim
creed if they could but understand that this is the right interpretation of it.
This proximity of God is implied in the verses: *He is with you wherever you are;
God sees all that you do* (Qur'an 57:4). *I am nearer to him than his jugular vein*
(Qur'an 50:15), and many similar passages both of the Qur'an and the *hadith*.

The foregoing arguments are intended specially to confine the opinion that
God is nearer to some men than others, namely, that the wise approach nearer
to Him than the ignorant. Their great object, however, is the inculcation of the
beautiful truth, that He is ever near to those who seek Him, while those only
are far from Him who by their actions fail to acknowledge that He is Omni-
present and Omniscient, knowing and seeing all they do.

Conclusion
The words quoted in the first chapter: 'I am a hidden treasure, and I would
fain be known', form the basis of the whole system of Sufi speculation.
Considering the entire universe merely as a manifestation of God, produced by
the agency of intelligence directly proceeding from Him, they rightly surmise
that this intelligence is the only means by which He can be known.

Now man being with them the most perfect entity in the universe, is clearly
the instrument by which the object of its creation is to be accomplished; but
this object is that God should be known, and He can only be known through
intelligence; therefore the attainment of this intelligence is the final aim of
man.

But as man sprung from the Intelligence which originated the universe, and
should, as has been just stated, tend to the same, the Sufis proceed to consider
his existence as a circle meeting in the intelligence which reveals the Godhead.
This circle they divide into two arcs, the former called descent, includes every
stage, from the first scintillation from the original intelligence to the full
development of man's reasoning powers; the latter arc, called ascent, includes
every stage, from his first use of reason for its true purpose to his final
reabsorption into the Divine intelligence. This is what is meant when they
speak of the origin and return of man.

The ascent, or upward progress, naturally presents itself to the Sufi mind in
the form of a journey, and the doctrines which profess to describe it are
accordingly called the road.

When a man possessing the necessary requirements of fully developed
reasoning powers turns to them for a resolution of his doubts and uncertainties
concerning the real nature of the Godhead, he is called a searcher after God.

If he manifest a further inclination to prosecute his inquiry according to
their system, he is called a *murid*, or one who inclines.

Placing himself then under the spiritual instruction of some eminent leader
of the sect, he is fairly started upon his journey, and becomes a *Salik* or
traveller, whose whole business in after-life is *suluk*, devotion, (or, as the word
signifies, the prosecution of his journey,) to the end that he may ultimately

arrive at the knowledge of God.

Here he is exhorted to serve God as the first step towards a knowledge of Him; this is the first stage of his journey, and is called service or worship.

When in answer to his prayers the divine influence or attraction has developed his inclination into love of God, he is said to have reached the stage called love.

This divine love expelling all worldly desires from his heart, leads him to the next stage, called seclusion.

Occupying himself henceforward with contemplations and the investigations of those metaphysical theories concerning the nature, attributes, and works of God, he reaches his next stage, which is that of knowledge.

Now this assiduous contemplation of startling metaphysical theories not unfrequently produces a stage of mental excitement. Such ecstatic state is considered a sure prognostication of direct illumination of the heart by God, and constitutes the next stage, ecstasy.

During this stage he is supposed to receive a revelation of the true nature of the Godhead, and to have reached the stage called the truth.

He is then said to proceed to the stage of direct union with God.

Further than this he cannot go, but pursues his habit of self-denial and contemplation until his death, which is, however, merely looked upon as a total absorption into the Deity, forming the consummation of his journey, the last stage designated extinction.

That stage in which he is said to have attained to the love of God is the point of view from which the Sufi poets love to discuss the doctrines of their sect; with them man is the lover, God the beloved one, and the journey above described is referred to allegorically as the distance which separates the lover from the object of his affection.

9 INTERPRETATIONS OF ISLAM IN THE MODERN WORLD

See 1.8. The success of Islam in the world is what all these authors desire. What kind of Islam that should be and where the crux of the problem is with present-day Islam is where they differ. Some see internal problems (9.1), others external (9.4). Compare 9.3 with 5.2. The document provided in 9.5 should be put in the context of various modern Muslim movements, especially that of 9.2.

9.1 SIR SAYYID AHMAD KHAN ON ISLAM AND SCIENCE

[(iii) A precedent to the present situation.] At the time when the reign of the

'Abbasid caliphs flourished and the star of the Muslims was at its zenith, Greek philosophy and natural science had gained popularity among the Muslims, with the result that doubts arose among the people concerning many questions regarding Islam. Because the very people who acknowledged the tenets of philosophy and natural science to be true, found a discrepancy between these and the contemporary teachings of Islam as they have been elaborated by independent judgement, and thus doubts about Islam arose among them. If one can rely on history, it emerges as an established fact that the period was one of hard attacks on Islam, and yet that Islam does not have to fear damage from the hardest attacks by its hardest enemies. All the *'ulama'* had to define Islam at that time. They made great efforts to protect Islam and to make it triumph. May God accept their efforts! They established three ways of protecting Islam. The first was to prove that tenets of Greek wisdom and philosophy which were against Islamic teachings were wrong. The second was to formulate such objections to the propositions of [Greek] wisdom and philosophy by which these tenets would themselves become doubtful. Third, to harmonise between the tenets of Islam and the tenets of wisdom and philosophy.

By pursuing this debate a new science originated among Muslims which they call *'ilm al-kalam*. Till this day the books of this science are part and parcel of the learning and teaching of the *'ulama'* of our religion, and they are quite proud of them. It was for this reason that many of the tenets of Greek philosophy and natural science of the third kind [i.e. that which could be harmonised] were incorporated by the Muslims into their religious books and that, step by step, they began to be accepted like religious tenets, whereas in fact they are by no means connected with the religion of Islam. It is no easy task today to separate them from it. Therefore, I think that since Islam is in the same state, attacked in the same way as then, we must make, to the best of our ability, the same efforts our elders made in former times.

My friends! You know well that in our time a new wisdom and philosophy have spread. Their tenets are entirely different from those of the former wisdom and philosophy [of the Greeks]. They are as much in disagreement with the tenets of ordinary present-day Islam as the tenets of Greek wisdom and philosophy were with the tenets of customary Islam during their time. Moreover, an especially difficult problem is posed by the tenets of Greek natural science. The erroneousness of these tenets is by now an established fact. Yet the Muslim scholars of that time accepted them like religious tenets, as I have just explained, and this has made things even more difficult.

[(iv) Former science and modern science.] My friends! Another problem is the big difference between critical research today [and its results] and the tenets of Greek wisdom of old, because the tenets of former wisdom were based on rational and analogical arguments and not upon experience and observation. It was very easy for our forbears, while sitting in the rooms of mosques and hermitages, to disprove teachings arrived at by analogous reasoning and to refute rational teachings by rational demonstrations, and not to accept them.

But today a new situation has arisen which is quite different from that [brought about] by the investigations of former philosophy and wisdom. Today doctrines are established by natural experiments [i.e. experiments in natural science] and they are demonstrated before our eyes. These are not problems of the kind that could be solved by analogical arguments or which can be contested by assertions and principles which the learned classes of former times have established. Take for instance the question of the piercing of the roof of heaven and the closing of [the doors of] heaven, which is a very big issue in the natural sciences of our tradition and which has lived on in our learning and teaching. Closely connected with this question are also the principles of natural science which have been accepted in the religion of Islam. But of what use is this doctrine [of the piercing and closing of the cupola of heaven] now and what utility is there in studying and teaching it, since it has been established that the way in which former philosophers and *'ulama'* decided upon the existence of heaven is wrong. What is needed now is to reflect upon what heaven means, and for this it is necessary to work out new principles and tenets instead of simply calling to memory the worn-out and obsolete doctrines. . . .

[(v) Need for a new *'ilm al-kalam*.] In the same way there are many other reasons for which in our time Muslims need to adopt new methods in controversy. The person who considers Islam to be true and believes firmly in it, his heart will testify that Islam alone is true – whatever changes may occur in logic, philosophy, and natural science, and however much the doctrines of Islam seem to be in contradiction with them. This attitude is sufficient for those who believe with a true and uncomplicated mind in Islam, but not for those who reject or doubt it. Furthermore, it is by no means a work of proper protection to confess just by the tongue that Islam is true, and to do nothing to strengthen it in its confrontation with the modern propositions of wisdom and philosophy. Today we need, as in former days, a modern *'ilm al-kalam* by which we either render futile the tenets of modern sciences or [show them to be] doubtful, or bring them into harmony with the doctrines of Islam. . . .

I happen to believe that there is nobody who is well acquainted with modern philosophy and modern natural science as they exist in the English language, and who at the same time believes in all the doctrines which are considered doctrines of Islam in present-day understanding. May the English-educated young men and students forgive me, but I have not yet seen anybody well acquainted with English and interested in the English sciences who believes with full certainty in the doctrines of Islam as they are current in our time. I am certain that as these sciences spread – and their spreading is inevitable and I myself after all, too, help and contribute towards spreading them – there will arise in the hearts of people an uneasiness and carelessness and even a positive disaffection towards Islam as it has been shaped in our time. At the same time I believe firmly that this is not because of a defect in the original religion but rather because of those errors which have been made, wilfully or not, to stain the face of Islam.

I am never entitled to claim that I could clean the luminous face of Islam from the black stains of these errors, or that I could take upon me the responsibility to undertake the work of protecting Islam. This is the duty and the privilege of other saintly and learned people. But since I have striven to spread among Muslims those sciences which, as I have just stated, are to a certain extent in discrepancy with contemporary Islam, it was my duty that, as far as it could be done by me, I should do, rightly or wrongly, whatever was in my power to protect Islam and to show forth to people the original luminous face of Islam. My conscience told me that if I failed to do so I should be a sinner before God. . . .

[(xii) The belief in the prophethood of Muhammad, in the modern context.] Now I want to deal a little with those subjects that are related to the affirmation of the prophethood [of Muhammad] and to those tenets of Islam that on first sight seem to be opposed to reason and science. A detailed treatment of these subjects would need a very long time and would probably not be finished in years. This is no matter of surprise. But it may not be out of place to succinctly deal with these subjects for the benefit of some English-educated young men, or for other people who desire to alter their outlook.

To be a Muhammadan (or what is synonymous with it), to belong to the circle of Islam, demands belief not only in the Unity of God but also in the divine mission of the Prophet, that is in prophethood. Two things put the English-educated or liberal-minded young man into doubt. Firstly, the belief in the prophethood; secondly, those tenets of Islam which seem to contradict contemporary wisdom and philosophy or reason, or which seem to be far removed from reason. The discussion of the prophethood along the principle of nature is a lengthy one. I am not going to open it up now. Instead I shall state a few points, as one does in a speech, concerning the truth of the prophethood of Muhammad – points which the heart can accept. Many great philosophers of the past and present, who have reached a very high rank in scholarship and have written many excellent books, accept, nevertheless, the teachings of basic Islam and the principles upon which it is built. But leave them aside and examine yourself how excellent, solid, and unrivalled the principles of basic Islam are, omitting the independent judgements and complex problems of the doctors of the law which do not correspond to the plain and simple principles of Islam. Even a man who all his life has investigated into the essence of philosophy, wisdom, the natural sciences, and human nature – even such a man would not be able to establish such principles. I therefore do not think it out of place to argue that a person who was born in a land full of sand and stones, who had become an orphan at a tender age, who had neither received training in a big *madrasa* nor heard the doctrines of Socrates, Hippocrates, or Plato, nor sat at the feet of an ustad, nor enjoyed the company of wise men, philosophers or men of political and moral science, but who spent forty years of his life among uneducated and rude camel drivers, who for forty years had seen nobody but a people addicted to idolatry, internecine warfare, and men and women who prided themselves on theft and fornication. Such a man, who all at once rose against all his own people and, albeit surrounded on four sides by idolatry, yet professed *La ilaha illa Allah* – who not only said it but made all his people say it, who for centuries had worshipped Lat and Manat and 'Uzza, who eradicated from his people all this bad behaviour and these immoral practices; who made them throw to the ground and break their idols and exalted the name and worship of God throughout the entire peninsula, the peninsula which, after Abraham and Ishmael, had been sullied by a thousand acts of impurity. Who then restored to it its original purity and the great religion of Abraham? Who, I ask, after forty years put light in man's heart, the light which has illumined not only the Arab peninsula but the whole world?

After teaching the *shahada* he gave the people precepts about the morals of religion. Could any philosopher have said more than what this illiterate man said? And not only did he pronounce these precepts but rather, by the influence of his pure heart and tongue, he implanted them in the hearts of people. This work was such that it could not have been achieved by any philosopher or any powerful political ruler. What was the thing in this orphan child which demonstrated not only to the Arab peninsula but to the whole world the wonder of divinity?

O my friends! The most hardened materialist and irreligious man, if he does not – God forbid – accept such a person as a prophet, surely he shall have, at least to acknowledge, that if after God there is any person as great, it is He alone. 'My spirit a sacrifice to you, O Messenger of God!' Thus whoever arrives at understanding the true nature of prophethood cannot but put his faith in the prophethood of the Messenger of God. These few words about our affirmation of prophethood will be fully sufficient to satisfy the mind of any person who possesses a little intelligence and understanding.

9.2 SAYYID QUTB FROM *THIS RELIGION OF ISLAM*

It might then be objected that humanity will not be able long to persist on this unique and lofty path of Islam. A group or community, having once established it for a period, will then abandon it and humanity will turn to other paths, which, while not causing it to attain the same summits, will not impose on humanity the same hard efforts.

At first sight this objection appears to be valid. Many writers have attempted to implant this idea in people's minds, to persuade them that the path of Islam is impractical and unrealistic, that it is too much for human nature to support for more than a time and that is only an idealistic summons to reach after unattainable horizons. They have had a cunning aim behind this attempt to spread despair at the possibility of reconstructing life in accordance with the path of Islam, and to frustrate efforts being made in that direction. These cunning ones have found in the disorders that began with the murder of

'Uthman, the subsequent conflict between 'Ali and Mu'awiya, and related events, a fertile ground for attempting to prove their vile contention, sometimes by implication and sometimes explicitly, as circumstances dictate.

They are unintentionally helped in this aim by those sincere believers who are disturbed by the fact that these events should have interrupted the rise of Islam in that glorious period of history. They involved, too, a deviation from the concept of government that prevailed in the time of the prophet and his first two successors. Similarly, the conduct of some leaders of the community thereafter deviated from Islamic norms. Because of their excessive sensitivity in this respect, they imagine that all forms of Islamic advance stopped after the brief period of the Caliphate. They propound this view with the utmost sincerity and out of their admiration for the summit of conduct attained by the prophet and the rightly guided caliphs.

The whole matter requires careful re-examination, however, with particular attention to the human factors involved. The nature of the faith should be understood as should faith's method for guiding the steps of humanity over a long period in different environments and circumstances.

First of all, it is not true that the path of Islam imposes on the soul of people exertions harder than these are able to bear or to endure for more than a short time. It is indeed a sublime path. But it is at the same time a natural path, and the capital on which it relies and which it spends is none other than essential human nature. Its distinguishing feature is that it knows from the very beginning how to obtain access to this capital.

From the outset it is able to find its way to the human soul. It knows how it may enter, and it does so gently. It knows the strength and capacities of the human soul, and it never exceeds them. It knows its needs and necessities, and responds to them. It knows too its pure, constructive potentialities, and it puts them to work for positive ends. Despite all its sublimity and loftiness, it is a path essentially for people, for people living here in this world. It takes into consideration the nature of people, with all its component parts and the composition of individuals also. When the soul is at one with its true nature, when its needs and necessities are fulfilled, when its constructive capacities are released, then with ease and without compulsion it will flow in natural harmony with life, will ascend to the lofty summit ordained for it. On its long path to this goal, it will find ease, security, and confidence.

Those who doubt and arouse doubt concerning the possibility of establishing the path of Islam are terrified by its morality, by the purity of the moral element in its make-up. They are scared by the duties of this morality, imagining them to be fetters and obstacles preventing individuals from striving for what they desire and what their natural instincts impel them towards. This, however, is an illusion arising from a misunderstanding of the essential nature of the Islamic faith. The morality of Islam does not consist of a mere collection of fetters, obstacles, and prohibitions. It is in its essence a constructive and positive force, a motive force for continual development and self-realisation in the course of that development. This development however is characterised by total purity.

Positiveness and activity have a moral aspect in the path of Islam. Idleness and negativism are immoral, since they contradict the purpose of human existence, as conceived of by Islam, namely the vicegerency of God on earth, and the use of all that God has subordinated to people for the purposes of constructive activity.

Effort expended towards the realisation of the good and the combating of evil is an ethical matter in which basic elements of the human personality are released. In the view of Islam, obedience to God represents the ethical aspect in a sublime manner.

When we take the ethical aspects which appear to be bonds and fetters, we find them in reality to be aspects of movement, liberation, and vitality. Let us take for example self-restraint from indulgence of forbidden sexual passion. It appears to be a bond and an obstacle. But in reality it represents a liberation from slavery to these passions, release from servitude to them, and the exaltation of human will, so that the indulgence of these passions may be chosen within the bounds of decency laid down by Islam and within the sphere of legitimate enjoyment decreed by God. . . .

We do not have the space to multiply examples. These must suffice to give an idea of the true nature of the moral bonds in the Islamic path. Islam regards sins and vices as bonds and fetters which imprison the human soul, weigh it down, and drag it into the abyss. It counts release from the ties of base desires as true liberation, and its entire moral system is based on this foundation. This is because it regards the basis of human nature as the disposition to good: humanity was created in the fairest of natures. It descends to the lower depths whenever it submits to a way of life other than that ordained by God: *We created humanity with the fairest of natures, and then caused it to descend to the lowest depths, except those who believe and perform good works* (Qur'an 95:4). Therefore, the way of life consonant with the individual's essential nature is that which helps that person to escape from the bonds which attach themselves to a virtuous disposition, and to be liberated from the fetters of the passions.

Islam aspires to lead human society in order to bring into being circumstances and conditions which will liberate people from perversions that have latched on to their essential nature, permit the virtuous and constructive forces within them to appear and establish their supremacy, and remove the obstacles which prevent their true nature from striving towards the good in which it was created.

Those who imagine that the morality of Islam makes of it a heavy burden for humanity so as to prevent its realisation in their lives, derive this belief from the tribulations undergone by the individual Muslim living in a society which is not governed by Islam. In such circumstances, the morality of Islam is in reality a heavy burden; it almost crushes those individuals who live with their pure Islam in the polluted society of ignorance.

This, however, is not the natural situation foreseen by Islam for it supposes its pure, sublime morality to be supreme. Islam is a realistic system and it therefore supposes that the people who live according to its path will be living in a society governed by Islamic principles. In such a society good, virtue, and purity will be well known and protected by the leaders of the community. Evil, vice, and impurity will be rejected and banished by the dominant forces in society. When matters are rectified in this manner, the Islamic way of life becomes an extremely easy one. In fact, opposition to this way of life on the part of individuals will become difficult; it will be difficult for them to indulge in base passions and to follow evil and vice. All the forces dominating society – in addition to the force of the true nature of humanity – will stand against them, and make their divergent path hard and difficult.

Hence Islam demands that the absolute control of human society belongs to God and the path laid down by God; it denies this control to any of God's creation, and to any path laid down by other than God. This it would consider complete infidelity and a clear ascription of partners to God, for, as we have already pointed out, Islam insists on attribution of divinity to God Almighty alone, and control of human society by His path alone. This is the direct meaning of bearing witness that there is none to be worshipped other than God.

Islam also prescribes the erection of an Islamic society in the aegis of which Muslims can live their religion in accordance with the character given them thereby. The Islamic concept of existence as a whole and of the aim of human existence in particular differs fundamentally from all human imaginings. These picture people in isolation from the guidance of God in all times and places. This is a basic difference concerning which no compromise is possible.

A specific environment is then indispensable for the life of this concept, an environment with its own specific values. This cannot be the environment of a system based on ignorance of defined guidance. It will live according to the concept of Islam and the way of life springing therefrom; it will breathe naturally in accordance with its own being, without internal obstacles to slow down or prevent this growth, and without external obstacles to crush it.

In such an environment the Muslim individual will live a natural and easy life, for that person will breathe naturally, find assistance in the performance of good deeds, and experience both inner and social comfort in following Islamic morality. Without this environment the life of the individual becomes impossible, or at least extremely difficult. Therefore whoever wishes to be Muslim should know that they cannot devote themselves to their practice of Islam except in a Muslim environment dominated by Islam. They are mistaken if they imagine that they can realise Islam on an individual basis lost in the midst of a society ignorant of divine guidance.

The Islamic path is easy when one lives in an Islamic environment. It presupposes such an environment to be indispensable and all its directives are based on this foundation.

It is, as well, untrue that Islam imposes on people more strenuous efforts than are necessary for people living according to systems emanating from other than God. Such systems – those adopted by humanity in isolation from the guidance of God at any time or place – are inevitably affected by the results of human ignorance, human weakness, and human folly, at the very best. Hence, in whole or in part they will conflict with human nature and the soul of humanity will suffer as a result. They are similarly characterised by partial cures and solutions for human problems. They will solve one aspect but aggravate another and this is a direct result of their deficient vision which fails to grasp all aspects simultaneously. When they cure the new illness that arose out of their cure of the first illness, yet another illness will arise, and so on indefinitely. Study of the changes and stages gone through by human-designed systems bears witness to this. Without doubt, this imposes on humanity exertions harder than those involved in that perfect and comprehensive system which is in accord with essential human nature, which regards problems from all their aspects, prescribes for them a complete and comprehensive solution, and arises from a complete and comprehensive vision.

Whoever studies the record of human suffering that has arisen from human-designed systems throughout history cannot dare to say that this divinely ordained path with its obligations and morality imposes on people exertions greater than those imposed by human systems. . . .

The path of Islam is easy and lenient. It encourages human nature to take one direction, discourages it from taking another direction, and strengthens it when it weakens. But it never breaks or destroys it, or attempts to do so. It is patient with it as the wise and the knowing are patient, like whoever is confident of the realisation of the long-term aim, which cannot be attained in one rush, or even in two, three, ten, a hundred, or a thousand! All that is demanded is the exertion of effort to progress along the path.

As the lofty tree grows after striking its roots deep in the soil, and its branches reach out and intertwine, so too this way of life grows in the souls and in the world. It expands slowly and softly, with assurance and confidence. Finally it will be what God has willed it to be.

Islam sows its seeds and stands guard over them, leaving them to grow in natural tranquillity, and being assured of the ultimate aim. Whatever slowness of retreat is observed, this is in accordance with human nature. Sometimes plants are covered over by the sand, consumed by worms, burnt by thirst, flooded with water, and afflicted with various catastrophes. But the intelligent cultivator knows that his plants will survive and grow and that ultimately they will surmount all catastrophes. That person does not panic or attempt to ripen them by unnatural means. Thus, too, Islam is characterised by ease, and its obligations sit light upon the souls of people.

We do not need at this point to speak of the sufferings inflicted upon people by the violence of human systems and their protagonists. The wretchedness it is experiencing all over the world is enough. Everywhere the intelligent are raising cries of alarm and warning.

Finally, it is not true that this system of Islam did not survive for long, as some say with cunning and others with pride! The spiritual, social, and political structure that was erected on the basis of this sublime, unique system, in the space of a single century or even half a century, has continued to resist all the catastrophes that have beset it and all the attacks to which it has been exposed, for more than a thousand years.

These terrible factors have insistently attacked and infiltrated its bases and behind them stand all the powers of the world ignorant of divine guidance. They have not been able to destroy it but with the passage of time, with concentration and watchfulness, with determination and persistence, they have been gradually eroding it and diverting it little by little from its principles, until eventually it has become weakened and seriously threatened. None the less, up to the present they have been unable to distort its doctrinal foundations and these doctrines are available for fresh investigation, to be embraced by a new generation. This is the basic distinction between the divinely ordained path and human paths.

There is indeed a period of excellence in the history of this path – and indeed in the history of all humanity – which is still the sublime summit towards which necks are craned and gazes directed, still there in its exalted place. The period of excellence is a short one indeed, however. It is not the whole of Islamic history, but a beacon erected by God so that people might reach up to it and try to attain it and might renew the hopes of arriving at the sublime summit by rising in upward ascent. God assigned to this period its place in the ascent, the place of a guiding beacon.

The fact is that this period was not the result of an unrepeatable miracle; rather it was the fruit of human exertion made by the first Muslim community. It can be achieved whenever that exertion is again made.

But that exertion undertaken by a select group of humanity can be a model for many generations of humanity to come, not merely one generation. Whether or not it will be successful in one generation or another depends on the will of God, so that the model may take on a realistic form and encourage its emulation. It is then left to succeeding generations of mankind to attempt again to attain it.

The path continued to play its role, after that period of excellence, in broad areas of human life; it continued to act upon the ideas, the history, and the situation of people for many centuries and it left many traces on the life of the whole of humanity. It is precisely this that enables us to hope that humanity today may again strive towards the summit.

9.3 MAWLANA MAWDUDI ON BIRTH CONTROL

The analysis we have done in the preceding chapters of the factors that contributed towards the popularisation of birth control and the grave consequences that have followed therefrom brings home the following two points:

First: the urge for birth control in the western peoples, and its popularity among them on such a wide scale, was not a natural demand and there was nothing inherently wrong with them: nor was there any innate abhorrence towards procreation. In fact the causes of their present attitudes must be sought in the socio-economic and cultural pattern of their life, as it developed during the last two hundred years. Their mode of thinking, their values, their outlook have all been so moulded that they willy-nilly adopt the course of escape from the responsibilities of parenthood and the inconveniences involved in procreation and the upbringing of children. Had they not been driven from the circumstances and conditions of life peculiar to the culture they find themselves in they too would have remained as indifferent and unresponsive to birth control as they actually were in the first half of the nineteenth century. This we say for the simple reason that human nature has not undergone any transformation now, and parents' urge to procreate and bestow love and care over their offspring is just the same today as it was before the advent of the movement.

Second: Another important fact that comes to light is that the disturbing results that were produced by resort to the practice of birth control have demonstrated in unmistakable terms that rebellion against the laws of nature is bound to be detrimental to man and society. Indeed the laws of life are so complex that any tampering with them only to suit whims and caprices cannot but wreak havoc. The ways of nature cannot be frustrated by such fiddlings with the socio-cultural phenomenon. It is against the very nature of man to interfere with the processes of procreation. What needs to be changed is not the natural mode of behaviour, but man's whims and complexes which induce him to resort to easy courses and a life of pleasure without responsibility. This is a sure road to destruction.

Islamic viewpoint: the fundamental principle

These above stated two lessons drawn from the western experience enable us to better appreciate the fundamental principle of Islam. Islam is the natural way of life: it is a natural religion for man. All the rules laid down by it, individual as well as collective, are based upon a fundamental principle: that man should behave and act in consonance with natural laws that he finds working in this universe; and that he should refrain from a course of life that might force him to deviate from the purposes for which nature is operating. The Holy Qur'an informs us that God Almighty has not only created everything that we find in the universe but has also endowed it with an instinctive knowledge of the ways by which it can most suitably perform the tasks assigned to it in the general scheme of things: *Our Lord is He Who gave every thing its peculiar form and nature, then guided it aright*, i.e. showed it the way following which it can fulfil the purpose for which its creation was due (Qur'an 20:50).

Everything that is there in the universe is engaged in the performance of its duty in complete submission to the will of God. That is how they must behave. No one has the power or capacity to go against the prescribed course. Only man is an exception in this regard. He has the freedom to choose a course different from the one set forth by nature. He can refuse to submit and obey and conform. With the help of his intellect and the faculty of reason he can carve out new ways and forms of behaviour and may tread them to his discretion. The freedom is there, but a misuse of this freedom is bound to produce bad results, in the same way as we are free to violate the rules of traffic, but the consequent accidents and collisions and the penalty of law we shall have to bear. If man chooses to violate the laws of nature and the guidance God has given for individual and social life this is bound to lead him astray from the right course and produce disturbing consequences here and hereafter. *And who is more erring than he who follows his desires (and caprices) without any guidance from Allah* (Qur'an 28:50).

This deviation from the right course may on the face of it seem quite attractive and fascinating and advantageous. But the fact is that straying away from the path laid down by the Creator and violating the limits set by Him, is bound to be harmful to man. By adopting such a course he would be unjust to himself. The reason is not far to seek. Every transgression of the limits laid by the Lord and every act of irresponsible behaviour must eventually be to the detriment of man, and the greater the violation the greater the penalty. The wages of sin is destruction. *And whoever transgresses the limits of Allah he indeed does injustice to his own self* (Qur'an 65:1).

This, according to the Qur'an, is so because to try to distort and disturb the scheme of things God has ordained and to violate the natural laws which govern and sustain the universe and all that it contains is bound to unleash forces of destruction – this is a fiendish act and not the one that behoves man. These violations are at the promptings of Satan who wants to deprive man of what God has bestowed upon him. *And the Satan said: I will enjoin the sons of Adam and they shall change Allah's (scheme of) creation* (Qur'an 4:119).

And Satan is man's enemy ever since the beginning of man's career in this universe. *And you should not follow the footstep of Satan; surely he is your enemy manifest; he only enjoins you (to pursue) evil and acts of indecency* (Qur'an 2:109).

Thus, the basic principle on which Islam rests the foundations of its social and economic order, and from which emanates its culture and civilisation, is that man should fulfil all the demands and urges of his nature in the laws of nature, – and make the fullest use of all his powers and capabilities in a manner desired by the Supreme Being. He should neither keep any of his faculties dormant and unexplored nor use them in an irresponsible manner unmindful of the Divine Guidance, nor should he allow himself to be misled by the suggestions and promptings of the forces of evil in persuading him to seek methods that are far removed from the straight path shown by nature. The wellbeing of man lies, not in deviating from nature, but in pursuing its course in the light of Divine Guidance.

Is birth control compatible with Islam?

If we view the problem in the light of the above discussed fundamental principle of Islam it becomes abundantly clear that the pattern of life that Islam builds can have no place for birth control as a national social policy. The Islamic culture strikes at the roots of the materialistic and sensate view of life and eliminates the motivating forces that make man abstain from fulfilling one of the most fundamental urges of human nature, that is, of procreation. As already seen, birth control is not an unavoidable demand of human nature. He does not need it for the fulfilment of his personality. Instead it is a product of certain cultural forces, of a peculiar social circumstance, of a value-pattern that makes man obsessed with his personal comforts and pleasures, to the neglect of the needs of the society and the race. It is then that procreation is discounted and artificial curtailment of the family gets premium. From this it can be legitimately inferred that if a people have a different socio-cultural set-up, and if the forces and conditions that led to the social movement of birth control in the western society do not obtain amongst them, the occasion for such a movement will not arise. When the motives and the causes are not there, the situation will be different. When the tree is not there, how could the fruits be? Naturally in such a social organisation all inducements to attempt to alter God's scheme, to transgress the limits prescribed by Him, and to violate the course of nature He has laid will cease to operate. This movement can have no place in such a society.

Let us look a little more deeply in the social system of Islam to see how it precludes the possibility of the emergence of tendencies that may give rise to a situation favourable to the movement of birth control or to any other unnatural tendency.

Islam's economic system has struck at the very roots of capitalism and the spirit of acquisitiveness. It forbids usury and interest, disallows monopoly, forbids speculation and gambling, discourages hoarding, and introduces such institutions and policies (zakat, an equitable law of succession and inheritance, fair wage, guarantee of basic necessities of life to all people, etc.) as lead to diffusion of wealth and wellbeing. Islam takes these and many other effective measures to remedy the ills that have been responsible for economic dislocation and disparity in the western society and for raising a system of economic exploitation of the many at the hands of the few.

The social system of Islam has given legal, economic, social, and judicial rights to woman. She has a share, by her own right, in the earnings of man, over and above the right to own and inherit property and invest capital in business and industry under her own name. Islam, however, clearly states that men and women have their own spheres of activities – a scheme of functional division in accord with their respective natural dispositions and inherent physical and physiological qualities and characteristics. Free mixing of the sexes is prohibited through *hijab*. That is how the doors of a number of social and economic ills have been closed, and the errands that might lead men and women away from the function that nature has assigned them have been blocked. The preservation and propagation of life is not left to chance arrangements, instead the entire scheme of social life is so arranged that on the one hand the demands of human nature may be fulfilled and on the other the task of procreation and rearing of new generations be accomplished in the best possible way.

The ethical teachings of Islam require man to lead a simple and morally chaste and unblemished life. Islam declares unlawful all forms of social misbehaviour including drinking, fornication, adultery, and other sexual vices. It discourages idleness and waste of time in useless pursuits and places, effective checks on irresponsibility, extravagance, and indulgences in those recreations and enjoyments that result in a care-free life and frittering of wealth on trifles. Islam wants man to live a balanced life – balance between work and rest, effort and enjoyment, material and moral, individual and social aspects of life. *Eat and drink but be not prodigal. Lo! Allah loveth not those who exceed the limits* (Qur'an 7:31), is the Qur'anic injunction. Islam's approach to spending is that wealth is a trust and should be spent only where necessary and up to an extent that is desirable. In the matter of dress, housing, and procuring comforts of life, one should exercise restraint and spend within reasonable limits. That is how not only through moral training and spiritual education but also through a set of social, moral, and economic regulations and directive principles Islam strikes at the roots of immorality, extravagance and insatiable hunger for luxury, and lust – the hall-marks of a society that takes to birth control, as was done in the West.

Islam also inculcates the spirit of mutual love and affection, fellow-feeling and sympathy. It stresses the right of the blood-relations and enjoins a policy of co-operation and help. It insists on compassion for neighbours and ordains *infaq fi sabil Allah*, spending in the way of Allah for the promotion of good and virtue in its widest sense. Islam develops a system of social responsibility and national solidarity and provides for the help of the poor and needy irrespective of their faith, colour, race, creed, religion, or country, and protects them from the selfishness, greed, and exploitation by the vested interests.

These, in brief, are some of the ways and means that inculcate in each man a sense of responsible individualism as well as develop a healthy and integrated society. It is a moral society for a moral man. Such a morally sublime atmosphere cannot breed any social tendency towards birth control.

Along with these social attitudes and a *modus operandi*, for their operation and flowering, Islam brings about a change in the heart of man – the seat of his personality. It assures that man is not alone in the universe. There is a God, the Creator, the Sustainer, the Lord. To Him it turns his face and thus brings him in line with the way all creation – and creatures – behave. Strive man must, but it should be done with faith and hope. Islam asks man to rely on his Creator and makes him realise that He alone is the Nourisher and the Provider of him as He is of all other organic beings in the universe. This realisation saves man from many a moment of false despondency or arrogance. He relies on himself and his resources; but he relies more on the Lord of the universe.

Summing up we find that the nature of Islamic faith, its spiritual and moral attitudes, its social laws and regulations, its code of ethical behaviour, and its over-all ideals and mission in life – all have contributed towards mitigating those forces that give rise to the movement of birth control and its adoption as a social policy. Islamic and the western civilizations, from this viewpoint, are poles apart. A really Islamic society can have no place for birth control as a national policy. If a person is a true Muslim in thought and deed he, in the ordinary course of circumstances, can neither feel any urge towards birth control nor would he be thrown in an amoral situation where violation of nature is forced upon him. He enjoys life by living with restraint. And that is the course most suited to human genius.

Does Islam forbid birth control?

So far we studied the problem in more general terms. We shall now look at the issue more directly and try to find out whether Islam forbids birth control or not.

The Holy Qur'an lays down a fundamental principle that effecting change in the scheme of God is a fiendish act. Changing God's scheme and creation signifies misuse of a thing, its utilisation for a purpose other than the one for which it was intended, or to use it in a manner that its real purpose is defeated. In the light of this fundamental principle let us see as to what is 'God's scheme' in the marital relationship of man and woman, i.e. what is the real natural purpose of this relationship and whether birth control changes it in the other direction. The Qur'an is not silent on this point. It has, on the one hand, forbidden sexual relations outside marriage, and on the other, laid bare the objective which matrimonial relations between men and women are to serve. These objectives are (a) procreation and (b) fostering of love and affection and promoting culture and civilisation. The Qur'an says: *Your wives are a tilth for you, so go into your tilth as you like and do good beforehand for yourselves* (Qur'an 2:223).

This verse expounds the first objective of marriage. The other one is referred to in the following verse: *And one of His signs is that He created mates for you from yourselves that you may find consolation in them and He ordained between you love and compassion* (Qur'an 30:21).

In the first verse by describing women as a tilth an important biological fact has been pointed out. Biologically man is a tiller and a woman a tilth and the foremost purpose of the interrelationship between the two is the procreation of the human race. This is an objective which is common to all – human beings, animals, and the world of vegetation. The tiller of the soil cultivates the land not in vain, but for the produce. Take away this purpose, and the entire pursuit becomes meaningless. Through the parable of the tilth this important fact has been stressed by the Qur'an.

The second verse refers to another purpose of this relationship, viz. the establishment of an organised social life. When husband and wife take up to live together as a family they in fact lay the foundation of culture and civilisation. Herein lies the unique function which man is to perform in God's creation and work towards the flowering of all that has been laid in man. This urge is latent in man's nature and seeks its fulfilment through promptings from within and without.

9.4 IMAM KHUMAYNI'S IRAN

9.4.1 The Sunni-Shi'i difference

In the Name of God, the Merciful, the Compassionate.

A group of Muslims are Shi'a and another group is Sunni. One group is Hanafi, another Hanbali, and another group is Akhbari. But emphasis on these differences was not a correct thing from the very beginning. These problems are not relevant in a society in which all people want to serve Islam. We are all brothers and must stand together. However the *'ulama'* of the Hanafis give one kind of *fatwa* (juristic opinion) about a matter, another group follows al-Shafi'i in their *fatwas* and call themselves Shafi'i, yet another group follows Hazrat Ja'far al-Sadiq in juristic matters and calls itself Shi'a.

However this is not any ground for differences and our disagreements should not lead to mutual conflict. We are all together brothers. The Sunni and Shi'a brothers must abstain from every kind of disagreement. Today our differences are only to the profit of those who believe neither in the Shi'a code nor the Hanafi code nor in any other code followed by Muslims. All they desire is that none of these codes may exist. Their weapon for our destruction is creation of disagreements between us.

We must concentrate our attention on the fact that we are all Muslims, we are all followers of the same Qur'an and believers in *tawhid*. Our ultimate aim should be to serve Qur'an and *tawhid*, to our utmost.

I am hopeful that you shall successfully serve Islam in this Islamic Republic which is yours and does not belong to any select section but to all Muslims.

As to these problems which are presently in Kurdistan and your region, these problems shall soon be solved. I pray for you all and hope that we all, under the standard of Islam and *tawhid*, will stand together firmly against those who kill our brothers (Imam Khumayni here refers to Marxists, Democrats, and other anti-Islamic groups who have created a year-long problem in

Kurdistan. Aided and backed by Iraq and American Imperialism, they have tried to do everything in their power to strike the Islamic Republic in Kurdistan). We have, however made this declaration that they shall be granted amnesty if they hand over their arms and return to the open arms of Islam. Once they lay down their arms, conflict shall end in Kurdistan. May God grant you success.

9.4.2 'Muslims must find Islam'

November 3, 1979, Imam Khumayni meets with a group of Saudi Arabian students who live in Iran on the occasion of *id-i-ghorban*. Imam Khumayni spoke about the following:

In the Name of God, the Merciful, the Compassionate.

The movement in Iran does not belong to itself alone because Islam is not special to any one group. Islam has come for mankind not for Muslims and not for Iran. The prophets and the Prophet of Islam were sent to human beings. They called out to the people and we who brought about the movement did so for an Islamic Republic. A movement for Islam cannot relate to one country and not even to all of the Islamic countries. Islam is, in fact, the movement which follows the prophets.

Our great prophet came from Saudi Arabia but this invitation did not belong to Saudi Arabia alone. It related to all of the world. A human being is a creature who at the beginning is like an animal and if he grows, he becomes a spiritual creature, who becomes higher than the angels of God and if he goes towards corruption, he becomes a creature lower than all of the animals.

Now you see those people who claim to be humanitarian and they support human beings and animals but I do not think that they will find an animal among all the animals who is more savage than they are. They are creatures who want to murder millions of human beings because of their own interests. Even if an animal is a flesh-eater, it does not kill more than that which fills its stomach and when it is full, it leaves the other animals alone. But these people are ready to kill multitudes of people for only a small profit.

Other people who do not wall their interests or at least, do not act to the other's advantage, their existence cannot be considered to be unimportant. Unfortunately, there are organisations among Muslim and eastern societies themselves, in your countries, who believe their words and they say, 'The east is backwards from the point of view of thought', or they do not believe them but they work for them. We must call them traitors.

They design these words in the midst of their own society. American media and the media which is directly under the influence of Zionism expresses that. These very expressed problems are spread to their own countries so that eastern and Muslim countries can no longer find Islam. They cannot have a noble existence. Muslims must find Islam. Islam has fled from their hands. We do not know what Islam is now. The West and these criminals have influenced our minds to such an extent that we have lost Islam. Even though every year in the great Mecca, which God, the Most Exalted, has determined to be the place of gathering of Muslims, Muslims gather there but they do not know what they are doing. They do not use it in an Islamic way and this political centre is changed into a centre where affairs neglect the problems of Muslims.

If Muslims know the politics for which the Pilgrimage was established, this would be sufficient in order for them to find their own independence. Unfortunately, we have lost Islam. They have completely separated it from politics. They cut off its head and gave the rest to us. They have created this situation for us. As long as Muslims remain in this situation, they cannot reach their glory. The glory of Islam is that which existed at the beginning of Islam. They destroyed two empires with their few numbers because they wanted to build human beings.

Islam does not conquer. Islam wants all countries to become Muslim, of themselves. That is, Islam seeks to make those people who are not human beings, human. They captured some people in a jungle. They tied them up and were taking them back when our great prophet said 'I must take them to paradise with chains'.

Islam exists to correct society and if a sword is unsheathed, it is unsheathed to destroy the corruptors who do not allow society to be corrected. In this way, the others can be corrected. I hope that if we are successful, it will gradually be corrected. We face many difficulties now. We need the prayers of all Muslims. May God confirm all of you.

9.5 EXTRACT FROM THE UNIVERSAL ISLAMIC DECLARATION OF THE ISLAMIC COUNCIL OF EUROPE

IV Framework for an Islamic order

1. State policy

Muslims are committed to the sincere and effective pursuit of the guiding principles of state policy as ordained by Allah and His prophet, which include the following:

(a) The *shari'a* is the supreme law of the Muslim community and must be enforced in its entirety in all aspects of life. Each and every Muslim country must explicitly make *shari'a* the criterion by which to judge the public and private conduct of all, rulers and ruled alike, the chief source of all legislation in the country.

(b) Political power must be exercised within the framework of *shari'a*. It is neither valid nor exercisable except by and on behalf of the community through the process of mutual consultation (*shura*). No one is authorised to arrogate to himself the right to rule by personal discretion.

(c) It is the obligation and right of every person to participate in the political process, and political authority is to be entrusted to those who are worthy of it according to the Islamic criterion of knowledge, trustworthiness, and capability.

(d) All political power, whether legislative, executive, or judicial, is exercisable within the limits set out by Allah and His prophet for the promotion and enforcement of the values prescribed by Islam.

(e) Obedience to the legitimately constituted authority is obligatory on people so long as it is in conformity with the *shari'a*.

(f) All persons in authority are bound by the rules of the *shari'a*, both in regard to their personal as well as public conduct.

(g) All citizens are equal before the law.

(h) People have the right to question the decisions of their rulers and to seek and obtain remedies for wrongs committed by them.

(i) The rights of people to life, liberty, honour, and property as guaranteed by Allah and His prophet can in no circumstances be abrogated or suspended.

(j) The civil and religious rights of minorities shall be upheld and protected.

2. Economic policy

The Islamic economic system is based on social justice, equity, moderation, and balanced relationships. It is a universal system embodying eternal values which safeguard man's rights while constantly reminding him of his obligations to himself and to society. It forbids all forms of exploitation and honours labour, encourages man to earn his living by honest means, and to spend his earnings in a rational way. Its salient features are:

(a) All natural resources are a trust (*amana*) from Allah and man is individually and collectively custodian (*mustakhlif*) of these resources. Man's economic effort and its reward are determined within the context of this framework of trust.

(b) Wealth must be acquired through effort and by lawful means. It should be saved, retained, and used only in ways approved by Allah and His prophet.

(c) Wealth should be justly distributed. When personal wealth has satisfied the legitimate needs of its owner, the surplus is required to satisfy the needs of others.

(d) All resources available to man in general and to the *umma* in particular, must always be put to optimum use; no one has the right to hoard them or to keep them idle, or to squander them or to use them for wanton display, be it the individual, the community, or the state.

(e) Development is an essential requirement, and participation in economic activity is obligatory on every Muslim. He must labour hard, and always seek to produce more than is necessary for his personal needs, because then alone would he be able to participate in the process of *zakat* and to contribute to the well-being of others.

(f) Every worker is entitled to a fair recompense for his or her work. There must be no discrimination based on race, colour, religion, or sex.

(g) The procurement of wealth and the production of goods must be lawful in terms of the *shari'a*. Usury (*riba*), gambling, hoarding, etc. are forbidden sources of income.

(h) The principles of equality and brotherhood require the just sharing of resources in prosperity as well as in adversity, *zakat, sadaqat, al-'afw*, and inheritance are some of the means for the equitable distribution of wealth and resources in society.

(i) Persons incapable of looking after their own needs, owing to permanent or temporary incapacity, have a just call upon the wealth of society. They are the responsibility of society which must ensure supply of basic necessities of food, clothing, shelter, education, and health care, to all of them irrespective of their age, sex, colour, or religion.

(j) The economic power of the *umma* shall be structured in such a way that there is co-operation and sharing within the *umma* and maximum self-reliance therein.

3. Educational policy

Education is an important corner-stone of the Islamic system. Pursuit of knowledge is obligatory for all Muslims, including knowledge of skills, crafts, and vocations. Some of the basic principles of Islamic educational policy are:

(a) There shall be universal basic education for all men and women in society, and adequate national resources shall be made available for this purpose.

(b) The purpose of education shall be to produce people who are imbued with Islamic learning and character and are capable of meeting all the economic, social, political, technological, physical, intellectual, and aesthetic needs of society.

(c) The two parallel streams of secular and religious education prevailing today in the Muslim world should be fused together so as to provide an Islamic vision for those engaged in education, and to enable them to reconstruct human thought, in all its forms, on the foundations of Islam.

4. Social policy

The social institutions of mosque, family, local community, social consultative bodies, socio-economic co-operatives, etc., are an integral part of the Islamic system, and should be established and strengthened on the Islamic principles of brotherhood (*ukhuwa*) and mutual help (*takaful*). The fundamental objectives of Islamic policy are:

(a) Affirmation, restoration, and consolidation of the dignity, integrity, and honour of the individual.

(b) Ensuring that women enjoy full rights – legal, social, cultural, economic, educational, and political – which Islam has guaranteed to them.

(c) Self-reliance, mutual consultation, social cohesion, and co-operation in all aspects of national life.

5. Defence policy

Defence of Islam and Muslim lands is the sacred duty of all Muslims. While Islam stands for peace, it also enjoins Muslims to be ever ready to deter and repulse aggression. To fulfil this duty, the Muslim countries should:

(a) Develop their defence potentials to the maximum.

(b) Strive for the earliest achievement of self-sufficiency in defence production.

(c) Establish the closest possible co-operation in every field of defence activity.

(d) Consider aggression against any Muslim country as aggression against the entire Muslim world.

V Co-operation among the Muslim states

Further co-operation among Muslim states requires that:

(a) The Muslim world should establish an Islamic Fund for Mutual Assistance (*bayt al-mal*), through which assistance to Muslim countries should be administered.

(b) The Muslim world should set up a monetary reserve of its own and take expeditious steps to establish a common currency system.

(c) A common market among Muslim countries should be established.

(d) The Muslim world should establish its own institutions to control and operate the 'service sector', viz. banking, insurance, travel, shipping, packaging, transport, advertising, and marketing, etc.

(e) The Muslim world should co-ordinate production policies and agreed programmes for improving and development the techniques and quality of agricultural and industrial production in different countries. The primary aim in this regard should be:

 (i) To create sufficient agricultural capacity and food reserves.

 (ii) To produce raw materials for consumption in the industrial sector.

(iii) To rationalise the development of industry, particularly heavy and basic industries, in order to make the Muslim world self-sufficient in essential supplies of capital goods and defence equipment.

(f) The Muslim world should formulate a joint approach to secure fair and stable prices for its raw material and natural resources. It must enjoy and exercise complete sovereignty with regard to their production, pricing, marketing and usage. The Muslim states may also establish a common fund in order to acquire effective capability for market intervention and price support.

(g) The Muslim world should seek a fundamental restructuring of the present international monetary and economic system so as to make its operation fair and equitable for the developing countries and to give them their due share in decision-making.

(h) The Muslim states should establish a Muslim World Court to resolve and/or adjudicate on all inter-state disputes.

(i) The Muslim states should establish a Permanent Commission to formulate information and educational policies for the Muslim world as a whole, and should develop the full range of expertise, techniques and production facilities in mass media.

(j) The Muslim world should take an active interest in the welfare of Muslim minorities in non-Muslim countries. It is incumbent upon it to see that they are not denied human rights, and enjoy full freedom to practise their Islamic way of life.

(k) Arabic, the language of al-Qur'an, should be developed as the lingua franca of the Muslim *umma* and every effort should be made to achieve this objective.

VI Liberation of Muslim lands

The subjugation of Muslim people and the occupation of their lands in certain parts of the world is a matter of grave concern to us. The most painful of these is the usurpation and occupation of the holy city of Jerusalem (al-Quds). It is the sacred duty of *umma* to mobilise itself fully and strive relentlessly to liberate Jerusalem and all other Muslim lands.

VII Unity of the *umma*

The people of the Muslim world should prevail upon their governments to adopt this framework as a principle of state policy, to be followed by statutory treaty arrangements leading to greater unity of the *umma* as envisaged by Islam.

Declaration and resolve

The affairs of *umma*, divided into nation-states, are presently in disarray because:

(a) In spite of public declarations of commitment to Islam, Islamic principles have not been implemented in the life of its people and institutions.

(b) Real power is, by and large, in the hands of people whose hearts are not imbued with the teachings of Islam and the spirit of Muslim solidarity, and who tend to put their own interests above those of the Muslim *umma*.

(c) The vast resources of the *umma* are being grossly wasted. In many cases they are being used for purposes held to be illegal and immoral by the Qur'an. Instead of being utilised for the removal of economic imbalance and social injustice in the *umma* wealth is used in a manner that benefits forces that are inimical to Islam and the Muslim *umma*.

We therefore, declare that the objectives of the Islamic Order can be achieved only IF:

(a) The Muslim *umma* dedicates itself to practising the principles of Islam at the individual and collective levels, and abolishes all forms of domination, exploitation, all distinctions, discriminations, and all un-Islamic systems, laws, and customs that have permeated Muslim society.

(b) A truly Islamic leadership emerges in the Muslim *umma* in all fields; capable of leading the people through the strength of its moral calibre and not through force, coercion, or manipulation; which trusts its people and is trusted by them; which regards itself as accountable to the *umma* and above all to Allah.

It is under such an inspiring leadership and with a clear commitment to Islamic principles that Muslims all over the world would be integrated into one organic community, and would be able to transform the mandate of Allah into reality.

NOTES

1. INTRODUCTION

1. On the throne as the first thing created, for example, see J. Knappert, *Traditional Swahili Poetry*, Leiden, 1967, pp. 68–9.
2. See Constance E. Padwick, *Muslim Devotions: a Study of Prayer Manuals in Common Use*, London, 1961, for a full discussion of popular prayer.
3. See Frederick M. Denny, 'The *adab* of Qur'an recitation: text and context', in A. H. Johns (ed.), *International Congress for the Study of the Qur'an*, Canberra, n.d., pp. 143–60.
4. Details of this are provided in Daiber's article, noted in the bibliography for 6.2. On Ibn Qudama's theological position in general see George Makdisi, *Ibn Qudama's Censure of Speculative Theology*, London, 1962.
5. Habib Taherzadeh (tr.), *Selections from the Writings of the Bab*, Haifa, 1978, p. 85.
6. Louis Massignon, *The Passion of al-Hallaj, Mystic and Martyr of Islam*, translated by H. Mason, Princeton, 1982, p. 90.
7. See Mervyn Hiskett, *A History of Hausa Islamic Verse*, London, 1975, pp. 74–7.
8. For an excellent study of a Kurdish Qadiri order and some vivid details of their *dhikr* and trance, the film 'Dervishes' in the series 'Disappearing World' (Granada TV) should be viewed.

2. SCRIPTURE, ITS VALUE AND INTERPRETATION

1. For the meaning of the 'mysterious letters' see the final paragraph of 2.2.1 and the overview given in M. S. Seale, 'The mysterious letters in the Qur'an', in his *Qur'an and Bible: Studies in Interpretation and Dialogue*, London, 1978, pp. 29–46.
2. The actual reference here is to what people shall be given to eat in the hereafter.
3. The emphasis here is on the root sense of 'similar' in the word *mutashabih*. In this view, 'unclear verses' is not the appropriate understanding of the word.
4. The point here is that each pair of Arabic phrases is of a similar meaning but employ different words.
5. See 3.2.3.2 where this anecdote appears in the context of *hadith* material.
6. That is: rather than 'Ask the inhabitants of the town'. Other theorists would classify this verse as metaphor rather than concision. Al-Rummani is early in the development of the literary analysis of the Qur'an and this fact is emphasised in this tentative working out of some of the terminology employed in the text.
7. See 2.1.1 for the Arabic text.
8. This analysis reflects al-Rummani's Mu'tazilite point of view which tends to see humans as authors/creators of their own deeds, as compared to the traditionalist attitude of God as the author/creator of all deeds.

9. Reference here is to a number of Mu'tazilite authors who developed this argument.

3. RELIGIOUS HISTORY

1. A number of the elements in these accounts are designed to explain rituals in the pilgrimage – e.g. the ritual slaughter and the casting of stones. See the map of the *hajj*, p 93. Note that al-Tabari makes no attempt here to resolve whether the son in question was Ishmael or Isaac.

2. Asiya is the handmaiden of Pharoah's daughter who, according to Islamic legend, testified to the existence of the one God in opposition to the Egyptian notion of the divinity of the Pharoah. For this she was boiled in a cauldron of oil along with her baby son whose last words were: 'There is no god but God'. God rewarded Asiya by giving her the status of a noblewoman in Islam. Mary is the mother of Jesus.

3. Traditionally said to be *jinn* or angels heard by travellers in the desert.

4. The author here demonstrates the uncertainty connected to the practice of circumcision which while universally applied in Islamic countries is not mentioned in the Qur'an or *hadith*.

5. That is, Khusrau I (531–79), king of Persia, last great ruler of the Sasanian dynasty.

6. Here Adam is being eternally punished for his sin of disobedience by watching many thousands of his children's children go to hell; he weeps most of the time therefore.

7. Also called the lote tree in Qur'an 53:14; it is the tree of life and death. Each of its leaves has a name written on it. As long as the leaf lives, the bearer of that name lives; as soon as it falls, that person dies.

8. The reality of God's existence is hidden behind many veils which protect human beings from the unbearable radiation of the divine presence. The mystics explain these veils as the numerous illusions of selfhood with which we surround ourselves and which prevent us from seeing God face to face. Muhammad was able to do just that on his heavenly journey, however, even though, in fact, God has no physical shape or substance. It was by a special miracle that Muhammad was able to see God, according to this legend therefore.

9. See above 2.2.2.

10. For further elaboration of this document see the items in the bibliography under 3.2.4.

4. RITUAL PRACTICE

1. Al-Baghdadi is famed for his book on the sects of Islam; his interest in this subject is reflected throughout this passage and also in 5.1.

2. Here will be recited surah 1 of the Qur'an plus other sections of scripture.

3. See above 2.2.1 and 2.1.5.

6. THEOLOGY

1. For further elaboration of this letter see the items in the bibliography under 6.1.

2. This would appear to be an error; the number is generally calculated as 6217 in the Medinan tradition.

3. Both of these verses should be taken as affirming God's existence and not His modality therefore.

4. That is, the Anti-Christ; see 3.3.

7. SECTARIAN MOVEMENTS

1. This letter is said to have been written by 'Ali in response to one from Mu'awiya, who the Shi'ites see as usurping the caliphate.

2. The translation of this passage of the Qur'an reflects the Shi'ite interpretation; Arberry translates: *But those related by blood are nearer to one another in the Book of God*. The context of the passage in the Qur'an places blood relatives closer to one

another than those who emigrated later to Medina are to those who were the original helpers of Muhammad in his *hijra*.

3. The 'lesser peace' is a traditional Sufi idea here used in a universal way. It refers to the Baha'i teaching that a lasting and complete peace will be attained in two major stages. The first is called the Lesser Peace and will be characterised by politi-

cal peace while the Most Great Peace refers not only to the cessation of war between nations but a deeper, more abiding spiritual peace which is the result of a universal raising of consciousness.

4. 'That which ye possess' means the faith of the Baha'i religion. That is, do not argue with people in trying to convince them of the truth of the Baha'i revelation.

BIBLIOGRAPHY

ESSENTIAL REFERENCE WORKS

Margaret Anderson, *Arabic Materials in English Translation: a Bibliography of Works from the pre-Islamic Period to 1977*, Boston, Mass., 1980.
David Ede and others, *Guide to Islam*, Boston, Mass., 1983, (An annotated bibliography.)
The Encyclopaedia of Islam. New Edition, Leiden, London, 1960–.
The Shorter Encyclopaedia of Islam, Leiden, 1974.

BASIC TEXTS ON ISLAM

Ignaz Goldziher, *Introduction to Islamic Theology and Law*, Princeton, 1981. (German original, 1910.)
Fazlur Rahman, *Islam, Second Edition*, Chicago, 1979.

GENERAL HISTORY

Carl Brockelmann, *History of the Islamic peoples*, London, 1949. (German original, 1939.)
Bernard Lewis, *The Arabs in History, Fourth Edition*, New York, 1966.
F. E. Peters, *Allah's Commonwealth: a History of Islam in the Near East, 600–1100 A.D.*, New York, 1973.

1.1 Qu'ran
Helmut Gatje, *The Qur'an and its Exege-*

sis: selected Texts with classical and modern Muslim Interpretations, Berkeley, 1976. (German original, 1971.)
Fazlur Rahman, *Major Themes of the Qur'an*, Minneapolis, Chicago, 1980.
John Wansbrough, *Quranic Studies: Sources and Methods of scriptural Interpretation*, Oxford, 1977.
W. Montgomery Watt, *Bell's Introduction to the Qur'an*, Edinburgh, 1970.
W. Montgomery Watt, *Companion to the Qur'an*, London, 1967.

1.2 Muhammad
Michael Cook, *Muhammad*, Oxford, 1983.
Annemarie Schimmel, *And Muhammad is His Messenger: the Veneration of the Prophet in Islamic Piety*, Chapel Hill, North Carolina, 1985.
John Wansbrough, *The sectarian Milieu: Content and Composition of Islamic Salvation History*, Oxford, 1978.
W. Montgomery Watt, *Muhammad, Prophet and Statesman*, Oxford, 1961.

1.3 Ritual
Frederick M. Denny and Abdulaziz Sachedina, *Islamic ritual Practices: a Slide Set and Teacher's Guide*, New Haven: Asian Religions Media Resources, 1983.
Gustav von Grunebaum, *Muhammadan Festivals*, New York, 1951.
Edward W. Lane, *The Manners and Customs of the modern Egyptians*,

London 1836. (Reprinted in Every-man's Library, London, New York, 1954.)

1.4 Law
N. J. Coulson, *A History of Islamic Law*, Edinburgh, 1964.
A. A. Fyzee, *Outlines of Muhammadan Law. Third Edition.* Oxford, 1964.
Joseph Schacht, *An Introduction to Islamic Law*, Oxford, 1964.

1.5 Theology
D. B. Macdonald, *Development of Muslim theology, Jurusprudence, and Constitutional Theory*, New York, 1903.
W. Montgomery Watt, *The formative Period of Islamic Thought*, Edinburgh, 1973.
A. J. Wensinck, *The Muslim Creed: its Genesis and historical Development*, Cambridge, 1932.

1.6 Sectarian movements
William S. Hatcher and J. Douglas Martin, *The Baha'i Faith: an emerging global Religion*, New York, 1984.
John Norman Hollister, *The Shi'a of India*, London, 1953.
Spencer Lavan, *The Ahmadiya Movement: a History and Perspective*, Delhi, 1974.
Bernard Lewis, *The Origins of Ismailism*, Cambridge, 1940.
Moojan Momen, *An Introductio . to Shi'i Islam: the History and Doctrines of Twelver Shi'ism*, New Haven, 1985.

1.7 Mysticism
A. J. Arberry, *Sufism*, London, 1950.
R. J. Nicholson, *Studies in Islamic Mysticism*, Cambridge, 1921.
Annemarie Schimmel, *Mystical Dimensions of Islam* Chapel Hill, North Carolina, 1975.

1.8 Modern period
Albert Hourani, *Arabic Thought in the Liberal Age: 1798–1939*, Oxford, 1970.
Edward Mortimer, *Faith and Power: the Politics of Islam*, New York, 1982.

2.1
The Arabic text of the Qur'an employed is that of the Royal Edition of Cairo, available in many prints. Another standard text, but with different verse divisions in some cases, is that edited by Gustav Flügel. The best English translation of the Qur'an, and the one upon which the version given here is greatly indebted, is Arthur J. Arberry, *The Koran Interpreted*, Oxford, 1964. The entire Qur'an is available on tape in various styles of recitation; Muslim Information Services, London, provides a number of versions.

2.2.1
Al-Tabari, *Jami' al-bayan 'an ta'wil ay al-Qur'an*, Cairo, 1374–88, VI, pp. 169–80. A French translation of some of this material is available (Paris, 1983–4); an abbreviated English translation is under way (Oxford, 1986–).

2.2.2
Muqatil ibn Sulayman, *Tafsir*, Cairo, 1969, pp. 9–12; reference has also been made to the manuscript copy of this work, Ahmed III, 74. On Muqatil, see Isaiah Goldfeld, 'Muqatil ibn Sulayman', *Bar-Ilan Arabic and Islamic Studies*, II, 1978, pp. xiii–xxx.

2.2.3
Ibn Kathir, *Tafsir al-Qur'an al-azim*, Cairo, n.d., III, pp. 492–4.

2.3
Al-Rummani, *al-Nukat fi i'jaz al-Qur'an*, published in M. Zaghlul Salam and M. Khalaf Allah, *Thalath rasa'il fi i'jaz al-Qur'an*, Cairo, 1956, pp. 73–113; the translation has most especially reduced the number of examples of each phenomenon given by the author.

3.1.1
Muhammad ibn Ahmad ibn Iyas, *Bada'i'*

al-zuhur fi waqa'i' al-duhur, Cairo, 1954, pp. 3–23, 36–9.

3.1.2

Al-Tabari, *Ta'rikh al-Tabari: ta'rikh al-rusul wa'l-muluk*, Cairo, 1967, vol. I, pp. 272–6. An English translation of this entire work is in progress.

3.2.1

Reprinted from J. Knappert, *Swahili Islamic Poetry*, Leiden, 1971, I, pp. 49–52.

3.2.2

Reprinted from J. Knappert, *Swahili Islamic Poetry*, Leiden, 1971, III, pp. 253–69 (odd numbered pages only).

3.2.3.1

Al-Bukhari, *al-Sahih*, bilingual Arabic–English edition, Ankara, 1976, VII, pp. 338–67.

3.2.3.2

Muslim, *Sahih Muslim*, Cairo, n.d., I, pp. 295–8; an English translation is available of the entire work, Lahore, 1976.

3.2.3.3

Abu Dawud, *Sunan*, Cairo, 1977, IV, pp 3–11.

3.2.4

Ibn Ishaq, *al-Sirat al-nabawiyya*, Cairo, 1955, I, pp. 501–4; an English translation of the whole work is available: Alfred Guillaume, *The Life of Muhammad*, London, 1955. On this text itself see: R. B. Serjeant, 'The "Constitution of Medina" ', *Islamic Quarterly*, VIII, 1964, pp. 3–16; *idem*, 'The *Sunnah Jami'ah*, pacts with the Yathrib Jews, and the *tahrim* of Yathrib: analysis and translation of the documents comprised in the so-called 'Constitution of Medina" ', *Bulletin of the School of Oriental and African Studies*, XLI, 1978, pp. 1–42; Moshe Gil, 'The constitution of Medina: a reconsideration', *Israel Oriental Studies*, IV, 1974, pp. 44–66;

F. M. Denny, 'Ummah in the constitution of Medina', *Journal of Near Eastern Studies*, XXXVI, 1977, pp. 39–47; Muhammad Hamidullah, *The first written Constitution in the World*, Lahore, 1975.

3.2.5

Qadi ibn Musa ibn 'Iyad ibn 'Amrun al-Yahsubi, *Kitab al-shifa' fi-ta'rif huquq al-mustafa*, Cairo, 1912; also found in Shaykh Sayyidi Muhammad ibn Sulayman, *Kitab dala'il al-khayrat*, Cairo, n.d., pp. 60–5; also see Hamadi ibn 'Abdallah al-Buhri, *Utenzi wa kutawafu nabii*, Kampala, 1956, pp. 34–42; J. Knappert, *Islamic legends*, Leiden, 1985, I, p. 30.

3.3

Hajji Chum of Zanzibar, *Utenzi wa nushuri*, unpublished Swahili manuscript, stanzas 1–200, summarized; see also Furati ibn Kutahia (d. 1580) *Kitabi hikayati kirk sual*, unpublished manuscript; J. Knappert, *Islamic legends*, Leiden, 1985, II, pp. 469–73; Mewla Furati, *Das Buch der vierzig Fragen*, Leiden, 1960, pp. 156–9.

4.1

'Abd al-Qahir al-Baghdadi, *Kitab usul al-din*, Istanbul, 1928, pp. 186–93.

4.2.1

The ritual prayer is available in many publications; one such is Sh. Muhammad Ashraf, *Salat, or Islamic Prayer Book*, Lahore, 1971, which provides the Arabic text and English commentary

4.2.2

These songs come from two poets of Kenya – Sayyid ibn Ahmad al-Qumri of Mombasa and Ahmad Shaykh Nabahani of Malindi; they were recorded from oral recitations.

4.2.3

Munshi Anis Ahmad, *Masnun al-du'a'ayn*, New Delhi, n.d., bilingual edition, Arabic–English, pp. 9–15.

4.2.4

Reprinted from J. Knappert, *Swahili Islamic Poetry*, Leiden, 1971, II, pp. 179–89 odd numbered pages only.

4.3

Abu Zakariya' Yahya ibn Sharaf al-Din al-Nawawi, *al-Tibyan fi adab hamalat al-Qur'an*, Cairo, 1977, pp. 49–57.

5.1

'Abd al-Qahir al-Baghdadi, *Kitab al-nasikh wa'l-mansukh fi'l-Qur'an*; this work is available only in manuscript, Berlin Staatsbibliothek Petermann 555, and Istanbul Beyazit 445. A. Rippin is in the process of editing this text.

5.2

Abu Hamid al-Ghazzali, *Ihya' 'ulum al-din*, Cairo, 1965, II, pp. 51–2. A rather poor English translation is available: *Imam Gazzali's Ihya ulum-id-din*, translated by Fazul-ul-Karim, Lahore, 1978.

5.3

Reprinted from Mia Brandel-Syrier, *The religious duties of Islam as taught and explained by Abu Bakr Effendi*, Leiden, 1971, pp. 117–21, 130–4.

5.4

Al-Marghinani, *al-Hidaya: sharh badayat al-mubtada*, Cairo, 1975, I, pp. 226–31 (sections only); an explanatory English translation is available: *The Hedaya or Guide: a Commentary on the Mussulman Laws* translated by Charles Hamilton (reprint, Lahore, 1957).

6.1

The text of this letter was published by Helmut Ritter in *Der Islam*, XXI, 1933, pp. 67–83; on the work see: Julian Oberman, 'Political theology in early Islam: Hasan al-Basri's treatise on qadar', *Journal of the American Oriental Society*, LV, 1935, pp. 138–62, and Michael Schwarz, 'The letter of al-Hasan al-Basri', *Oriens*, XX, [for] 1967, [pub.] 1969, pp. 15–30 – the translation presented here (of about the first half of the full document) is greatly indebted to the work of Schwarz.

6.2

The text, along with helpful analysis has been published in Hans Daiber, 'The creed ('Aqida) of the Hanbalite ibn Qudama al-Maqdisi: a newly discovered text', in W. al-Qadi (ed), *Studia Arabica et Islamica: Festschrift for Ihsan 'Abbas on his sixtieth Birthday*, Beirut, 1981, pp. 105–12.

6.3

Muhammad ibn Muhammad al-Fadali, *Kifayat al-'awamm fima yajibu 'alayhim min 'ilm al-kalam*, Cairo, n.d., chapter 1; see Martin Horten, *Muhammedanische Glaubenslehre*, Bonn, 1916, pp. 5–45. Also see Ernst Dammann, 'Ein Shafiitischer Traktat in Suaheli', *Der Islam*, XXIII, 1936, pp. 189–91, and J. Knappert, 'Swahili theology in the form of an utenzi', in H. J. Greschat and H. Jungraithmayr (ed.), *Wort und Religion Kalima na dini, [Festschrift] Ernst Dammann*, Stuttgart, 1969, pp. 282–93.

7.1.1

Al-Sharif al-Radi *Nahj al-balagha*, ed. Muhammad Abduh, Beirut, n.d., pp. 82, 141–3, 266–7, 321–2 and 545–51. Several English versions are available of the work including that of Askari Jafery, published under several different titles (*Peak of Eloquence* or *Nahjul Balagha Sermons*) and published in numerous prints in the Muslim world.

7.1.2

Hamadi ibn 'Abdallah al-Buhri, *Utenzi wa Seyidina Huseni*, Dar es Salaam, 1965; also see J. Knappert, *Islamic Legends*, Leiden, 1985, II.

7.1.3

Charles Virolleaud, *La passion de l'imam Hosseyn*, Paris, 1929. Also see Sir Lewis Pelly, *The Passion Plays of Hasan and Husain*, London, 1879; P. J. Chelkowski (ed.), *Ta'ziyeh: ritual and drama in Iran*, New York, 1979; Mahmoud Ayoub, *Redemptive Suffering in Islam: a Study of devotional Aspects of 'Ashura in Twelver Shi'ism*, The Hague, 1978.

7.2.1

This material comes from unpublished sources in the possession of J. Knappert.

7.2.2

A Khutba of Aga Khan Karim 'Ali, Mombassa, 1957, pp. 45–9.

7.3.1

Reprinted from *Selections from the writings of the Bab*, translated by Habib Taherzadeh, Haifa, 1978, pp. 41–2.

7.3.2

Reprinted from *Basharat (Glad-Tidings): Tablets of Baha'u'llah revealed after the Kitab i-Aqdas*, translated by Habib Taherzadeh, Haifa, 1978, pp. 19–29.

7.3.3

Reprinted from 'Abbas Effendi ('Abdu'l-Baha), *Some answered Questions*, ed. Laura Clifford Barney, Wilmette, reprint, 1981, pp. 138–9.

7.3.4

Reprinted from Shoghi Effendi, *The World Order of Baha'u'llah: selected Letters*, Wilmette, reprint, 1982, pp. 188–204, extracts.

7.4

Reprinted from Mirza Ghulam Ahmad, *The Philosophy of the Teachings of Islam*, London, 1979, pp. 99, 104–8.

8.1

Ibn Hanbal, *Kitab al-zuhd*, Beirut, 1976, pp. 3–6.

8.2

Paul Nywia, *Trois oeuvres inédites de mystiques Musulmans*, Beirut, 1973, pp. 35–6.

8.3

Mtungaji Mwinyi H. Mzale, *Sayyid Abdul Kadir na karama zake*, Zanzibar, 1968, pp. 1–24. Javanese versions of these legends are published in G. W. J. Drewes and R. Ng. Dr. Poerbatjaraka, *De mirakelen van Abdoelkadir Djaelani*, Bandoeng, 1938; also see J. Knappert, *Islamic Legends*, Leiden, 1985.

8.4

Al-Hajji Isma'il ibn Sayyid Muhammad Sa'id al-Qadiri, *al-Fuyudat al-rabbaniyya fi'l-ma'thira wa'l-awrad al-Qadiriyya*, Singapore, n.d., pp. 141–3; other texts were copied for J. Knappert by a pupil of Mu'allim Salimin in Mombasa in 1969.

8.5

Hendrik Kraemer, *Een Javaansche prim-bon uit de zestiende eeuw*, Leiden, 1921, pp. 153–91, condensed.

8.6

Reprinted from E. H. Palmer, *Oriental Mysticism: a Treatise on Sufiistic and Unitarian Theosophy of the Persians*, reprinted London, 1969, pp. 4–7, 22–7, 64–7; the passages have been modified slightly to match the style of this book.

9.1

Reprinted from C. W. Troll, *Sayyid Ahmad Khan: a reinterpretation of Muslim Theology*, Delhi, 1978, pp. 310–15, 322–4.

9.2

Sayyid Qutb, *Hadha'l-din*, eighth edition, Beirut, 1983, pp. 29–41. An English translation, to which the translation provided here is greatly indebted, is available under the title *This Religion of Islam* under many publishers' imprints, including International Islamic Federation of Student Organizations, Kuwait, 1977, and Markazi Maktaba Islami, Delhi, 1974. On Sayyid Qutb, see Yvonne Y. Haddad, 'Sayyid Qutb: ideologue of Islamic revival', in John L. Esposito (ed.), *Voices of Resurgent Islam*, Oxford, 1983, pp. 67–98.

9.3

Reprinted from Abul A'la Maududi, *Birth Control: its Social, Political, Economic, and Religious Aspects*, Karachi, 1968, pp. 74–87. On Mawdudi, see Charles J. Adams, 'Mawdudi and the Islamic state', in John L. Esposito (ed.), *Voices of Resurgent Islam*, Oxford, 1983, pp. 99–133.

9.4.1

Reprinted from *The Message of Peace* (published by Hamdami Foundation, Tehran) II, 3, no date, p. 20. On Khumayni, see Michael M. J. Fischer, 'Imam Khomeini: four levels of understanding', in John L. Esposito (ed.), *Voices of Resurgent Islam*, Oxford, 1983, pp. 150–74.

9.4.2

Reprinted from *Selected Messages and Speeches of Imam Khomeini*, Tehran, *c.* 1980, pp. 48–9.

9.5

Reprinted from Salem Azzam, *Islam and contemporary Society*, Harlow, Essex, 1982, pp. 260–6.

GLOSSARY

'Abbasid, dynasty of caliphs ruling from 750, coming to a final end in 1258 although it had lost any meaningful power several centuries earlier.

Abu Hanifa, lived 700–67; eponymous founder of the Hanafite school of law and theologian.

Ahmad ibn Hanbal, lived 780–855; eponymous founder of the Hanbalite school of law and a theologian.

Akhbari, Shi'ite group who as a school of law and theology rely on traditions (*akhbar*) from the *imams* rather than speculative reason.

'Ali ibn Abi Talib, cousin and son-in-law of Muhammad; fourth caliph after the death of his uncle; the first *imam* for the Shi'a, died 661.

Allah, Arabic for God.

Ansar, the helpers of Muhammad in Medina.

Dajjal, name given to the anti-Christ figure appearing at the time of the end of the world.

dhikr, 'mentioning' or 'remembrance'; term used for chants in Sufi meditations.

faqir, 'one who needs'; devotee of Sufism, same as dervish.

fatwa, a legal opinion given by an expert in response to a question submitted.

firman, edict of the ruler, in origin referring to the Ottoman Sultan.

hadith, a tradition or written report embodying an aspect of the *sunna* of Muhammad.

hajj, pilgrimage of Mecca done in the month of *Dhu'l-hijja*; one of the 'Five Pillars'.

Hanafi, follower of the school of law of Abu Hanifa.

Hanbali, follower of the school of law of Ahmad ibn Hanbal.

haram, the area of Mecca; also something forbidden.

Hashimite, members of the family to which Muhammad belonged.

hijab, 'screen'; separation between women and men.

'id-i-ghorban, Persian name for festival generally called *'id al-adha'*, the sacrificial feast on 10 *Dhu'l-hijja* during the pilgrimage.

ihram, state of sacredness adopted for the pilgrimage; also the actual clothes worn for the ritual.

'ilm al-kalam, the science of theology.

imam, (1) the prayer leader in the *salat*; (2) the leader of a school of law, a renowned scholar or a political leader; (3) the semi-divine source of authority in *Shi'ite* Islam who is a descendant of 'Ali and who takes the place of the *Sunni* caliph.

inshallah, Arabic for 'if God wills'.

isnad, chain of authorities through whom an oral tradition (e.g. a *hadith*) has passed.

Jahmiyya, early literalist sect in Islam believing in predestination and anthropomorphism.

Ja'far al-Sadiq, 700–56, sixth of the twelve Shi'ite *imams*, celebrated for his knowledge of traditions.

jinn, the genies of *Arabians Nights* fame.

Ka'ba, the black cube building in the middle of the mosque in Mecca.

kafir, unbeliever.

Kharijites/Khawarij, puritanical sect of early Islam who believed in absolute devotion as the mark of a true Muslim, all others being unbelievers.

La ilaha illa Allah, 'there is no god but God', part of the *shahada*.

madrasa, religious school.

mahdi, Messiah figure expected at the end of time.

Malik ibn Anas, lived 715–95; eponymous founder of Maliki school of law.

mawla, a 'client'; someone who has become aligned with a certain clan.

mawlid, 'birthday'; those of Muhammad

and of many Sufi saints are often celebrated.

minbar, pulpit of a mosque.

Mu'awiya, first caliph of the Umayyad dynasty who fought against 'Ali in the first civil war of Islam for the right to rule the community; ruled 661–80.

Murji'a, early theological party holding to a *status quo* position.

Mu'tazilites, developers of a school of thought in early Islam stressing human free will and the justice of God.

Qadarites, precursors of the Mu'tazilites who argued for human free will.

qibla, the point towards which one faces in prayer (towards Mecca), marked in the mosque by the *mihrab*.

rak'a, 'bowing, prostration'; refers to the entire series of actions which are accompanied by various liturgical formulae in the *salat*.

sadaqa, charity.

salat, the prescribed five prayers a day; one of the 'Five Pillars'.

sawm, fasting; one of the 'Five Pillars'; performed during Ramadan.

al-Shafi'i, lived 767–820; eponymous founder of the Shafi'ite school of law and a major jurist.

shahada, 'witness to faith'; saying (in Arabic) 'There is no god but God and Muhammad is the messenger of God'; one of the 'Five Pillars'.

shari'a, the religious law.

Shi'a, the religio-political party believing the claims of 'Ali and his heirs to rightful leadership of the community and to his status as *imam*.

sira, the biography of Muhammad.

sirat, the bridge in the hereafter across which the souls must pass on their way to paradise.

sunna, 'custom'; the way Muhammad acted which is then emulated by Muslims.

Sunni, those who follow the *sunna*, as opposed to the *Shi'a* who, although they follow the example of Muhammad, also abide by the rulings of the *imams*.

surah, a chapter in the Qur'an.

tafsir, commentary on the Qur'an.

takbir, praising God by saying *Allahu akbar*, 'God is great'.

tasmiya, saying 'In the name of God'.

tawhid, the oneness of God; theology.

'ulama', the learned class, especially those learned in religious matters.

Umayyad, the first dynasty of caliphs ruling in Islam from 661 to 750.

umma, community, nation.

'umra, the lesser pilgrimage or 'visitation'.

'ushr, tithe, generally one-tenth, paid on land owned by Muslims.

wadi, a valley through which a river will run generally only after rain storms.

wird, form of private prayer in addition to the *salat*.

witr, supererogatory prayers said at night of the same type as the *salat*.

zakat, alms tax; one of the 'Five Pillars'.

INDEX